# *Tabligh – e – Deen*

## The Forty foundations of the Religion

## Imam Ghazali

Translated by

Maulana Moosa Kajee

*Tabligh-e-Deen*

*Translated By: Maulana Moosa Kajee*

*First Edition: Dhul Hijjah 1436, November 2015*

# Table of Contents

بسم الله الرحمن الرحيم

Foreword to English translation of Tabligh-e-Deen
By Al-Haaj Ibrahim Tasbihwala Saheb (دامت بركاتهم) (Batley, England)

Khalifa Majaaz-e-Bay'at of Hadhrat Maseehul Ummat

Moulana Maseehullah Khan Saheb &

The request by a *Sufi* Master of the calibre of Hadhrat Hakimul Ummat Mujjadid-ul-Millat Moulana Ashraf Ali Saheb Thanwi &, to a dedicated friend, to have this particular Arabic work of Hujjatul Islam, Imam Muhammed Al-Ghazali &, translated into Urdu for the benefit of the masses who are conversant with the language, is sufficient to highlight the paramount importance of implementing the prescriptions, as penned by Imam Ghazali & (one would not be erring in referring to him as The Sage of his age), for the sincere seeker, treading the path of Sulook/Tasawuff towards the Beloved Creator, Allah &.

It is a concise, yet comprehensive treatise, that guides and assists the sincere seeker in developing amongst others, the noble qualities of taqwa, parhez-ghaari, ta'alluq ma'Allah, ikhlas etc. Inorder to gain maximum benefit from this literary masterpiece, it is the advice of experienced kaamil masheikh of Sulook/Tasawuff, that a particular frame of mind be adopted, that is mentally one should regard Imam Ghazali & as one's own affectionate beloved Sheikh, rendereing sincere advice from the bottom of his heart, based on deep knowledge and experience, inorder to accelerate the progress of the beloved mureed entrusted to him.

The sincerity of Imam Ghazali & in serving Islam, is legendary, in that, when questioned about his motivation in seeking Islamic knowledge by the Sultan

5

who was the patron of the institution of learning where Imam Saheb was enrolled, he answered that it was only for the Pleasure of Allah ﷻ. Incidently, this motivated the Sultan to keep the institution running, as the corrupt intentions of the other students present, prompted the Sultan to consider shutting it down completely.

The principle that operates in this world is that, inorder to obtain peak performance, everything **must** be used according to the manufacturer's instructions. Similarly, this is Allah ﷻ's Kingdom, which also has Divine rules, regulations and instructions directly from the Creator, knowledge of which we should ambitiously seek and implement .This book is full of barakaat and azmat, to the extent that any true seeker with talab for Allah ﷻ, who follows the instruction herein, will InshaAllah reach the desired goal of tazkiyah, and in the experience of many , Wilayat.

Note: Due to significant physical weaknesses prevalent amongst people of this age, the elders and pious of this era strongly advise against practising on the severe dietary restrictions mentioned in the section related to food and drink. These were relevant in the age in which they resided. It was prior to the current era of physical, moral and spiritual decline. A person should always consult with the elders of his era before undergoing any spiritual exertions, as they can cause destruction to a person instead of benefit.

# Preface

Our sincere appreciation is extended to Ml. Moosa Kajee for undertaking the enormous task of translating these priceless advises from the Urdu version, Mufti Siraj Desai for painstakingly proof reading and editing, and all others that have assisted in anyway in bringing this project to fruition. May Allah ﷻ grant you all Jaza-e-Khair and make this a means of earning His Pleasure & Acceptance. Ameen.

بسم الله الرحمن الرحيم

# SECTION ONE

# TEN PRINCIPLES OF OUTWARD ACTIONS

# FIRST PRINCIPLE

# SALÂH

**Allâh** ﷻ states, "And establish salâh for My Remembrance."
*Rasulullâh* ﷺ said, "Salâh is a pillar of dîn (religion)."[1]
Understand well that during salâh, you are conversing with your Creator and Sustainer. Therefore watch carefully how you are performing your salâh. **Allâh** ﷻ has commanded 'iqâmate-salâh' i.e. correcting and perfecting of one's salâh. This means that one should be vigilant with regards to his salâh and all the necessary acts related to salâh. Therefore complete care should be taken in the following three matters:

1) Before salâh, be careful with regards to your wudu. The method of acquiring this is to fulfil all the *Sunnah* and mustahab actions, and to recite the duâs mentioned in the hadith at the time of washing each limb.[2]

---

[1] Shuabul Imân (2550), Musnad Firdaws (3795)

[2] Before wudhû, recite:

اللَّهُمَّ أَنِّي اَعُوذُ بِكَ مِنْ هَمَزَاتِ الشَّيَاطِينِ وَ اَعُوذُ بِكَ رَبِّ اَنْ يَحْضُرُوْنَ

"O Allâh! I seek Your Protection from the whisperings of the shayateen, and I seek Your Protection from them coming close to me."

Thereafter recite Bismillâhir Rahmânir Rahîm.

Whilst washing the hands recite:

اللَّهُمَّ أَنِّي أَسْأَلُكَ الْيُمْنَ وَ الْبَرَكَةَ وَ اَعُوذُ بِكَ مِنَ الشُّوْمِ وَ الهَلاكَةِ

"O Allâh! I ask You for felicity and blessings, and I seek Your Protection from misfortune and destruction."

Whilst gargling recite:

اللّٰهُمَّ أَعِنِّي عَلَى تِلَاوَةِ كِتَابِكَ وَ كَثْرَةِ الذِّكْرِلَكَ وَالشُّكْرِلَكَ

"*O Allâh!* Assist me to recite Your Book, and to make Your zikr and gratitude in abundance"

When placing water in the nostrils, recite:

اللّٰهُمَّ أَرِحْنِي رَائِحَةَ الْجَنَّةِ وَ اَنْتَ عَنِّيْ رَاضٍ

"*O Allâh!* Allow me to smell the fragrance of Jannah, whilst You are Pleased with me."

When removing water from the nostrils, recite:

اللّٰهُمَّ أَنِّي اَعُوذُ بِكَ مِنْ رَوَائِح النَّارِ وَ مِنْ سُوْءِ الدَّارِ

"*O Allâh!* I seek Your Protection from the foul smells of the Fire. and from the Abode of evil."

Whilst washing the face recite:

اللّٰهُمَّ بَيِّضْ وَجْهِي يَوْمَ تَبْيَضُّ وُجُوهُ أَوْلِيَائِك وَلا تُسَوِّدْ وَجْهِيْ يَوْمَ تَسْوَدُّ وُجُوهُ أَعْدَائِك

"*O Allâh!* Brighten my face on the day You Brighten the faces of Your *Awliyâ* ﷺ, and do not blacken my face on the day You Blacken the faces of Your enemies."

Whilst washing the right hand recite:

اللّٰهُمَّ أَعْطِنِي كِتَابِي بِيَمِينِي وَحَاسِبْنِي حِسَابًا يَسِيرًا

"*O Allâh!* Grant my book of deeds in my right hand, and grant me an easy reckoning"

Whilst washing the left hand recite:

اللّٰهُمَّ أَنِّي اَعُوذُ بِكَ أَنْ تُعْطِيَنِي كِتَابِي بِشِمَالِي أُوْ مِنْ وَّرَاءِ ظَهْرِي

"*O Allâh!* I seek Your Protection from receiving my book of deeds in my left hand, or from behind my back."

Whilst making masah of the head recite:

اللّٰهُمَّ اجْعَلْنِي مِنَ الَّذِينَ يَسْتَمِعُونَ الْقَوْلَ فَيَتَّبِعُونَ أَحْسَنَهُ اللّٰهُمَّ اسْمِعْنِيْ مُنَادِيَ الْجَنَّةِ مَعَ الْأَبْرَارِ

"*O Allâh!* Make me among those who carefully listen to Your Speech, and thereafter follow that which is the best. *O Allâh,* let me hear the caller of Jannah with the righteous."

Whilst making masah of the nape recite:

اللّٰهُمَّ فَلَّ رَقَبَتِي مِنْ النَّارِ وَ اَعُوذُ بِكَ مِنَ السَّلَاسِلِ وَ الاَغْلَالِ

"*O Allâh!* Free my neck from the Fire, and I seek Your Protection from its chains and shackles."

Whilst washing the right leg recite:

9

Together with this, keep in mind that one's clothing, one's body, and the water used for wu<u>d</u>u must be pure. However, do not be so overly cautious, that it reaches a stage where one is afflicted by wasâwis (thoughts and doubts), for these are from shaytân; shaytân wastes away the time of many a pious servant in doubts and confusion.

## A UNIQUE WISDOM IN TAHAARAT

Understand well that the example of the clothing of a person who performs salâh, is like the outer skin of a fruit. The body is like the inner skin and the heart is similar to the kernel and core of the fruit. It is obvious that the object is core or kernel. Similarly the aim of this external cleanliness is to purify the heart and to make it effulgent. Perhaps you may

---

اللَّهُمَّ ثَبِّتْ قَدَمَيَّ عَلَى صِرَاطِكَ الْمُسْتَقِيْمِ

"*O* Allâh! Keep my feet firm on Your straight path."

Whilst washing the left leg recite:

اللَّهُمَّ أَنِّي اَعُوذُ بِكَ أَنْ تَزِلَّ قَدَمَيَّ عَلَى الصِّرَاطِ يَوْمَ تَزِلُّ اَقْدَامُ الْمُنَافِقِيْنَ فِي النَّارِ

"*O* Allâh! I seek Your Protection from my feet slipping on the Bridge, on the day the feet of the hypocrites will slip into the Fire."

After wudhu, stand and recite the following duâ:

أَشْهَدُ أَنْ لاَّ إِلهَ إِلاَّ اللّٰهُ وَحْدَه لاَ شَرِيْكَ لَه وَ أَشْهَدُ أَنَّ مُحَمَّدًا عَبْدُه وَ رَسُوْلُه سُبْحَانَكَ اللَّهُمَّ وَ بِحَمْدِكَ لاَّ إلهَ إِلاَّ أَنْتَ عَمِلْتُ سُوْءً وَ ظَلَمْتُ نَفْسِيْ اَسْتَغْفِرُكَ وَ أَتُوْبُ إِلَيْكَ فَاغْفِرْلِيْ وَ تُبْ عَلَيَّ إِنَّكَ أَنْتَ التَّوَّابُ الرَّحِيْمُ اللَّهُمَّ اجْعَلْنِيْ مِنَ التَّوَّابِيْنَ وَاجْعَلْنِيْ مِنَ الْمُتَطَهِّرِيْنَ وَاجْعَلْنِيْ مِنْ عِبَادِكَ الصَّالِحِيْنَ وَاجْعَلْنِيْ عَبْداً صَبُوْراً شَكُوْراً أَذْكُرُكَ ذِكْراً كَثِيْراً وَ أُسَبِّحُكَ بُكْرَةً وَّ أَصِيْلاً

I testify that there is none worthy of worship besides Allâh. He is Alone. He has no partner, and I testify that Muhammad ﷺ is His Servant, and Messenger. *O* Allâh, You are Pure, all praises are solely for You. There is none worthy of worship besides You. I have committed evil, and I have oppressed myself. I seek Your Forgiveness and I turn towards You, thus forgive me and accept my repentance, for verily You are the Most Forgiving, the Most Merciful. *O* Allâh, *make me from amongst those who are repentant, make me from amongst those who are pure, make me from amongst Your pious servants, and make me a servant who exercses an abundance of patience and gratitude, I make abundance of zikr and I sing Your Praises morning and evening."*

Thereafter recite Surah Qadr thrice. (Translator)

doubt, that how can the heart become cleansed by the cleanliness of clothing. Therefore, understand that **Allâh** ﷻ has kept a special relationship between the inward and outward, due to which, the effect of outward cleanliness definitely has an effect on inward cleanliness. Judge for yourself ! After completion of wudu, you will find such a feeling of purity and expansion in the heart, which was not found before performing it. It is apparent that this is the effect of the wudu, which transcends the body and reaches the heart.

## DEFINITE BENEFIT IN PERFORMANCE OF SALÂH, EVEN THOUGH ITS SECRETS ARE NOT KNOWN

2) Fulfil all the actions of salâh, whether they are *Sunnah* or mustahab, or whether they are tasbîhât or dhikr, as they ought to be performed. Remember that just as the outward cleanliness of the body had caused an effect on internal purity, similarly, in fact, to a greater extent, the actions of salâh have an effect on the heart, and create effulgence. Just as a sick person taking medication definitely benefits by it, even though he is not aware of the effects of the ingredients of the medication, similarly by fulfilling all the postures of salâh, you will definitely attain benefit, even though you are completely unaware of its wisdoms and secrets.

## THE SOUL AND BODY OF SALÂH

Understand well, that just like living creations, **Allâh** ﷻ has granted salâh an outward form, and a soul. Thus the soul of salâh is intention, sincerity and presence of heart; the posture of standing and sitting are the body of salâh; ruku' and sujud are the head and limbs of salâh, all the adhkar and tasbîhât in salâh are the eyes, ears, etc., understanding their meanings are the sight of the eyes, and the ability to hear, etc., and performing all the postures of salâh with humility and concentration is the beauty of salâh i.e. its beautiful colour and form.

In short, by completing all the postures and actions of salâh with presence of heart in this manner, a most beautiful and beloved structure of salâh is created. As for the closeness the one performing salâh attains to **Allâh** ﷻ, understand it by means of the following example. A servant presents a beautiful slave girl to the king as a gift. At this time, he will achieve closeness to the king. Thus, if there is no sincerity in your salâh, then it is as though you are presenting a dead and lifeless slave girl. It is apparent that this is so disrespectful and insolent, that if such a cheeky person is killed, it won't be surprising. If there is no ruku' and sajdah, then it is as though he is presenting a slave girl void of limbs. If there is no <u>dh</u>ikr and tasbîh, then it is as though the slave girl does not possess eyes, ears, etc. if all are present, but one does not understand its meaning, and the heart is not concentrating, then it is as though the slave girl possesses all her limbs, but there is no movement and feeling in them i.e. the eye is there, but there is no sight, the ear is present, but cannot hear, the hands and feet are present but are ineffectual, and devoid of feeling. Now will such a defective slave girl be accepted as a royal gift or not? Perhaps it may occur to you that once a person has performed the fardh and wâjib of salâh, the ulamâ have passed a ruling of the salâh being correct, whether one understands the meaning or not. And when the salâh is correct, then the objective has been obtained. This shows that it is not necessary to understand the meaning. Therefore understand that the ulamâ are like doctors. Thus if a doctor has to see any slave girl who is paralyzed and full of defects, but she has life in her, he will definitely say, "She is alive, not dead."

## THE RULING OF THE ULAMÂ ON THE CORRECTNESS OF SALÂH WITHOUT PRESENCE OF HEART, AND THE ANSWER TO THIS DOUBT

Similarly, with the presence of the soul of salâh and its vital limbs, the ulamâ will pass the verdict that the salâh is correct, and not invalid. In such a case whatever the doctor and the scholar have stated, according to their position, is correct. However, salâh is a royal offering and an action whereby one attains divine closeness. It is understood that a defective slave girl, even if she is alive, is not worthy of being presented as a royal offering. In actual fact, presenting such a slave girl as a gift is disrespectful and worthy of royal censure. Similarly, if one desires divine closeness by a flawed salâh, then it is not surprising if it is returned like an old, torn piece of cloth and flung onto the face.[1]

---

[1] Contents of a <u>h</u>adîth mentioned in Shuabuil Imân (2871) and Tabrânî in Awsat (3119)

In short, since the objective of salâh is honouring and glorifying **Allâh** ﷻ, according to the amount of deficiency there is in the *Sunnah* and mustahab postures, as well as the etiquettes of salâh, this amount of deficiency will be present in one's honour and respect.

## THE SOUL AND LIMBS OF SALÂH

3) Take extra care of the soul of salâh i.e. from the beginning till the end of salâh maintain full concentration and sincerity. Whatever you utter with the tongue, and whatever actions you perform with the limbs, bring its effect into the heart as well. This means that when your body bends for ruku', then bend the heart with humility, when you utter **Allâhu-akbar** (**Allâh** ﷻ is the Greatest) with the tongue, then this feeling should pervade the heart, that definitely there is nothing greater than **Allâh** ﷻ, when you recite الْحَمْدُ لِلّٰهِ (All praises are solely for **Allâh** ﷻ), then your heart should be filled with gratitude for **Allâh** ﷻ's favours, and when إِيَّاكَ نَعْبُدُ وَإِيَّاكَ نَسْتَعِينُ (Only You do we worship, and only You do we seek assistance) emerges from your tongue, then at that time you should admit to your feebleness, worthlessness, and neediness, i.e. this feeling should be found in the heart that besides **Allâh** ﷻ, neither do I, nor anyone else, have control of anything.

## HEART AND TONGUE BEING IN CONFORMITY IN SALÂH

In short, all the adhkâr, tasbîhât, postures and conditions of salâh, should be in conformity inwardly and outwardly. Remember that only that portion of salâh is written in the book of deeds, which is read with understanding and thought. Thus whichever portion is recited without understanding is not included.

## THE METHOD OF ACQUIRING PRESENCE OF HEART

Yes, it is obvious that in the beginning, you will find extreme difficulty in establishing presence of mind in totality. However if you train yourself, then gradually, it will become a habit. Therefore turn your attention towards this. Increase this concentration gradually. For example, if you had to perform four raka'ts of salâh, then see how much of presence of heart is found. If we assume that you could concentrate for two raka'ts, and in two raka'ts you were completely unmindful, then do not count these two raka'ts. Thereafter perform so many raka'ts of nafl in which you will gain presence of heart that is equal to two raka'ts. The more heedlessness there is, offer as many raka'ts of nafl, so much so that in ten raka'ts of nafl, concentration equal to that of four fardh raka'ts are found, then have hope that **Allâh** ﷻ will complete the shortcomings of the fardh, by means of the nawâfil, only through His ﷻ Grace and Kindness, and He ﷻ will accept the amends of the deficiency by nawâfil.[1]

# SECOND PRINCIPLE

# ZAKÂH, SADAQAH AND OTHER CHARITY

**Allâh** ﷻ states, "The example of those who spend their wealth in the path of **Allâh** ﷻ is like a grain that has grown seven ears, within each ear there is one hundred grains."

*Rasulullâh* ﷺ said, "Those who possess a lot will be destroyed, except he who spends his wealth in the path of **Allâh** ﷻ abundantly, on all sides."[2]

Since charity fulfils the needs of the creation, and it removes the poverty of the needy ones, it is therefore a pillar of Islam. The wisdom behind this, is that since **Allâh** ﷻ has commanded us to love the creation, and the Muslims also claim to love **Allâh** ﷻ, so **Allâh** ﷻ has made the spending of wealth a scale and criterion to test one's love, so that the claims of the truthful claimants of *imân*, can be differentiated from the false ones. It is an accepted maxim, that one is prepared to sacrifice all his beloved possessions for the beloved, whose love has permeated his heart. Thus spending a beloved commodity like wealth for the sake of **Allâh** ﷻ, is a sign of love for **Allâh** ﷻ, and stinginess is a proof of not possessing love for **Allâh** ﷻ. The believers who spend charity are divided into three categories:

---

[1] Hâkim (1/262), Abû Dâwûd (864) and Tirmidhî (413) has narrated this subject matter.
[2] Ahmad (32/535)

1) The strong ones - These are the ones who spend all that they own, and do not keep anything for themselves. They have shown themselves true in the covenant they have pledged with **Allâh** ﷻ. An example of this is AbuBakr Siddique ؓ when he brought all the wealth which he possessed to *Nabî* ﷺ. When *Nabî* ﷺ asked him, "What have you kept back for your family?" he replied, "**Allâh** ﷻ and his *Rasûl* ﷺ." On the same occasion, Umar Farûq ؓ also brought wealth. When Nabi ﷺ asked him, "What have you kept back for your family?" he replied, "I have kept back the same amount that I have brought". *Rasulullâh* ﷺ remarked, "The difference in your rank is apparent by your answers."[1]

2) The intermediate ones – These are the ones who are unable to spend all their wealth at once. However, together with this, they do not spend on themselves more than necessity. They wait for the opportunity to spend on the needs of impoverished people. As soon as they find some avenue to spend, or see some needy person, they spend their wealth without any anguish. These people do not suffice on their zakâh i.e. the fardh (obligatory) amount, but they have intention to spend all their wealth for **Allâh** ﷻ's sake. Thus the object of keeping wealth is to spend in **Allâh** ﷻ's path, however they are waiting for the opportune moment.

3) The lowest level – The weak Muslims who suffice on fulfilling only their compulsory duty of zakâh. If they do not give anything more than the compulsory amount, they also do not give anything less than required. The difference in rank of these 3 groups, and the level of their love for **Allâh** ﷻ can be understood from their spending. If you are unable to reach the first or second group, then strive to reach the lowest level of the second group, by giving more than compulsory amount, even if it be a small amount, because sufficing on only the compulsory amount, is the rank of the stingy. Ensure that no day passes by without giving some optional charity, even though it be a piece of bread, by which you will remove yourself from the category of the stingy.

If you possess nothing, then remember that charity is not restricted to the wealthy, so you are not excused. Spend in the path of **Allâh** ﷻ whatever you are able to spend i.e. honour, comfort, speech, actions e.g. visiting the

---

[1] Mukhtârah (80) and Hakim (1/414), etc.

sick, accompanying the bier (janâzah), assisting a person in need (lifting someone's load or supporting someone, interceding for someone, speaking good words like giving encouragement, or consoling someone etc.) All of these will be written as charity in your book of deeds. These are such actions of charity, for which wealth is not a requirement.

In zakâh and other charities, one should take extra precaution in five matters:

1. Give in secrecy – A hadith sharîf states "Verily, giving charity in secret extinguishes the anger of **Allâh** (ﷻ)."[1] The Muslim who spends with his right hand in such a manner that his left hand does not know what it (the right hand) spent, will be among one of the seven groups of people whom **Allâh** ﷻ will grant shade on the day when there will be no shade but His.[2]

**Allâh** ﷻ states," And if you conceal it, and give it to the poor then it is better for you." The wisdom behind this is, that the object of giving charity is to remove the evil quality of stinginess. However, in the action of giving charity, there is fear of developing the dangerous disease of giving in order to show others. By giving secretly, one will be saved from show and ostentation. When a person is placed in the grave, *riya* (show) personified as a snake, and stinginess personified as a scorpion, will inflict pain on one. Thus by not spending, and by being stingy, one is sending forth a scorpion to his grave to torment him.

If however, one spends, but his object is to show others, then it is as though he has made the scorpion food for the snake. In this case, he will attain salvation from the scorpion, but the poisonous effect of the snake will increase, because by fulfilling the demands of stinginess, the power of the scorpion will increase, and by fulfilling the demand to show others, the power of the snake will increase.

2. Abstain from boasting/broadcasting of your favour to others. Do not feel that you have favoured the person to whom you have given charity to. The sign of this is, for example, you anticipate that he shows gratitude to you, or if he has dealt with you in an unfavourable manner, or has love for

---

[1] Hâkim (3/568), Shuabul Imân (3168), Tabrânî in Kabîr (8/261)and Awsat (3474)
[2] Bukhari (660) and Muslim (1031)

your enemy, then you become angry to such an extent, that if he had done this without you giving him something, you would have not become so angry. This clearly shows that you feel that you have favoured this poor person; therefore you became upset with his conduct.

**The Cure:** Regard the poor person you are spending upon, as your benefactor, who by accepting your wealth, is releasing you from the right **Allâh** ﷻ has placed over you. He has become the cure for your ailment of stinginess, since you know that one of the objectives of zakâh and charity is to remove stinginess. Thus zakâh acts as a cleanser or remover of stinginess. It is for this reason that *Rasulullâh* ﷺ would not accept zakâh (for personal use), and he would say, "Verily zakâh is the filth of people's wealth."[1] So tell me, have **you** favoured the poor Muslim who takes your wealth, or has **he** favoured you? If any surgeon operates on you, free of charge and removes from your body blood etc. that causes harm to you, will you not regard him as your benefactor? In like manner, a person who, at no cost, removes the corrupt matter of stinginess from your heart, matter that will cause harm to your life of the Hereafter, should be regarded as your benefactor and well-wisher, to a greater extent.

3. You should spend from your purest and best wealth, because how can it be appropriate to spend that which you dislike for **Allâh** ﷻ's sake? You have already read, that the object of spending is to expose the level of your love. You will be able to gauge the level of love you possess for **Allâh** ﷻ, according to what you spend for His ﷻ sake.

4. You should give charity happily, and with a smiling face as *Rasulullâh* ﷺ said, "One dirham surpasses one hundred thousand dirhams."[2] What *Rasulullâh* ﷺ meant is that one dirham spent happily, with a good intention and from one's best wealth, is more virtuous than one hundred thousand dirhams spent unhappily.

5. Seek an appropriate avenue when giving charity i.e. give it to a pious scholar, who by using it will gain strength to obey **Allâh** ﷻ and his taqwâ (piety) will increase, or give it to a pious family man who has a large

---

[1] Muslim (1072), Abû Dawud (2985), Nasâî (5/105)
[2] Nasâî (5/59), Hâkim (1/416), Ibn Hibbân (3347), Ibn Khuzaimah (2443)

number of dependants. If these qualities are not found in one person, then give it those who possess even one of these qualities. Consideration for piety is the most important matter, as the worldly possessions have not been created except as a conveyance here, and to be utilized as provision for the Hereafter. Thus, spend on those travelling towards the Hereafter; on those who consider this world as a path needed to be crossed, in order to reach the Hereafter. *Rasulullâh* ﷺ said," Do not eat except the food of the pious, and let only the pious eat of your food."[1] *Rasulullâh* ﷺ also said, "Feed your food to the pious, and show good conduct to the believers."[2]

# THIRD PRINCIPLE

# SAUM (FASTING)

*Rasulullâh* ﷺ said, "**Allâh** ﷺ states, 'Every good action is multiplied by 10 to 700, except fasting, which is especially for Me, and I will give the reward for it.' "[3]

*Rasulullâh* ﷺ said, "Everything has a door, and the door of worship is fasting."[4]

Fasting possesses these specialities due to two factors :

1. Fasting refers to abstinence from eating, drinking and sexual relations. This is a hidden action which no one except **Allâh** ﷺ is aware of. Other forms of worship like salâh, zakâh, tilâwah, hajj etc. are such that can be seen by others. Only that Muslim will fast, who does not desire to be referred to as an âbid (worshipper) and zâhid (abstinent) by people, and who does not love show and ostentation.

2. The second factor is that it overpowers the enemy of **Allâh** ﷺ i.e. shaytân. The enemy cannot become strong except by means of one's *nafs*âni (egocentric) desires, which become forceful with a full stomach. Hunger crushes all these desires, which are the instruments of shaytân. For

---

[1] Abu Dawud (4832, Tirmidhi(2395), Hâkim (4/128)

[2] Abu Ya'lâ (1332), Ibn Hibbân (616, Ahmed (3/55)

[3] Muslim (164,1151), Nasâî (4/162), MuattaImâm Malik (1/310)

[4] Musnadul-Firdaus (4992), Zuhd of Ibnul Mubârak (1423)

this reason *Rasulullâh* ﷺ said," Verily shaytân flows in the children of *Adam* like blood."[1] Some commentators have said, "Thus close its avenues by hunger." This is the wisdom behind the above statement of *Rasulullâh* ﷺ.

With the onset of Ramadân, the doors of *Jannah* are opened, the doors of Hell are closed, the shâyatîn are chained, and a caller calls out."*O seeker of good, advance. O seeker of evil, desist.*"[2]

Know well that fasting is of 3 types with regards to its quality, and of 3 types with regards to its quantity.

As regards its quantity, the lowest level is that one suffices with fasting only in the month of Ramadân. The highest level is Sawm-e-Dâwûd i.e. to fast every alternate day. A hadith sharîf states, "This is more virtuous than continuous fasting."[3] and "This is the most virtuous form of fasting."[4]

The reason behind this is that, by continuous fasting, one becomes accustomed to it. Once fasting is a habit, one will then not feel humility, purity of heart and weakening of desires, because the carnal desires are affected by that which is tedious, and not by that which it is accustomed to. The doctors also prohibit a person from continuously drinking medicine, when not seriously ill. They state that continuous medicinal intake will result in that medicine losing its effect, and will not work when the person really falls seriously ill. When one's temperament becomes accustomed to something, it is not affected by it.

It is for this reason that *Rasulullâh* ﷺ said to Abdullah Ibn Amr ﷺ, when asked by him about fasting, "Fast for one day, and do not fast the next." He ﷺ said, "I have the strength to do more." *Rasulullâh* ﷺ said, "There is no rank higher than this."[5] Once, *Rasulullâh* ﷺ was informed of a person

---

[1] Bukhârî (2038), Muslim (2174)
[2] Nasâî (4/129), Musannaf Abdur Razzâq (4/176), Ahmad (4/312)
[3] Bukhârî (1979), Muslim (1159)
[4] Bukhârî (4765), Muslim (1159)
[5] Bukhârî (1976), Muslim (1159)

who kept continuous fasts. *Rasulullâh* ﷺ said "Keeping such fasts and not keeping them is the same."[1]

The intermediary level is that you fast a third of your life. Therefore, it is appropriate that besides the month of Rama<u>d</u>ân, weekly, you should fast on Mondays and Thursdays. This will amount to about 4 months and 4 days annually. However, since fasting on the 2 Eid days and Ayyâmut Tashrîq (3 days after Eidul-A<u>dh</u>a) is prohibited, and it is quite possible that the 2 Eids fall on 1 of these 2 days, and 1 of the days of Tashrîq will definitely fall either on a Monday or a Thursday, thus 4 months and 1 day remain. This is only 1 day more than 1/3 of 12 months (1 year).One can understand this calculation easily. It will be inappropriate (for those having the capacity) to fast less than this, as this can be done with ease, and it carries immense rewards.

As for the quality of fasts, they are also of 3 types:

1. To suffice with abstaining from eating, drinking, and fulfilling sexual desires. However, one does not prevent his limbs from engaging in sin. This is the fast of the general masses. This type of fasting is restricted to name only.

2. Together with abstaining from the above, one prevents one's limbs from any action contrary to the laws of Islam. Thus one controls his tongue from backbiting, his eyes form looking at strange women, and all other limbs as well.

3. Together with the above, to protect the heart from evil thoughts and evil whisperings, and keep the heart occupied with **Allâh** ﷺ only. This is the level of perfection. This is the fast of the elite. Since every person cannot attain such perfection, the least one can do, is break one's fast with halâl and pure food, in which there is no doubt whatsoever, and abstain from filling the stomach to the point where lustful desires are increased, which will result in the benefit of the fast being lost. This will lead to laziness, and the inability to wake up for Tahajjud. At times one might miss Fajr salâh as well. One should abstain from eating so much at the time of Iftâr, that it covers up for the food missed during the day.

---

[1] Muslim (1162), Hâkim (1/435)

# THE FOURTH PRINCIPLE

# HAJJ

**Allâh** ﷻ states," It is compulsory on people, for **Allâh** ﷻ's sake, to make Hajj of Baitullah (the House of **Allâh**), for those who have the ability to do so."

*Rasulullâh* ﷺ said, "Whoever passes away, and he has not performed Hajj, then let him die, if he wishes as a Jew or a Christian."[1]

In another hadith, *Rasulullâh* ﷺ has also stated, that Hajj is one of the five pillars of Islam.[2] We have mentioned the outward fundamentals of Hajj in *Ihyâ ul Ulûm*. Here we will only mention the etiquettes and hidden secrets of Hajj.

There are 7 etiquettes of Hajj:

1. Seek a pious companion as well as pure, wholesome, and halâl wealth for the journey. Halâl provisions will create nûr (effulgence) in the heart, and a pious companion will encourage you to perform righteous actions and prevent you from evil.

2. Remove any thought or intention of conducting business during the journey, as this will result in one's thoughts being diverted. One's intention must remain clean and pure.[3]

3. Be generous with food on the journey, and speak softly and kindly to travel companions, servants and hired assistants. Keep them happy.

4. Abstain from vulgar, immoral, futile, and worldly speech, and fighting. After fulfilling one's necessary needs, one should keep one's tongue moist with <u>dh</u>ikrullâh and tilâwah of Qurân Sharîf.

---

[1] Dârimî (1826), Bayhaqî in Kubrâ (4/334)

[2] Bukhârî (8), Muslim (16)

[3] The thought that Imam Ghazâlî ﷺ is advising against something for which the Qurân gives permission, should not be entertained, as he has not prohibited business per- se, and secondly, unlike the Sa<u>h</u>âba ﷺ, who conducted business in order to strengthen the dîn, people now perform Hajj in order to buy and sell and make profit during the journey.

5. Travel on a simple conveyance so as to avoid showing one's status. One should present oneself in the Court of **Allâh** ﷻ in a forlorn, dishevelled and dusty state with no beautification. One should be in the guise of a beggar, so that one is not written amongst the proud.[1]

6. At times, (if travelling by animal) descend from the conveyance, and walk. This will please the owner, and give some comfort to the animal. The activity will also keep your limbs feeling lively. Do not burden the conveyance with more than it can bear. Be as considerate as possible.

7. Be happy and pleased with whatever money is spent, and with whatever tiredness and loss one has to endure. One should regard this to be the effect of the acceptance of Hajj, and hope to receive reward for this.

## THE PHILOSOPHIES OF HAJJ

There is much wisdom underlying the actions of Hajj. Here we will only further elaborate on two points:

1. Hajj is a substitute for monasticism which was found in the past nations. A narration states that **Allâh** ﷻ made Hajj an act of monasticism for the ummah of *Rasulullâh* ﷺ. First **Allâh** ﷻ honoured Bait-e-Atîq (The Ancient House, i.e. the Ka'bah) by attributing it to Himself (calling it Baitullâh). He created it as a place where worshippers must proceed. He demarcated the area around it as Haram (sanctified place). He made Arafât like the courtyard of His Haram. He then emphasized the sanctity of the area by prohibiting hunting and cutting of plantations. It is apparent that **Allâh** ﷻ is free from place. He ﷻ is not in need of any house or residence. He ﷻ encompasses everything, and no place can encompass Him ﷻ.

By attributing the Ka'bah to Himself ﷻ, and commanding people to make tawâf (circumambulation) thereof, the underlying wisdom is to make apparent the servitude of His ﷻ servants, and to test them. Obedient servants will come from far, in huge numbers, to visit in a manner that their hair will be dishevelled, and they will be covered in dust, humbling

---

[1] Ml.Ashraf Alî Thânwî ﷺ explains that this is advised as to avoid showing one's social status as a means of pride. If this does not apply, there will be no harm if comfortable means are used in order to ease the journey.

themselves before **Allâh** ﷻ, and His Grandeur ﷻ, together with admitting that His Wholesome Being ﷻ, is Pure of any house or place surrounding Him ﷻ, so that this can be a great show of their servitude and slavery. For this reason **Allâh** ﷻ has stipulated some peculiar acts of worship, which is not in keeping with ones' nature and intellect, so that their actions can be based on mere servitude and obedience, having no other contaminating objective.

For this reason *Rasulullâh* ﷺ uttered, "*O* **Allâh**, we are present for Hajj, to make our servitude and bondage apparent."[1]

2. This journey has been made similar to the journey of the Hereafter. The person intending to perform Hajj should remember that every action of his, is similar to one stage of the Hereafter. For example, when one is bidding farewell to one's family at the commencement of the journey, one should think of bidding them farewell at the time of one's death. When leaving one's country, think of the separation from this world; when being carried by the conveyance, think of how you will be carried in the bier (janâzah); when wrapping oneself in the i<u>h</u>râm, think of being wrapped in the kafan; when crossing the desert into the boundaries of the <u>H</u>aram, think of crossing the valley of this life to the Hereafter i.e. the grave; at the time of fear of attack by highway robbers, think of the questioning by Munkar and Nakîr; when passing ferocious animals during the journey, think of the scorpions and insects in the grave; when separated from one's family and friends, think of the loneliness and dread of the grave; when reciting the *talbiyah* (Labayk Allâhumma labbayk), then think of all the people answering the caller of **Allâh** ﷻ at the time of resurrection. One should do this in every action. In every action there is wisdom, a lesson and a reminder for the Hereafter, which every servant according to his ability, purity of heart, and endeavour for the fulfilment of the compulsions of dîn, will be able to understand.

---

[1] Târikhe Baghdâd of Khatîb(14/218), Târikhe Dimashq of Ibn Asâkir (38/45)

# FIFTH PRINCIPLE

# TILÂWAT OF QURÂN SHARÎF

## VIRTUE OF TILÂWAT

*Rasulullâh* ﷺ said, "The most virtuous act of worship for my ummah is the recitation of the Qurân."[1]

In another hadith, *Rasulullâh* ﷺ said, "If the Qurân is placed in a leather bag, the fire will not burn it."[2]

*Rasulullâh* ﷺ also said, "On the Day of Judgement, there will not be a greater intercessor, than the Qurân, neither a *Nabî* ﷺ, nor an angel, nor anyone else."[3]

In a Hadith-e-Qudsî, **Allâh** ﷻ states, "Whoever is so pre-occupied with recital of Qurân, that he cannot ask of Me, then I will give him more than that which I will give to those who ask."[4]

## EXTERNAL ETIQUETTES

There are 3 outward/external etiquettes to be observed when reciting the Qurân Sharîf:

1. Whilst reciting, one's heart should have honour and reverence for the speech of **Allâh** ﷻ. Since the outward has a great effect on the inward, if one adopts an outward form of reverence and respect, then reverence and respect will also present itself in the heart. The outward form of reverence is that after performing wudu, one should sit motionless, lowering the head slightly, facing the direction of the Qiblah in the tashahhud position (not sitting cross-legged, leaning or lying down), just as if you were sitting in front of your ustadh (teacher). Recite the Qurân according to the laws of tajwîd, with every letter being pronounced from its correct makhraj. Read distinctly, without rushing. Ibn Abbâs ﷺ said," My recitation of

---

[1] Shua'bul Imân (1865)

[2] Shua'bul Imân (2443), Ahmad (4/151), Sunan of Dârimî (3353)

[3] Abdul Malik ibn Habîb has narrated it in a mursal form from Saîd ibn Salîm

[4] Shua'bul Imân (1860), Du'afâ of Uqualî (4/1214)

Surah Qadr and Al Qâria'h whilst pondering over its meaning, is more beloved to me, than reciting Surah Baqarah and Âle-Imrân very hastily."[1]

(Note: By reciting hastily, the words are usually not understood. Disrespect is thus apparent. However, if one recites the words of the Qurân Sharîf correctly, and does not understand the meaning, then this does not constitute disrespect, but will earn one reward.)

2. At times you should aim to attain the greatest virtue of tilâwah, as you have come into this world for the commerce of the Hereafter. Therefore, wherever possible, make an effort to attain the maximum profits. Most definitely, tilawah of the Qurân Sharîf is full of virtue, whether recited whilst walking, sitting or lying down, with wudu or without wudu (i.e. from memory, without touching the text or pages), in solitude, and in public. However, the greatest benefit is when one recites Qurân Sharîf at night, especially in the masjid, whilst performing salâh.

Ali ﷺ said," Whoever recites the Qurân whilst standing in salâh will receive 100 rewards for every letter. Whoever recites the Qurân whilst sitting in salâh, will receive 50 rewards for every letter. Whoever recites the Qurân out of salâh, in the state of wudu will receive 25 rewards, and whoever recites the Qurân without wudu (from memory), will receive 10 rewards."[2]

Now why should one not become a businessman of the Hereafter, and be desirous of attaining the greatest benefit?

3. Keep in mind the amount of tilawâh made. The lowest level is to make one khatam (complete recital) every month, and the highest level is to make one khatam every three days (which equals to 10 khatams in a month). *Rasulullâh* ﷺ said, "Whoever recites the Qurân in less than 3 days, has not understood it."[3]

The moderate level is to make a khatam every week. As far as completing a khatam every day is concerned, this is against the preferred (mustahab)

---


[1] Shua'bul Imân (1971)
[2] Fawâid of Tamâm Râzi in a marfu' form (301)
[3] Abû Dâwûd(1394), Tirmidhi(2949), Nasâî in Kubrâ(8013).

method. Do not think that since tilâwah of **Allâh** ﷻ's speech is beneficial, the more tilâwah that is made, the more the reward. This deduction (*qiyâs*) of yours is incorrect. Understanding the wisdoms and secrets of **Allâh** ﷻ is the work of the *Ambiyâ* ﷺ. Now when *Rasulullâh* ﷺ has stated that to make a khatam in less than 3 days is not preferred, then it is necessary upon you to follow him. To now use your opinion is an act of foolishness, and shows a lack of understanding.

You know that medicine benefits a sick person. However, if you give a patient more than the dose prescribed by the doctor, will his illness increase or decrease? In the like manner, even though salâh is the core of all other acts of worship, it is not permissible to perform salâh at sunrise, midday, and sunset, and it is makrûh (abhorred) to perform it after the fardh of Fajr and Asr. When a person accepts the prescription of a physical doctor wholeheartedly, then what is the reason for him not considering the 'dose' prescribed by the spiritual (rûhâni) doctor? How can he use his intellect and ask, "Why is it not permissible to complete a khatam in less than 3 days?"

## INTERNAL ETIQUETTES

There are 5 internal etiquettes to be observed when reciting the Qurân Sharîf:

1) Just as one possesses the Awe and Majesty of **Allâh** ﷻ in his heart, similarly, he should possess the Awe and Majesty of **Allâh** ﷻ's speech in his heart. For example, when one thinks of **Allâh** ﷻ's Creation i.e. the Arsh (Throne), the Kursi (Chair), the Lowh (Protected Tablet), the Qalam (Pen), the heaven and earth, animals and human beings, the jinn, the forestry and plantation, and the minerals, then one will be forced to accept the fact that the Creator ﷻ of this universe, the One ﷻ who is Alone and possesses no partner , is very Powerful ﷻ and is such a Fashioner ﷻ, whose Power ﷻ has no limits. The existence of the entire universe and beyond, is based only on His ﷻ Grace and Kindness. To obey such a lofty and Majestic Sovereign ﷻ, is compulsory. Thus how much of respect and honour should one not possess for the Qurân Majîd? Remember, just as it is necessary to be in a state of purity and wu<u>d</u>u to touch the Qurân, it is also necessary for one's heart to be in the state of purity, and to be free

from all evil qualities, in order to understand the real meaning and essence of the Qurân, and to welcome it into the heart. How can a heart soiled with internal filth and impurities comprehend the realities of this Honourable Royal Edict? For this reason Ikramah ﷺ many a times would fall unconscious on opening the Mus'haf (Qurân Sharîf). He would repeat, "This is the speech of my Sustainer, this is the speech of my Sustainer"[1]

## WISDOM OF CONCEALING THE DIVINE SPEECH IN THE APPAREL OF WORDS

It is **Allâh** ﷺ's Great Mercy that He ﷺ has handed over the radiance and light of His Majestic Speech to you, cloaked in the apparel of words. Otherwise, no human can bear or withstand its illuminated rays. Note, even a mountain like Tûr was unable to bear the illuminating power (Tajalliyât) of Divine Speech, and as a result it was pulverized. If **Allâh** ﷺ had not kept Mûsâ عليه السلام firm, he too, would not have been able to hear His ﷺ speech, which is free from the cloak of letters and sounds.

2) Recite the Qurân Sharif without haste, pondering over its meaning. If you understand the meaning of the Qurân Sharif, then do not read even one verse without understanding it, because the 'tartîl' that we are commanded to observe in the Qurân Sharif, is so that one can ponder deeply and contemplate.

Ali ﷺ said, "There is no goodness in that act of worship in which there is no understanding, and in that recitation in which there is no contemplation"[2] Do not worry about increasing the number of khatams without understanding. Your recitation of one verse the entire night, pondering over it, is better than making two khatams. Note, *Rasulullâh* ﷺ once repeated بسم الله الرحمن الرحيم 20 times.[3] Abu <u>Dh</u>arr ﷺ states, "Once *Rasulullâh* ﷺ recited a verse over and over. The verse was :

---

[1] Tabrânî in Kabîr (17/371, Majmauz Zawâ'id (9/388)

[2] Sunan of Dâramî (305), Hilyah of Abû Nu'aym(1/77)

[3] Abu <u>Dh</u>arr Al-Harawî in his Mu'jam narrates from Abû Hurairah ﷺ with a <u>d</u>a'îf sanad

$$\text{إِن تُعَذِّبْهُمْ فَإِنَّهُمْ عِبَادُكَ وَإِن تَغْفِرْ لَهُمْ فَإِنَّكَ أَنتَ الْعَزِيزُ الْحَكِيمُ}$$

*"O **Allâh** ! If You punish them, then they are your servants; and if You forgive them, then verily You are the Most Powerful, the Most Wise."*[1]

Once Tamîm Dâri ﷺ stood the whole night in salâh reciting the following verse

$$\text{أَمْ حَسِبَ الَّذِينَ اجْتَرَحُوا السَّيِّئَاتِ أَن نَّجْعَلَهُمْ كَالَّذِينَ آمَنُوا وَعَمِلُوا الصَّالِحَاتِ سَوَاءً مَّحْيَاهُمْ وَمَمَاتُهُمْ سَاءَ مَا يَحْكُمُونَ}$$

*"Do those who commit evil think that We will make them like those who believe and do good actions?"*

Saî'd ibn Jubair ﷺ one night recited the following verse, till the morning

$$\text{وَامْتَازُوا الْيَوْمَ أَيُّهَا الْمُجْرِمُونَ}$$

*"O Sinners! Be separated today."*

One ârif said, "One khatam I finish weekly, one khatam I finish monthly, one khatam I finish yearly, and my one khatam is such that I have been busy reading it for the past 30 years, and I have not as yet completed it." These differences are due to the time spent in pondering and contemplation, since one's mental strength is fluctuating, and it is not always in the same state, thus is it not always possible to delve into the depths of Qurânic knowledge. Therefore, if one khatam is kept especially for this purpose, whereby you ponder while reciting, and you recite only at a time when you are able to ponder, when your heart is completely unoccupied at that time, and you can thus understand the meaning properly, then this would be excellent, as there will be no harm caused to your normal khatam recital and you will gain the above as an additional virtue.

3) One should strive to recognize the special meaning of each verse. Whilst pondering, harvest the fruits of *ma'rifat* (Divine recognition) from its different branches. Every fruit comes from a different branch. Every mineral is found in a different mine. Do not seek a remedy from the place where gems are sought, and do not seek gems from a place where musk

---

[1] Hâkim (1/241), Nasâî(2/177), Ahmed(5/149), Ibn Mâjah(1350)

and amber are extracted. Similarly, strive to attain the recognition of the Qurânic verses, for which they were revealed. For example, where **Allâh** ﷻ has mentioned His ﷻ Pure Being, Attributes and Actions, gain the recognition of His ﷻ Grandeur and Greatness. Where mention is made of being guided to the straight path, gain the recognition of His ﷻ Mercy, Compassion and Wisdom. Where mention is made of the destruction of His ﷻ enemies, gain the recognition of His ﷻ Independence, Power and Control ﷻ. As for the verses in which the *Ambiyâ* عليهم السلام are mentioned, gain the recognition of His ﷻ Bounties, Grace and Kindness. In short, according to the subject matter mentioned, gain that recognition.

4) One should try and remove all such impediments which hinder one from the understanding of the Qurân. For those of weak îmân, desires of the *nafs* and shaytâni whispers (those which are intentionally entertained in the heart) become a barrier, as their souls are joined to their temporal attachments, and their hearts are soiled with doubts and misgivings. These cover the heart resulting in one being unable to understand the subtle, and finer meanings of the Qurân Majîd. Make an effort to remove these. As for those whose îmân is strong, whose love for **Allâh** ﷻ is growing in their hearts, and they begin attaining pleasure in His ﷻ obedience, they too are affected by whispers in their hearts e.g. whilst in salâh their hearts become focussed on the type of intention they had made, and as to whether the sincerity they possessed at the commencement of salâh is still intact or not.

Another example is that of one doubting whether he correctly pronounced the letters from their makhârij, following which, he continuously repeats the verse in order to correct the recitation, whereas this is also a barrier for the heart. To be completely engrossed in the letters and in correcting them, and well as being absorbed in their makhârij i.e. the teeth, lips, palate and throat, (for example, worrying about where the letter emerges from, and whether it has emerged correctly etc.) this is not the work of the one who desires to traverse the higher realms and witness angelic matters.

5.) Together with recognition, one should establish qualities and their effects as well. One should not suffice with the recognition and tajalliyat (manifestation) of the verses of the Divine Speech only. Its effects should also be visible on one; e.g. if you read a verse in which His Mercy ﷻ is mentioned, and Forgiveness is promised, then engender the quality of happiness within yourself. When His ﷻ Anger and Punishment is mentioned, then you should shiver and tremble. When the Name of **Allâh** ﷻ is taken and His ﷻ Grandeur and Majesty is mentioned, then lower yourself and feel insignificant, as if you are annihilated due to beholding His ﷻ Grandeur. When the nonsensical behaviour of the disbelievers are mentioned, such as attributing sons and a wife to **Allâh** ﷻ, then lower your head due to shame, and you should lower your voice as well, as if it is difficult for you to even utter it.

In short, according to the subject matter of the verse, establish the relevant condition in your heart, and leave such an effect on the body that when verses of fear are mentioned, tears should flow from the eyes; when shame is mentioned, perspiration should ooze from the forehead; when terror is mentioned, the hairs should stand on end; and when glad tidings are mentioned, happiness should be present in the voice, on the tongue and limbs.

# SIXTH PRINCIPLE

# <u>DH</u>IKR OF ALLÂH ﷻ IN ALL CONDITIONS

**Allâh** ﷻ states, "Make the <u>dh</u>ikr of **Allâh** ﷻ in great abundance so that you may be successful."
*Rasulullâh* ﷺ said, "The <u>dh</u>ikr of **Allâh** ﷻ morning and evening is better than brandishing swords in the path of **Allâh** ﷻ, and giving wealth in great abundance."[1] From this we learn that no action is more virtuous than the <u>dh</u>ikr of **Allâh** ﷻ. The <u>dh</u>ikr of **Allâh** ﷻ has a core and three coverings. The core is the object, and the coverings are desired and beloved, as they are the medium through which the core is reached.

The outermost covering is mere verbal <u>dh</u>ikr. The second covering is <u>dh</u>ikr with the heart, and forcefully becoming accustomed to it. One should not leave the heart unattended, as it will become perturbed due to falling into

---

[1] Ibn <u>Sh</u>âhîn from Ibn Umar ﷺ in a marfû' manner, Musnad Firdaws (5402) etc.

different thoughts and notions. Therefore, it is appropriate that it be handed its most beloved i.e. dhikr-e-îlâhî, so that solace could be attained.

The third covering is when dhikr with the heart becomes so entrenched, that it becomes difficult for one to leave it. This means that just as it was difficult to become accustomed to the dhikr mentioned in the second covering above, it will become more difficult to abstain from remembering **Allâh** ﷻ in the third stage.

## THE REALITY OF FANÂ AND FANÂ-UL-FANÂ

The fourth level which is the seed and actual objective, is when the name and signs of dhikr do not remain in the heart, only the Madhkur (One being remembered) i.e. **Allâh** ﷻ alone remains. One's attention is not to the heart, not towards the dhikr, neither to one's self, nor to anything else, in short, one becomes completely absorbed in **Allâh** ﷻ's Being. This condition is referred to as fanâ.

When one reaches this stage, the servant is neither aware of his outward actions, nor of his inner situation. Eventually, the awareness of him being annihilated too, does not even remain, because this also ghairullah, i.e. something other than **Allâh** ﷻ. Thinking of anything other than **Allâh** ﷻ, is contamination and a blemish. When one reaches this stage, even knowledge of fanâ is distant and soiled. In this condition, together with annihilation of one's existence, one's annihilation is also annihilated.

To understand such engrossment seems difficult. In fact, outwardly it seems impossible, and a claim without any proof. However, if by chance you become enamoured with some beautiful woman, or you see someone madly in love, then it will not be difficult for you to understand this condition. Does an infatuated person not remain so engrossed and immersed in the thoughts and remembrance of his beloved that at times, he utters something which he himself does not understand? He wants to place his foot in one place, but it lands elsewhere. A person walks past him, his eyes are open, yet he does not see the person walking past. Another person speaks to him, but he does not hear. If he is asked, "What have you seen? What have you heard?" he is unable to even give an answer! He is so engrossed, that he possesses no knowledge of his engrossment. He has become mad, and to such a degree that he is unaware of his madness. This is the effect of being completely absorbed in the thoughts of this desirable beloved of his.

An example that is even easier to understand, is that you have love for your wealth and self respect. If, **Allâh** ﷻ forbid, your enemy attacks these, then imagine how angry and incited you become. Your condition is one of unawareness. In anger, you neither think of yourself nor anyone else. You become so unaware, that at that moment you have no clue of this unawareness of yours. So why the astonishment if a servant becomes so engrossed in the thoughts of his Master ﷻ, that he even forgets his engrossment?

We have mentioned these examples by way of illustration. The reality is that when one, through **Allâh** ﷻ 's Grace, reaches this stage, then only will one understand the actual reality of fanâ and fanâ-ul-fanâ.

# SEVENTH PRINCIPLE

# SEEKING HALÂL SUSTENANCE

**Allâh** ﷻ has linked the consumption of halâl and pure food with worship. **Allâh** ﷻ states, "Eat from the pure foods and perform good deeds." *Rasulullâh* ﷺ said, "Seeking of halâl sustenance is a compulsory duty on every Muslim, after the other compulsory duties (i.e. *imân* and salâh)."[1] Abdullah Ibn Umar ؓ said, "If you perform salâh until you become bent like a bow, and you fast so much that become thin like gut, **Allâh** ﷻ will not accept this from you, without such piety that prevents you from harâm." Making ibâdah together with consuming harâm is like building a house on excrement.

Remember, pure food has a great influence in purifying the heart and enlightening it. Thus, it is of utmost importance that one abstains from harâm wealth and adopts taqwâ (piety).

Taqwâ (piety) has four levels:

---

[1] Tabrânî in Kabîr (10/74), Bayhaqî in Kubrâ (6/128)

1.Do not use such things or wealth that the jurists and ulamâ have declared harâm (forbidden), as using these will result in one becoming a fâsiq (open rebellious sinner), and his testimony will be rejected in court. This is the level of piety of the common Muslim.

2. The second level of piety is that of the sulaḫâ (pious). This means that one should abstain from doubtful things, even though the Muftis, based on outwards circumstances, have declared them to be halâl. However, these items are such, that there is a possibility of ḫurmat (prohibition, thus they become doubtful. The sulaḫâ abstain from such type of food.

*Rasulullâh* ﷺ said, "Leave that in which there is doubt, for that in which you do not have doubt."[1]

3. The third level is that of the atqiyâ (those having taqwâ/abstinent). *Rasulullâh* ﷺ said, "A person cannot reach the rank of the muttaqin (those having taqwâ), until he does not leave out the harmless things, for fear of getting engaged in those things in which there is harm."[2]
Umar ؓ used to say, "We used to leave out nine-tenths of halâl, out of fear of falling into harâm."[3] Based on this principle, some of **Allâh** ﷻ's pious servants would only suffice on 99 dirhams when they were eligible to receive 100. When they had to fulfil anyone's right, they would give extra. When claiming their right, they would take less![4]
Umar bin Abdul Aziz ؓ would cover his nose, when musk was weighed in his presence in the Baitul-Mâl (public treasury).When asked regarding this, he remarked, "The benefit of it is in its fragrance."[5]

This is the reason for abstaining from delicious halâl food, and permissible forms of beautification. There is fear that once habituated to it, one's *nafs* will overpower a person, and thereafter lead him to prohibited desires. The

---

[1]Ibn Hibbân(722), Tirmiḏhi (2518), Hâkim (2/13)
[2] Tirmiḏhi (2451), Hâkim (4/319), Ibn Mâjah (4215)
[3] Musannaf of Abdur Razâq (8/152)
[4] Note, this extra amount is not regarded as interest, since there was no condition of paying anything extra attached to the loan when it was granted.  This is merely an act of kindness and favour, that one grants to another, without the receiver having any claim to it, i.e. the extra is a gift.
[5] Abu Nua'ym in Hilyah, Bayhaqî in Az-Zuhdul Kabîr (919), Taârikhe Dimishq (28/64)

prohibition of the Qurân of longingly gazing at the abundance of wealth and material chattels of the disbelievers, and towards their status and honour, is because the beauty and lustre of one's îmân diminishes, due to this outward glamour. When the love and desire of worldly wealth and goods overtakes one, the love of îmân does not remain in the heart. A pious person once said, "He whose clothing is thin, his dîn is also thin." In short, according to the abstinent, only that wealth which is halâl, is presently devoid of any form of doubt, and devoid of any possibility of causing harm in future, is worthy of consumption.

4. The fourth level is of the siddiqîn i.e. they abstain from eating all such foods from which one does not gain strength to perform acts of worship and obedience. An incident is mentioned of a sage who drank some medicine. His wife asked him to take a small walk. He answered, "I do not see a need for such a futile action. I take stock of my every move." Similarly, it is necessary in this stage, to abstain from anything that has been contaminated by sin, prior to it reaching you. Once, Zunnun Misri ﷺ was unjustly imprisoned. Finding him hungry, a pious woman sent him some food, which was prepared from her halâl wealth. The prison guard gave the food to him. He did not eat from it, and returned it saying, "Even though the food is halâl, the plate is impure," referring to the hands of the prison guard, as he was guilty of enforcing the unjust imprisonment. That food that has been contaminated by the touch of the oppressor, was now unfit for consumption. Bishr Hâfî ﷺ would not drink water from canals dug by oppressive rulers. When the slave of a pious man once lit his lantern at the house of an oppressor, the pious man extinguished it saying, "It is not appropriate to take benefit from a lamp lit from the lamp of **Allâh** ﷻ's disobedient servants."

The essence of the matter is that these pious people practice on the verse :

$$\text{قُلِ اللَّهُ ثُمَّ ذَرْهُمْ فِي خَوْضِهِمْ يَلْعَبُونَ}$$

*"Say **Allâh**, then leave all else,"*

in its entirety. They would never use anything in which **Allâh** ﷻ's Pleasure was not intended.

Since reaching this rank is not easy, the least one should endeavour to attain is the rank of the trustworthy Muslims, i.e. do not indulge in those things that the ulemâ have declared harâm. However, with regards to this, one should keep two points in mind:

1) Do not turn your attention to some loopholes that some jurists have mentioned regarding some masâ'il. For example, before the end of one year, you hand over all your money to your wife and she hands over all her wealth to you. Since your wealth has not remained in your possession for one full year, zakâh does not become compulsory. Never use loopholes of this sort. Since the speciality of the fuqahâ (jurists) is administration and regulation of laws, the meaning of passing a fatwa stating that obligation for zakâh will be waived, is understood in the context where a Muslim ruler will demand zakâh on zakaatable wealth in one's possession for a full year. However, in the above case, the zakâh collector will not call on this wealthy Muslim, as the wealth was not in his possession for a full year, since it was transferred to his wife's ownership. However, since this affair is directly linked with His Creator ﷻ, and He ﷻ, is fully aware of what transpires in the hearts, this type of deception will be of no benefit in the Hereafter. The object of zakâh is to expel the evil habit of stinginess. How can the stinginess be removed if one abstains from paying zakâh, by seeking loopholes? In fact, stinginess has now become your leader, whom you regard as worthy of obedience, since you have accepted it to such an extent, that you regard it as a means of salvation, and you are prepared to present it before **Allâh** ﷻ. Thus, in this case, you have not attained the objective of zakâh at all. You have not turned your attention to the benefit that **Allâh** ﷻ has placed in it. In fact, you have done the complete opposite, in that instead of ejecting stinginess, you have caused it to flourish.

Another example is that of a man who ill-treats his wife, until eventually she excuses him from paying her the mahr or dowry that is due to her. When this poor woman, in order to obtain relief from this torment, is terrified and utters the words of forgiveness, then the husband becomes satisfied, and regards such exemption as being valid, and believes that the retained mahr is halâl for himself.

How can such wealth ever be halâl for him? **Allâh** ﷻ clearly states:

فَإِن طِبْنَ لَكُمْ عَن شَيْءٍ مِّنْهُ نَفْسًا

This means that if she happily exempts her husband from paying the dowry, then it is halâl for him. If the dowry was waived in order to obtain relief from ill-treatment, can this be regarded as happy consent?

## FINE DIFFERENCE BETWEEN HAPPINESS OF THE HEART AND HAPPINESS OF THE *NAFS* (SELF)

Happiness of the heart and happiness of the self (*nafs*) are two different things. Cupping, taking bitter medicines, venesection, cauterising boils and sores, etc. are such difficulties which are distasteful to the self, but pleasing to the heart. The *nafs* desires things that grant it immediate enjoyment. However, the heart prefers those things, which even though presently cause difficulty, will eventually lead to attainment of future benefit. The self is not willing to undergo any difficulty, irrespective of future comfort. If the wife, due to her husband's pressure, becomes afraid of her husband causing further difficulty to her, decides to forgive the dowry, keeping in mind the future benefits and comforts, that will be a result of this action, then this is due to the pleasure of the heart, and not the self. However, the verse mentioned takes into consideration the happiness of the self and not that of the heart, when waiving the dowry. By means of the above loophole, no ruler or king can demand that he pay the dowry, but how secure will he be in front of **Allâh** ﷻ? What answer will he offer the Ruler ﷻ of rulers, when the question will be posed to him, "Why did you consume the right of this weak and helpless lady, contrary to Our Permission?"

In the like manner, do not stretch out your hands before anyone, since begging is an evil habit. If at the time of extreme necessity, one is forced to ask then never ask in a gathering. Generally, in such conditions, the one who gives will do so to save himself from embarrassment and disgrace in front of others present in the gathering. This is not happiness of the self. Money given in this manner cannot be used. There is no difference in extorting money from someone by physically whipping them and extorting money using the whip of shame on his conscience. Both are extortion.

Do not make your religion a means of your livelihood. For example, do not don the garments of the pious with the intention of being regarded as a pious person, and as such, become the recipient of their monetary favours, whereas, in fact, you are completely useless and your heart is contaminated with filth. Remember, the wealth given to you by others is only halâl when your internal condition is not so bad that if the giver comes to know of it, he will abstain from giving. Thus, if you have imitated the outward form of the pious, and your heart is inundated with sensual desires, it is obvious that the giver has only considered your external and is completely unaware of your spiritual contamination, thus even though the ulamâ will regard it as halâl, since they rule on the external matters, the person of insight will regard it as harâm, and will not allow one to make use of it.

## NECESSITY OF SEEKING A RULING FROM THE HEART

The second point that must be kept in mind is that you should not suffice on the fatwa of the ulamâ. Peek into your heart and see what it says. *Rasulullâh* ﷺ said, "Seek a verdict from your heart, even though the Mufti has given a verdict."[1] The reason is that sin will definitely prick the conscience of a believer. Anything which causes harm to one, will certainly result in the heart being overcome by anxiety. Thus, that thing which in reality is harâm, or that action which is actually a sin, will not be accepted by your heart, without apprehension. In this way, one can come to know the ruling of the origin of everything, according to the verdict of the heart.

## ABSTENTION FROM EXTREMISM

However, do not be too hard on the self (*nafs*). For example, you say to yourself," Where can one find such wealth that is not doubtful, and which has not passed through the hands of an oppressor or sinner?" When one does not acquire such wholesome wealth, one either suffices on grass, or if he cannot manage this, he becomes audacious, eating any and everything. Such a thought is deviant and erroneous. Remember, halâl is clear and harâm is clear. In between the two, are such things that are doubtful. You are only liable for acquiring wealth that is halâl according to the Shariah. If

---

[1] Sunan of Dârimî (2575), Ahmed (4/228), Abû Ya'lâ in his Musnad (1586)

you are unaware of any outward cause of it being impure or harâm, then regard it as halâl, and make use of it. *Rasulullâh* ﷺ once made wu<u>d</u>u with water from the leather bag of a polytheist, and Umar ﷺ used water from the pitcher of a Christian woman. Had they been thirsty, they would have drunk from it. From here, we come to know that to have unnecessary doubts, regarding whether something is pure or impure, permissible or impermissible, is not correct. In the absence of a clear outward factor making it impure or impermissible, regard it as pure and permissible. Similarly, whatever object you find in the hand of a person whose condition is unknown to you, regard it as pure and hold good thoughts of your Muslim brother. Think that whatever wealth is in the possession of the Muslims, will definitely be from pure and halâl sources. Therefore accept his invitations as well. This will apply to a greater degree if the Muslim is pious and noble as well. Yes, one should not consider halâl that wealth which reaches you from an oppressive ruler, or person who deals with interest, or sells alcohol, until you ascertain as to where he obtained the wealth.

After investigation, if you are satisfied that it is not from these sources then it would be permissible to take it. If the majority of a person's wealth is halâl, and a small portion is harâm, then too, it will be permissible to consume from it. However, abstention therefrom is regarded as a level of piety. An associate of Abdullah ibn Mubârak ﷺ in Basrah wrote to him, asking whether he could transact with a person who had dealings with an oppressive ruler. The learned scholar replied, "If he deals with the ruler only, then do not deal with him. If he deals with others as well, then you may deal with him."

In short there are six groups of people and the law regarding each one is different:

1) Those people whose condition of piety and impiety, as well as their manner of earning is unknown to you. Such people's wealth is permissible, and it is not necessary to abstain from it. However, due to caution if one does not consume from it, it will be included in taqwâ.

2) Those people whose piety is known to you. To have doubts on this wealth is satanic whisperings. If abstaining from this wealth causes hurt to

such a person, then this abstinence is a sin and harâm, due to causing undue hurt to, and having bad thoughts about a pious man.

3) Those people whose wealth, either all of it, or most of it (more than 50%) has been procured by oppression, interest, or selling of any harâm items. Their wealth is harâm, and it is binding upon one to abstain from it.

4) Those people whose wealth is tainted with harâm. The majority of their money is halâl e.g. a person has two halâl means of income. One is his business, and the other is some property from which he earns an income, which he had acquired through inheritance. However, one avenue of his income is harâm e.g. he is also employed by an oppressive ruler, and receives a salary from him. The money earned from the other two avenues is more than the latter. Since the majority of his wealth is halâl, his wealth will be regarded as halâl. However, if one abstains there from then this will also be included in taqwâ.

5) Those people whose means of income are unknown; however the signs of oppression are apparent on them e.g. they don the clothing, or the appearance of an oppressive ruler's government. Since this outward sign shows that their wealth was most likely received in an oppressive manner, it should not be regarded as halâl without investigating first.

6) Those people upon whom the signs of oppression are not seen. However, the effects of sin are visible on them e.g. a shaved beard, long moustache, un-Islamic hair-cut, uttering vulgarities, talking or gazing at strange women (women with whom one is not permitted to speak to freely in the Shariah). Even though all these actions are prohibited in the shariah, since they have no bearing on how the wealth was earned, the wealth will not be regarded as harâm. If you come to know that it was attained through inheritance or some other permissible means, then regard it as halâl. *Rasulullâh* ﷺ did not regard the water of a polytheist to be impure. When Christianity and Fire-worshipping do not make water impure or doubtful, then how can a Muslim's wealth become impure merely do to him sinning and transgressing? However, if you are unaware of him having any permissible avenues of earning, then you should be cautious in eating from his wealth. (However, it will not be regarded as harâm)

After having mentioned the above we advise that one should seek a verdict from his heart. If one feels uneasy, he should never utilize that wealth. However, by acting on the verdict of your heart and choosing taqwâ, ensure that the person concerned is not hurt or upset.

## SUCH INVESTIGATION WHICH CAUSES HURT TO A MUSLIM IS IMPERMISSIBLE

If there is a fear of causing any distress, then such taqwâ is not permissible e.g. a Muslim person whose condition is unknown to you presents a gift to you or invites you for meals. Due to your piety you begin investigating the source of his wealth. It is obvious that you will either ask him regarding it, or enquire from others secretly. If you ask him directly, he will feel hurt. If you have to ask others, and he comes to know about it, then besides causing him distress, you have entertained an evil thought of a Muslim brother, and there is a fear of falling into backbiting and false accusations, all of which are prohibited. To abstain from taqwâ is not harâm in this context. Thus, at such occasions to please the heart of a Muslim is compulsory. Without any second thoughts, *Rasulullâh* ﷺ ate the food of his slave girl, Barîrah ؓ which some Muslims had given to her as charity. He neither asked her about the wealth nor the condition of the one who had given the charity. However, when *Rasulullâh* ﷺ arrived in Madinah Munawwarah, he would enquire regarding that which was presented to him, whether it was a gift or charity. The reason was that the wealth of charity was not permissible for him, and there was no fear of causing distress by asking. Charity and gifts have the same external form - the only difference lies in the intention of the giver, and to who it can be given. *Rasulullâh* ﷺ did not ask more than this e.g. how and from where it was attained. It was *Rasulullâh* ﷺ's habit to accept the invitation of every Muslim. There is no record of *Rasulullâh* ﷺ asking "From where did you acquire your wealth?" Occasionally, when there was a strong doubt, then only *Rasulullâh* ﷺ investigated.

## ITEMS IN THE MARKET ARE HALÂL

During their journeys, *Rasulullâh* ﷺ and the Sahâbah ؓ would buy and consume all their necessities from the local market places, even though they were aware that in the market places were usurers, usurpers and those who have embezzled booty. Then too, they dealt with them **without** investigation. They regarded all the wealth and items to be halâl, due to the majority of it being halâl. However, if in any city or market place items obtained through prohibited means are sold in great abundance, then it will not be permissible to buy and use the goods without prior investigation.

# EIGHTH PRINCIPLE

# FULFILLING THE RIGHTS OF MUSLIMS AND DEALING FAVOURABLY WITH THEM

This is an important branch of dîn, since dîn means to travel to **Allâh** ﷻ, and an important fundamental of travelling, is to be considerate of one's fellow travellers. All of creation is also travelling, their lives moving with them, just as a ship moves with its passengers.

The condition of man is one of the following:
1.) Isolated and alone
2.) With the creation in general
3.) With one's close associates such as family, friends, neighbours, etc

It is necessary for one to fulfil the rights that are due from him, and to deal favourably with others in all the above conditions.

## THE RIGHTS OF A PERSON IN ISOLATION

It is necessary for man to reform himself, and to fulfil the rights of the internal army which **Allâh** ﷻ has created in this minor universe (âlame asghar) i.e. his own body. Since our objective is brevity, we will suffice by mentioning the commanders of this army, so that one can be vigilant in protecting and guarding them.

The faculty of desire has been created with every person, due to which one will make an effort to acquire anything beneficial and favourable. The faculty of anger has been created to repel every disliked and harmful thing.

The faculty of intellect has been created, by which one can manage one's affairs and ponder over its result. By means of the intellect, man can control all those subservient to him.

Regard your anger as a dog, your desire as a horse, and your intellect as the king. Understand that these three faculties have been placed under your control so that you can establish equilibrium between them, fulfil their rights and seek assistance from them so that you may attain eternal bliss.

If you discipline the horse, train the dog and subjugate them to the king, it will become simple for you to attain success in your endeavours. If on the other hand you use the intellect to seek loopholes, in order to fulfil the desires of the dog with its anger and fighting, and the horse with its greed and craving, then instead of reaching your goal, you will attain nothing. You will be referred to as a zâlim (oppressor), because zulm (oppression) refers to placing something in a place where it doesn't belong.

When your faculty of desire wishes to acquire something, or your faculty of anger desires to repel something, then ponder using your faculty of intellect as to what would the consequences thereof be. If the result is good, then the intellect should allow them to act accordingly. If the result is harmful, it should never grant permission, but should command its other subordinates to arrest it; e.g. if the desires of the *nafs* become unrestrained, then command anger to attack it, and to chain this foolish servant. If anger is inflamed and desires to wander unrestricted, then command the desire to attack it to cool it down, so that it does not give vent to its thoughts. If you did not ask your intellect, or you asked it, but did not obey it, you have made it the slave and the servant of its slave. Your intellect now plans how to fulfil its slave's wishes. You have inverted the natural system and have done a great injustice with regard to those matters in which **Allâh** ﷻ commanded one to be fair and just. On the day of judgment when all intangible objects (a'râd-things which do not physically exist by themselves e.g. anger, forbearance, colour and actions) will be personified: the faculty of desire will be in the form of a horse, the faculty of anger will be in the form of a dog, and the faculty of intellect will be donned in royal apparel, the reality will be made apparent, and one will say "Oho! What oppression we have committed! We made the king prostrate before the dog and horse. O, if only we used this dog and horse at the time of necessity, like a hunter who does not make them run unnecessarily. He does not take work from them contrary to intellect, nor does he leave them unrestrained. They are made completely subservient to his intellect, so that whenever he wishes, he uses them; otherwise they remain motionless as if they are non-existent."

## FULFILLING THE RIGHTS OF CREATION

When meeting with people, the least you can do is not to cause any form of harm to them. *Rasulullâh* ﷺ said, "A true Muslim is he from whose tongue and hands other Muslims are safe."[1]

A higher level is to benefit people. *Rasulullâh* ﷺ said, "All of creation is the family of **Allâh** ﷻ . The most beloved of them in the sight of **Allâh** ﷻ is the one benefits His family most."[2]

A higher level than this is to bear their difficulties and in spite of this, to be kind to them. This is the level of the ṣiddiqîn (very high level of saints). *Rasulullâh* ﷺ advised Ali ؓ, "If you wish to reach the rank of the ṣiddiqîn, then join ties with those who break them, give to those who deprive you, and forgive those who oppress you."[3]

Here we will suffice on mentioning twenty rights of the creation:

1. Love for others what you love for yourself. *Rasulullâh* ﷺ said, "Whoever wants to be saved from the Fire, then let his death come to him while he testifies that there is none worthy of worship besides **Allâh** ﷻ, and Muhammad ﷺ is the messenger of **Allâh** ﷻ, and let him treat people as he would like to be treated."[4]

2. Humble oneself before others, because **Allâh** ﷻ does not like any proud and arrogant person. If another person acts arrogantly with one, then one should bear this patiently. **Allâh** ﷻ states, "Adopt the quality of forgiveness, command righteousness and turn away from the ignorant."

---

[1] Bukhâri (10), Muslim (41), Ibn Hibbân (180), Abû Dâwûd (2481)
[2] Shua'bul Imân (7045), Tabrânî in Awsat (5537) and Kabîr (10/86)
[3] Shua'bul Imân (7723), Musnad Firdaws (8307), Ahmad(4/158) from Uqbah Ibn Amir ؓ
[4] Tabrânî in Awsat (4738), Hilyah (4/122)

3. Respect the elders and show mercy on the young. *Rasulullâh* ﷺ said, "He who does not show mercy on our young nor on our elders, is not of us."[1] Another hadith states, "Whichever young person honours an old person due to his age, **Allâh** ﷻ will create people who will honour him in his old age."[2] In this hadith an indication is given of the glad tidings of a long life for such a person.

4. Meet every person with a cheerful countenance, since *Rasulullâh* ﷺ has given such a person the glad tidings of being safe from Jahannam (Hell),[3] and becoming the beloved of **Allâh** ﷻ.[4]

5. Mend relations between Muslims. The Shariah has on such occasions granted permission to even speak lies, if there is a necessity to do so, in order to join hearts.[5] This action is regarded to be more superior than optional salâh, charity and fasting.[6]

6. Never listen to the speech of those who carry tales of others, and create mutual enmity amongst Muslims, by conveying stories from one side to the other. *Rasulullâh* ﷺ said, "The tale-bearer will not enter *Jannah*."[7]

7. If you are displeased with any person, do not stay away from him for more than three days.[8] *Rasulullâh* ﷺ said, "Whoever overlooks a Muslim's faults, **Allâh** ﷻ will overlook his faults on the Day of Judgement."[9]

8. Be kind to every person, whether he is worthy of it or not. *Rasulullâh* ﷺ said, "Do good to those who are deserving of it, and also to those who are undeserving. If you have done good to one who is deserving, then he is

---


[1] Abû Dâwûd (4943), Tirmidhi (1919), Hâkim (1/62)

[2] Tabrânî in Awsat (5899), Tirmidhî (2022), Shu'abul Imân (10485)

[3] Tabrânî in Awsat (4887), Tirmidhî (2488), Shu'abul Imân (7774), Ibn Hibbân (470)

[4] Shua'bul Imân (7697), Musnad Firdaws (574)

[5] Bukhâri (2692), Muslim (2605), Ibn Hibbân (5733), Tirmidhî (1938)

[6] Tirmidhî (2509), Ibn Hibbân (5092), Abû Dâwûd (4919)

[7] Bukhâri (6056), Muslim (105), Ibn Hibbân (5765), Abû Dâwûd (4871)

[8] Bukhâri (6056), Muslim (2559), Ibn Hibbân (5669), Abû Dâwûd (4910)

[9] Ibn Hibbân (5030), Abû Dâwûd (3460), Hâkim (2/45)

deserving of your kindness. If you do good to one who is not deserving, then you are deserving of such an act."[1]

9. Treat people according to their rank. Perfection and knowledge which is found in the ulamâ, should not be sought for in a foolish person. Do not expect the layman to possess the understanding and insight of the elite. Dâwûd ﷺ made the following duâ, "O **Allâh**! Show me that path by means of which people will love me, and You would be pleased." **Allâh** ﷺ commanded him, "O Dâwûd, treat the people of the world, with the character of the world, and the people of the Hereafter, with the character of the Hereafter."[2]

10. Keep in mind the rank and status of people when dealing with them. Honour a person of status, even if it be of worldly status. *Rasulullâh* ﷺ spread out his honourable shawl for some respectable people, and remarked, "When an honourable person of any community comes to you, then honour him."[3]

11. Conceal the faults of Muslims. A person who conceals the weakness of a Muslim will enter *Jannah*.[4] Do not backbite about him and do not search for his faults. If you search for a Muslim's faults today, tomorrow **Allâh** ﷺ will expose your faults, and disgrace you.[5] If **Allâh** ﷺ disgraces one, then how can one be saved?

12. Abstain from visiting such places which could lead to accusations, thus saving people from harbouring evil thoughts about you, and from backbiting. Since you were the cause of them falling into this evil, you will also be sinful, because the cause leading to a sin, is also a sin. Once, *Rasulullâh* ﷺ was talking to one of his pure wives. A man walked passed him and greeted him. *Rasulullâh* ﷺ called this man and said, "O so-and-so, this is my wife Safiyya." The man remarked, "O *Rasulullâh* ﷺ, how can I ever harbour ill thoughts of you?" *Rasulullâh* ﷺ remarked, "Verily, shaytân

---

[1] Musnadush Shihâb (747)

[2] Ad-Durrul Manthûr

[3] Hâkim, Ibn Mâjah (3712), Bayhaqî in Kubrâ (8/168)

[4] Tabrâni in Awsat (1503) and Kabîr (17/288)

[5] Tirmidhî (2032), Ibn Hibbân (5763), Abû Dâwûd (4880)

flows in the veins of a person like blood."[1] i.e. It is possible that an evil thought arises in your heart, which can lead to your destruction. Therefore, it is necessary for me to inform you.

13. Make an effort to fulfil the needs of Muslims, even if it be by means of intercession. *Rasulullâh* ﷺ said, "Intercede by me, you will be rewarded. I at times intend something, but I delay it, so that you may intercede by me, and thus be rewarded."[2] *Rasulullâh* ﷺ said, "Whoever walks to fulfil the needs of his brother, whether it be for a short while in the day or night, whether he fulfils it or not, it is better for him than making i'tikaaf for two months."[3]

14. Try to make salâm first, and be the first to shake hands. *Rasulullâh* ﷺ said, "When two Muslims meet and shake hands, then seventy portions of mercy are distributed to them, sixty nine for the one who initiated the shaking of hands."[4]

15. Help ones Muslim brother, even in his absence. One should thus look after his Muslim brother's health and honour. *Rasulullâh* ﷺ said, "If any Muslim helps his brother in a place where his honour is being tarnished and harmed, then **Allâh** ﷻ will help him when he is in need. If any person does not help a Muslim when his honour is being tarnished, then **Allâh** ﷻ will not help him when he is in need."[5]

16. Be courteous with an evil person, with this intention that you want to be safe from his evil. Aisha ﷺ says, "Once a person sought permission to meet *Rasulullâh* ﷺ. *Rasulullâh* ﷺ remarked, "Grant him permission, he is a very evil person." When he arrived, *Rasulullâh* ﷺ spoke so affectionately to him, that I eventually thought that *Rasulullâh* ﷺ possessed great regard for him. When he went away, I asked *Rasulullâh* ﷺ regarding this. *Rasulullâh* ﷺ said, "*O Aisha*, verily the worst of people in status in the sight of **Allâh** ﷻ on the Day of Judgement will be the one who people shun, out of fear for

---

[1] Bukhâri (2039), Muslim (2174), Ahmad (3/156)
[2] Abû Dâwûd (5132), Nasâî (5/78)
[3] Hâkim (4/269)
[4] Tabrânî in Awsat (7668) has narrated similar wording.
[5] Abû Dâwûd (4884), Bayhaqî in Kubrâ (8/167), Shu'abul Imân (7226), Ahmad (4/30)

his evil."[1] In another hadith, *Rasulullâh* ﷺ said, "In whichever manner a person saves his honour, it will be counted as charity for him."[2]

*Rasulullâh* ﷺ once advised, "Mingle with people outwardly, but stay away from them within the heart."[3]

17. Abstain from the company of the wealthy, and visit the poor regularly. *Rasulullâh* ﷺ made the following duâ, "O **Allâh**(ﷻ), let me live with the poor, die with the poor, and let me raised amongst the poor."[4] Despite Sulaiman ﷺ's status, when he would see a poor person in the masjid, he would sit by him and say, "A poor person sitting by another poor person." Once Mûsâ ﷺ asked, "O **Allâh**(ﷻ), where can I find you?" **Allâh** ﷻ replied, "By those whose hearts have been broken for My Sake."[5]

18. As far as possible, sit in the company of those who you can benefit, or from whom you can benefit. As for the negligent ones, remain aloof from them. *Rasulullâh* ﷺ said, "Solitude is better than an evil companion, and a good companion is better than solitude."[6] Consider the following: a person comes to you regularly, and each time he pulls out one strand of your beard, or he removes one stitch from your clothing. Will you not stay far away from him, fearing that if he continues with this, soon you will be left beardless or naked? Similarly, if in the company of any person there is the slightest harm to ones religion, then one should stay far away from him, fearing that soon ones whole dîn can be destroyed.

19. Visit ones Muslim brother if he falls ill, accompany his bier, visit his grave, convey rewards to him (*ithâle thawâb*), seek **Allâh** ﷻ's forgiveness on his behalf, and make duâ for him in his absence

20. If he sneezes and says '*Alhamdulillah*', then reply by saying '*YarhamukAllâh*', and if he consults with you, advise him appropriately.

---

[1] Bukhâri (6054), Muslim (2591), Abû Dâwûd (4792)

[2] Hâkim (2/50), Dâraqutnî (3/28), Shu'abul Imân (3221)

[3] Dârami as the statement of Alî ﷺ, Zuhd of Hannâd (1247)

[4] Hâkim (4/322), Tirmidhî (2352), Ibn Mâjah (4126),

[5] Abu Nuaim in Hilyah (2/364)

[6] Hâkim (3/343), Shu'abul Imân (4639)

In short, benefit others to the extent that you would like to be benefited yourself.

## THE RIGHTS OF FAMILY MEMBERS AND CLOSE ONES

Included in these rights are ones immediate family members, in-laws, neighbours and slaves. *Rasulullâh* said, "The first case to be presented on the day of Judgement will be of neighbours."[1] Therefore, give due importance to the rights of neighbours. If you happen to throw a stone at your neighbour's dog, it would be regarded as having caused harm to him. A woman used to perform abundant optional salâh and fasts. However, she would cause distress to her neighbour. *Rasulullâh* said, "She is in the Fire."[2]

Once *Rasulullâh* asked the Sahâbah, "Do you know what is the right of a neighbour? If he seeks your help, assist him. If he seeks a loan, grant it to him. If he becomes poor, spend on him. If he becomes sick, visit him. If he passes away, follow his bier. If some goodness comes to him, congratulate him. If a calamity afflicts him, console him. Without his permission, do not build your house to such a height that negatively affects his ventilation. If you buy fruit, then send some to him as a gift. If you cannot do so, then take it secretly into your home (so that he does not see and desire it). Do not allow your child to take it outside, since his children will desire and long for it (thus causing him grief). Likewise, when putting up a pot of food, send one scoop to your neighbour as well. Do you know what the right of your neighbour is? By that Being in whose control my life lies, only that person can fulfil the rights of his neighbour on whom **Allâh** showers His Mercy."[3]

### RIGHTS OF THE FAMILY MEMBERS

*Rasulullâh* said, "**Allâh** says, "I am Rahmân (the Most Merciful). Rahm (family ties) I have extracted from My Name. Whoever

---

[1] Tabrânî in Kabîr (17/303), Ahmed(4/151)
[2] Ahmed (2/440), Ibn Hibbaan (5764), Hâkim (4/166)
[3] Shu'abul Imân (9113), Musnad Firdaws (2336)

joins family ties, I (ﷻ) will maintain ties with him, and whoever breaks it, I (ﷻ) will sever ties with him."[1] *Rasulullâh* ﷺ said, "Joining of family ties increases life."[2] In another hadith *Rasulullâh* ﷺ said, "The fragrance of *Jannah* can be perceived at a distance of five hundred years. Its fragrance will not reach the one who is disobedient to his parents, and the one who severs family ties."[3]

*Rasulullâh* ﷺ said, "Kindness to parents is more virtuous than salâh, fasting, Haj, Umrah and Jihâd in the path of **Allâh** ﷻ."[4]
*Rasulullâh* ﷺ said, "The rights of the mother is double that of the father."[5]

Regarding children, *Rasulullâh* ﷺ said, "Observe equality in the distribution of gifts to your children."[6]

## RIGHTS OF SLAVES

*Rasulullâh* ﷺ said, "Fear **Allâh** ﷻ regarding your slaves, feed them from that which you eat, clothe them from that which you wear, and do not burden them with such work which they cannot bear. Realise that **Allâh** ﷻ has granted you control over them. If He wishes, He can grant them control over you (i.e. make you their slaves).[7]

*Rasulullâh* ﷺ said, "When one of your slaves prepares your food, and has borne the heat and attained its fragrance, and then presented it to you, then seat him down and eat with him. If not, then at least take one morsel, place it in his hand, and say with love, "Eat this."[8] *Rasulullâh* ﷺ was asked, "How many times should we forgive our slaves daily?" He ﷺ replied, "Seventy times."[9] The summary of his rights is to feed him, clothe him,

---

[1] Abû Dâwûd (1694), Ibn Hibbân(443)
[2] Shu'abul Imân (3168), Tabrânî in Kabîr (8/261) and Awsat (947)
[3] Tabrânî in Awsat (5660) and Musnad Firdaws (3260)
[4] Abu Ya'lâ (2760), Shu'abul Imân (7451),
[5] Bukhâri (5971), Muslim (2548)
[6] Baihaqi in Kubrâ (6/177), Sunan Saî'd ibn Mansûr (293), Tahâwi
[7] Extracted from various aḥâdith from Muslim (3014), Ibn Hibbân (6605), Baihaqi in Kubrâ (8/36) and Abdur Razzâq in his Musannaf 9/440)
[8] Bukhâri (2557), Muslim (1663), Abû Dâwûd (3846)
[9] Abû Dâwûd (5164), Tirmidhî (1949)

not to burden him with more than what he can bear, forgive his errors, do not look at him with pride and disdain, and teach him the necessities of dîn.

## RIGHTS OF THE WIFE

Her rights are much more than those mentioned for a slave. Together with fulfilling her rights, it is compulsory to speak kindly to her and to live amicably with her. *Rasulullâh* ﷺ said, "The best of you is the best to his family. I am the best to my family."[1] *Rasulullâh* ﷺ was the most jovial person with his wife and children.[2] The ahâdith proving this point are too numerous to be enumerated.

## VIRTUE OF LOVE AND FRIENDSHIP FOR ALLÂH ﷻ

Amongst the principles of dîn regarding friendship, is to choose friends only for **Allâh** ﷻ's Pleasure. *Rasulullâh* ﷺ said, "On the day of Judgement **Allâh** ﷻ will proclaim 'Where are those who loved one another due to My Grandeur (ﷻ)? Today, I will grant them My Shade (ﷻ) when there is no other shade beside My Shade (ﷻ)."[3] *Rasulullâh* ﷺ said, "Around the Arsh (Throne) will be pulpits of effulgence, upon which will be a group of people whose clothing and faces will be illuminated. They will not be from amongst the *Ambiyâ* or the martyrs. The *Ambiyâ* ﷺ and martyrs will envy them."[4] The Sahâbah ﷺ exclaimed, "What quality did they possess, *O Rasulullâh* ﷺ?" He ﷺ replied, "They loved one another for **Allâh** ﷻ's Sake, sat with one another for **Allâh** ﷻ's Sake, and visited one another for **Allâh** ﷻ's Sake."[5]

---

[1] Ibn Hibbân (4177), Tirmidhî (3895), Ibn Mâjah (1977)

[2] Tabrânî in Awsat (6357), Ibn Asâkir in Târikhe Dimishq (4/37)

[3] Muslim (2566), Ibn Hibbân (574), Sunan of Darimî (2799)

[4] At times, those higher in status can envy those lower in status. An example of this is a land owner who envies a menial servant working on his land without any worries, whilst he is worried about responsibilities such as an inspector coming to inspect his property. Similarly, the Ambiyâ ﷺ will be concerned about their followers. Those who are lower than them in status, will be freed from such concern. Thus the Ambiyâ ﷺ will envy them.

[5] Ibn Hibbân (573), Abû Dâwûd (3527), Hâkim (4/170)

Know well, that every love which cannot be fathomed without belief in **Allâh** ﷻ and the Last Day, is love for **Allâh** ﷻ's Sake. However, there are two levels in this:

1. You love a person so that you may attain something in this world from him, which will benefit you in the Hereafter. An example is that of a student who loves his ustâ<u>dh</u>, due to attaining knowledge from him. A disciple loves his spiritual mentor, due to learning the path of tasawwuf from him. An ustâ<u>dh</u> loves his student, since his knowledge will increase and spread, by teaching him. A master loves his servant who cleans his house and washes his clothing so that his heart may be free to worship and involve himself in **Allâh** ﷻ's obedience. A person loves one who spends his wealth on him, so that he can be free for **Allâh** ﷻ's worship. All of these are love for **Allâh** ﷻ's Sake, since no worldly objective is desired from this love.

2. This is a higher level; you love a person solely as he is the beloved of **Allâh** ﷻ and loves **Allâh** ﷻ, even though you do not attain any worldly or religious benefit from him. This is because when love dominates, it spreads to everything which has a relationship with the beloved, to such an extent that a man loves those who love his beloved, as well as those whom his beloved loves. Even the dog which passes the path of the beloved is different from other dogs. It is not possible for one who loves to meet **Allâh** ﷻ, that he does not love those who are beloved to Him. This steadily grows until one begins to treat them like his own self, in fact, he begins to give preference to them over himself. Their status in his eyes will be according to his rank and love for **Allâh** ﷻ.

## HATRED FOR ALLÂH ﷻ'S SAKE

Similarly, one should hate those who disobey Him ﷻ, and act contrary to His ﷻ commands. Whoever attains this level, his condition will be such that he will abstain from sitting and speaking with **Allâh** ﷻ's disobedient servant, and even avoid looking at him.

*Rasulullâh* ﷺ made the following duâ:

اللهم لاتجعل لفاجر علي يدا فيحبه قلبي

*"O **Allâh** (ﷻ), do not allow any sinner to do a favour for me causing my heart to love him."*[1]

This is what is referred to as love and hatred for **Allâh** ﷻ's Sake. Whichever Muslim does not possess that amount of love for his Master ﷺ that makes the beloved servants of **Allâh** ﷻ's beloved unto himself, and that makes **Allâh** ﷻ's enemies his own enemies, then he should regard his îmân as weak, and his love to be deficient.

# NINTH PRINCIPLE

# INVITING TOWARDS GOOD AND PREVENTING EVIL

**Allâh** ﷻ states, "Let there be amongst you a group which calls towards virtue, commands good and prevents evil. They are the successful ones."

*Rasulullâh* ﷺ said, "When people become involved in sin, and amongst them are such people who are able to stop them, but do not do so, then very soon **Allâh** ﷻ will send a general punishment over all of them."[2]

Aisha ؓ said, "Punishment was sent onto a group of people who numbered eighteen thousand. Their actions were like that of the *Ambiyâ* ﷺ. However, they would not become angry for **Allâh** ﷻ's Sake, they did not command righteousness, and they did not prohibit evil."

If you have to witness any evil and do not prohibit it, but rather remain quiet, then you will be regarded as an accomplice to this evil. Thus those who listen to backbiting will be equal in sin to the one who backbites. This applies to all sins. Just as the one who wears silken clothing, or a gold ring is a sinner, so too are those Muslim acquaintances of his who see him

---

[1] Musnad Firdaws of Dailami (2011)
[2] Abû Dâwûd (4338), Tirmidhî (2168), Ibn Mâjah (4005)

wearing this, and do not prohibit him from doing so. Sitting in such places where pictures are hung on the walls, participating in such gatherings in which innovation is occurring, or attending such debates wherein there is vulgar language and futility are all sins. Merely abstaining from the place of sin is not sufficient. As long as one does not advise and prevent people from sinning, he will not be free from his responsibility. For this reason, it is preferable to stay in solitude, since in abundant mixing, sin will definitely occur even if one is pious; unless one abstains from mudâhanah (flattery), and does not fear the criticism of any person, and takes stock of himself.

A person is absolved of the compulsion of commanding righteousness and prohibiting evil in the following two conditions:

1. One knows that if he has to prohibit a sin, people will not pay attention to him, the sin will not be stopped, and he will be looked at with scorn and derision. Generally, this occurs in those sins in which the ulamâ and those who regard themselves as pious are involved. In such a condition, keeping quiet is permissible. However, if one is unable to prevent it in any other way, to verbally prohibit, will be musta<u>h</u>ab (commendable), thus making apparent the features of dîn. Even though it is permissible to keep quiet, it is not permissible to voluntarily remain in that place. To voluntarily witness a sin, is also a sin. Thus, one should immediately vacate the following places: where alcohol is being served, backbiting occurs, sitting with one who wears silk, interest and harâm is being consumed, etc.

2. One knows that he is able to prohibit an evil e.g. he sees a container in which there is alcohol and is able to break it. Similarly, he can snatch musical instruments from someone and destroy them. However, he knows that he will be beaten, or have some harm inflicted upon him. In this condition, it will be musta<u>h</u>ab (preferable), and not compulsory, to prohibit it. If a person does so, and harm is caused to him, there is a great reward for him. In short, the compulsion will not be waived unless there is a fear of harm being caused to one physically, monetarily or to one's honour by being disgraced or embarrassed.

If a person fears that the other person will not like him, say something evil to him, have enmity for him, or in future will try to cause some harm to him, or it will create a barrier from one attaining greater goodness in future, then it is not permissible to keep quiet on such occasions, as these have no basis in the shariah.

## THE PREREQUISITES FOR ONE TO BE ABLE TO COMMAND RIGHTEOUSNESS AND PROHIBIT EVIL

1. It is necessary for him to be soft-natured and forbearing. If a person gives advice to others just to show off his own piety or merely to object, then the end-results will not be positive. This attitude will upset people, and they will become more persistent in the sin instead of abstaining there-from.

If someone causes any harm to this person and he does not possess noble character, he will become angry and will not prohibit solely for **Allâh** 's Pleasure; instead it will only be to cool the anger burning in his heart, thus becoming a sinner himself. If is preferable that one not be keen on reproaching others, hoping that the person will leave the sin due to someone else's advice. If a person loves to be an objector, this is due to ones desire for respect, which is contrary to sincerity.

A lecturer advised Ma'mûn  harshly. Ma'mûn remarked, "Advise with compassion, because **Allâh**  sent one who is better than you (i.e. Mûsâ ) to one who was worse than me (i.e. Fir'awn) and commanded him to be compassionate. **Allâh**  advised,

فَقُولَا لَهُ قَوْلًا لَّيِّنًا لَّعَلَّهُ يَتَذَكَّرُ أَوْ يَخْشَى

*"(O Mûsâ and Hârûn ), speak to him gently, perhaps he will accept the advice or fear."*

Abu Umâmah  states that a young man came to *Rasulullâh*  requesting permission to commit fornication. People began reproaching him. *Rasulullâh*  said, "Leave him, leave him." Turning to the youngster, he  said, "Come here." When he came closer, *Rasulullâh*  said, "Would you like it if someone fornicates with your mother?" He replied, "No, may **Allâh**  sacrifice my life for you." *Rasulullâh*  explained to him, "Similarly, people will not like it with their mothers." Thereafter *Rasulullâh*  asked, "Would you like it if someone fornicates with your daughter?" He replied in the negative. *Rasulullâh*  said, "Similarly, people will not like it with their daughters." *Rasulullâh*  then asked him about his sister and maternal and paternal aunts. When he replied in the negative,

*Rasulullâh* ﷺ said, "Similarly, people will not like it." Then he ﷺ placed his hands on the man's chest and said, "*O* **Allâh**(﷾)! Purify his heart, forgive his sin, and protect his private parts." After this there was no person who detested fornication more than this man.[1]

Once in a gathering someone complained to Fu<u>dh</u>ail ibn Ayâdh ﷦, "Sufyân ibn Uyaynah accepts gifts from the kings." He replied, "He took from them less than his due right." He then called Sufyân ﷦ in private and gently advised him. Sufyân ﷦ said, "*O* Abu Ali, if we are not from the pious, then verily we love the pious."

2. The person giving advice should first reform himself, since advice has an effect when one practices on it, or else people will mock at him. However, this is not a condition. Even a sinner may prevent evil. Anas ﷦ asked *Rasulullâh* ﷺ, "Should we only command righteousness once we have implemented good actions, and should we only prohibit evil once we abstain from all evil?" *Rasulullâh* ﷺ replied, "Continue commanding righteousness, even if you do not practice upon all of it; and continue prohibiting evil even though you do not abstain from all of it."[2]

<u>H</u>asan Ba<u>s</u>ri ﷦ said, "Shaitân desires to overpower you with this thought i.e. you will not command righteousness until you practice upon all of it." In other words, this will lead to the closing of the doors of correcting and reforming, as there is no one who is free from sin. Remember well that commanding righteousness is a compulsory act. It is permissible for even a sinner to give advice to others. But, to practice on one's knowledge, and to act on that which one advises others and remain steadfast on it, is a separate obligation on lecturers and advisors. If one leaves out one compulsory action (i.e. one does not practice on what one preaches), then it will not be permissible to leave out a second compulsion (i.e. preaching to others and advising them).

---

[1] Tabrânî in Kabîr (8/162) and Musnad ash Shâmiyyin (1066), Ahmad (5/256), Shu'abul Imân (5032)

[2] Tabrânî in Awsat (6624), Shu'abul Imân (7163), Musnad Firdaws from Abû Huraira ﷦ (6526)

# TENTH PRINCIPLE

# FOLLOWING THE *SUNNAH*

The key to success is to follow the *Sunnah* and lifestyle of *Rasulullâh* ﷺ in all actions. *Rasulullâh* ﷺ's actions are of two types:

1. Ibâdât (Outward forms of worship) e.g. salâh , fasting zakâh, hajj, etc.

2. Âdat (habits) e.g. eating, drinking, sleeping, standing, etc.

It is necessary for a Muslim to follow both of the above, since **Allâh** ﷻ has commanded us to follow *Rasulullâh* ﷺ without any restriction. "Whatever the messenger gives you, accept it, and whatever he prohibits you from, abstain." Mu<u>h</u>ammad ibn Aslam ﷺ never ate watermelons in his life, since he did not know the manner in which *Rasulullâh* ﷺ ate them. Once, a saint erred by wearing his left sock first. He expiated this by giving away a huge amount of wheat. From the above we learn that complete success lies in following all the habits of *Rasulullâh*ﷺ, since there are countless benefits in this. To be deprived of such a great bounty due to negligence, is the height of foolishness. We will now mention the benefits one will attain in total obedience:

1. You are aware that the heart and limbs have a special connection. The effect of all actions performed by the limbs, reach the heart. Therefore, as long as the movements of ones limbs do not reach the level of moderation, the heart cannot attain complete illumination and potential, since the heart is like a mirror. A mirror can only truly reflect the light of the sun, when three factors are found:

a. It is polished

b. Its surface is illuminated

c. Its surface is completely smooth, not warped.

Similarly, when these three qualities are found in the heart it will become a reflection of **Allâh** ﷻ's Tajalliyât (Special Mercies).

a. It is polished by abstaining from lustful desires and evil character.

b. It is illuminated by dhikrullâh and the ma'rifah (recognition) of **Allâh** ﷻ.

c. Its warped nature is removed by bringing the actions of the limbs into equilibrium.

## THE WISDOM AND BENEFITS OF FOLLOWING THE *SUNNAH*

Equilibrium (*I'tidaal*) refers to placing everything in its proper place. For example, of the four directions **Allâh** ﷻ has given honour to the direction of the Qiblah. For this reason, all good actions, whether they be dhikr, tilâwah, wudu or duâ, should all be done facing the Qiblah. Those actions which are regarded as lowly, such as passing of urine and stool, sexual intercourse, etc. should be done by turning away from the Qiblah. Thus, by establishing the honour of the Qiblah, one remains in equilibrium. **Allâh** ﷻ has honoured the right hand over the left. Therefore, keep its honour in mind at all times. For example, raise the Qurân Sharîf, eat food, drink, etc. with the right hand; and lowly work e.g. istinjâ (purification after passing urine or stool), cleaning ones nose or placing ones hand on an impure object should be done with the left hand. Begin wearing your clothing and shoes from the right. Enter the masjid with the right foot, and emerge with the left foot. In short, keeping in mind the status of everything is referred to as equilibrium. By this external equilibrium, the heart becomes balanced. If you cannot understand this, then try it out. You must have already witnessed that those who are in the habit of speaking the truth, have truthful dreams. Those who speak lies, have false dreams. The reason for this is that truthfulness causes equilibrium, steadfastness and rectitude to enter the heart; and through lies the heart becomes warped. Poets are accustomed to speaking lies and futility. Therefore, their hearts become warped. Hence, as far as possible, do not give place to lies and futile thoughts, or else equilibrium will not remain within the heart.

2. Medication is of two types. Some medication is such, that its effect and reaction are compatible with reason. For example, since honey is hot, it will cause harm to people of hot temperaments, and it will benefit people

of a cold temperament. However, these types of medication are few. Most medication is such, that its effect and reaction are not understood through reason alone; it is a special characteristic peculiar to that medicine which causes healing. The characteristics of everything are known either through ilhâm (inspiration), or wahî (revelation) or experience e.g. scammony is a laxative, and draws bile from the veins. The specialty of a magnet is that it attracts metal. The effects of these two are known through experience.

In this way, the effects of actions are of two types:

(a) There is a clear relationship in some actions and their effects, e.g. fulfilling ones bestial desires and hankering after worldly pleasures is harmful, because at the time of death one will definitely undergo sorrow, due to having to part from these pleasures. Thus there is a clear relationship between these pleasures and their harms.

Another example is that of dhikrullâh which is beneficial. By means of dhikr, ma'rifah (recognition) is attained. Due to ma'rifah, love of **Allâh** ﷻ in created in the heart. The result of Divine Love is that one will have enthusiasm and intense desire for the everlasting pleasures. Thus, when leaving the world, there will be no sorrow. One will depart laughing and happily, desiring to meet his Beloved ﷻ. Thus, the relationship between dhikrullah and its fruits and effects, is apparent.

(b) There is an unknown relationship in other actions and their effects. Regarding this second type, the characteristics of these can only be learnt via revelation (wahî) and the light of nabuwwat. Most of the injunctions of shariah are of this type. When one finds that *Rasulullâh* ﷺ has given preference to one permissible action over another, despite having the ability to do both, e.g. it is possible to make istinjâ with the right hand. When *Rasulullâh* ﷺ used the left hand instead of the right, this is a sign that he did so knowing its intrinsic characteristic. Without doubt there is a special benefit in this, the wisdom of which is beyond the understanding of most people. It is amazing that the characteristics of stones and medication as explained by the doctor Muhammad ibn Zakariyya Râzî, is accepted without any reservations. However, the specialties of a'mâl (actions) mentioned by the most virtuous of mankind, Muhammad ﷺ, through the means of the illumination of nubuwwah and divine revelation, is not believed, and is regarded to be contrary to intellect. *O* Muslims! Be convinced that whatever the spiritual doctor does, there is definitely benefit therein, even though its benefit cannot be understood by you.

3. Man has not been created free like animals. He is the most honourable of creation. He has been commanded to follow the Divine Law. Therefore, it is appropriate that whatever you do, you should do it according to the *Sunnah*, so that the *nafs* is made to be obedient and ruled; and you can then imbibe the qualities of angels. Understand that servitude means humbleness. It is thus necessary for a servant that whatever action he does, he should do so with the intention of following *Rasulullâh* ﷺ and obeying his command. In doing so the effects of servitude will be apparent at all times, and one will attain the reward of being perpetually obedient. Being constrained is such a condition, that if any person has to hand over all his affairs to an animal, it will be better than that of a person who only follows his desires.

The last-mentioned benefit will be attained by implementation of shari' laws, no matter how the command is established, since the actual objective is to be bound in a specific manner. This is attained by following any system and way of life. Thus even though there have been different codes of law sent to different *Ambiyâ* ﷺ, this special benefit was found in all. This is contrary to the other benefits, whose wisdoms and specialities are something specific, and they do not change in all the different shariahs.

If you have understood these benefits, the importance of following the *Sunnah* in all your actions will become evident.

## ABSTINENCE FROM THE *SUNNAH* IN ACTS OF WORSHIP WITHOUT ANY VALID REASON

What has been mentioned above, serves as encouragement to follow the *Sunnah* in day-to-day matters of habit and natural routine. As for those actions related to acts of worship, in which reward is mentioned, then besides subtle kufr or plain foolishness, we cannot find any other explanation for omitting the *Sunnah* method. For example, *Rasulullâh* ﷺ said, "Performing salâh in congregation is twenty seven times more virtuous than performing salâh individually."[1] After accepting this, if any Muslim, without any reasonable excuse, does not perform salâh in congregation; the reason can either be foolishness or insanity. If a person gives R2 in exchange for R1, people will regard him as insane. Here, a person is leaving out twenty seven virtues, and sufficing on one. Even worse than this (**Allâh** ﷻ protect us!) is when a person thinks that *Rasulullâh* ﷺ's statement is only based on encouragement, so that people are inclined to gather together, since there does not seem to be any affinity between the number twenty seven and salâh in congregation. If a person possesses such a thought, then this is kufr; and so subtle, that he himself does not know of it. The condition of people is such, that if any doctor, astrologer or fortune teller says anything, then whether they understand it or not, they accept it immediately. However, they seek explanations for *Rasulullâh* ﷺ's statements. If any astrologer says that after twenty seven days a calamity will befall you, since there is a twenty seven degree distance between Saturn and your star, and each day it becomes one degree less, thus if you desire good fortune, sit in your home, and do not emerge. On hearing this, you will definitely remain within the precincts of your house, and will not even attend to your business. If a person says to you, "What is the affinity between one degree and one day? What relationship is there in Saturn and misfortune? What connection is there in not emerging from your home and the calamity being averted? These are all deception of astrologers, and are nonsensical. Don't worry about it." you will not accept his word; in fact you will regard him to be foolish, insane and a denier of astrology. Then how sad it is that you wish to understand all the wisdoms behind the actions shown by *Rasulullâh* ﷺ, and if you do not understand it, you become a denier and one who is unfaithful. Tell me, is this not denial of Risâlah (Divine appointment) and open kufr, whereas the effects of these acts of worship are already known by experience? It is also not vital that every person understands all the benefits, and affinities in the teachings of *Rasulullâh* ﷺ. I ask you: if a doctor gives some medication and does not mention its purpose; or if an astrologer passes a judgment on a future event, and he does not explain the reason, will you not accept this? How sad it is that when *Rasulullâh* ﷺ gives us any spiritual prescription, and does not inform us of its speciality and effects, then you are not prepared to

---

[1] Bukhârî (645), Muslim (650), Tirmidhî (250), Nasâî (2/103)

accept it. The only reason is, that since the astrologer and doctor are prescribing matters relating to ones physical life, which you love, you do not have any thought of asking the reason of an impending calamity or sickness. In fact, you begin preparing, and are concerned with calamities which will appear after ten years, whereas this is merely conjecture, and has been mentioned by such people, whom you have seen telling lies thousands of times. A *Nabî* ﷺ is a spiritual doctor. He thus shows the cure for spiritual ailments, and explains the method of attaining everlasting good health. However, you have no concern, worry and care for this. The conviction which one is supposed to possess regarding the everlasting life of the Hereafter, has not been attained. Therefore, they ask for the proofs. May **Allâh** ﷻ save us from such negligence that even in acts of ibâdah we do not follow *Rasulullâh* ﷺ.

## PRACTICING ON DAÎF (WEAK) AHÂDITH IS PREFERABLE WITH REGARD TO CERTAIN A'MAAL

The quality of a Muslim is that if a hadith has been narrated relating to a particular command, he should follow it whole heartedly e.g. *Rasulullâh* ﷺ said that there is a fear of being afflicted with leprosy, if one does cupping on a Saturday or Thursday.[1] A scholar of hadith , considering this hadith as daîf, intentionally did cupping on a Saturday, and was afflicted with leprosy. After a few days, he was honoured by a vision of *Rasulullâh* ﷺ in a dream. He complained of his illness to *Rasulullâh* ﷺ. *Rasulullâh* ﷺ said, "You have suffered the consequences of your action. Why did you do cupping on a Saturday." He answered, "O *Rasulullâh* ﷺ, the narrator of this hadith is weak." *Rasulullâh* ﷺ said, "However, the words he narrated were mine." On hearing this, he said, "O *Rasulullâh* ﷺ, I have erred. I repent."

In a similar manner, *Rasulullâh* ﷺ said, "If a person sleeps after Asr, there is a fear that a person might lose his intellect."[2] Another hadith states, "Whoever's shoelace breaks, then as long as he does not repair it, he should not walk around with one shoe."[3] A third hadith states, "The first type of food that a woman should eat immediately after giving birth is

---

[1] Hâkim (4/409), Baihaqî in Kubrâ (9/340), Musannaf Abdur Razzâq (11/29)
[2] Musnad Abû Ya'lâ (4918)
[3] Muslim (2099), Ibn Khuzaimah (98), Ibn Hibbân (5459)

moist dates, and if not then dry dates. If there was anything better, then **Allâh** ﷻ would have fed it to Maryam ﷞, after she had given birth to Îsa ﷶ."[1]

*Rasulullâh* ﷺ said, "If someone brings sweetmeats to you, then eat some portion of it. If he offers perfume, then apply it."[2] In this way whatever the spiritual physician (i.e. *Rasulullâh* ﷺ) says, one should abstain from seeking proofs. It should be accepted whole-heartedly, as in every command there are countless secrets and benefits which are beyond the understanding of most people.

# CONCLUSION

From the above-mentioned acts of worship, some can be performed together e.g. salâh, fasting and tilâwah of Qurân Sharîf. A fasting person can recite Qurân Sharîf in salâh. Hence, at one time, three acts of worship are being executed. Some acts of worship are such, that they cannot be performed together e.g. A person cannot make tilâwah of Qurân Sharîf and dhikrullâh at the same time. Nor can a person perform salâh and fulfil the rights of others simultaneously. It is thus appropriate that the various acts of worship be divided over a period of twenty four hours. By following a programme, there will be ease, and the objective of ibâdah will be attainted i.e. enjoying the remembrance of **Allâh** ﷻ, and creating an aversion and dislike for this temporary life.

Remember, this world is a cultivating field for the Hereafter. The object behind creating this world is, so that man becomes attached and gains the Love of **Allâh** ﷻ, the result being that he can attain success in the Hereafter. Since love cannot be attained without *ma'rifat* (divine recognition), *ma'rifat* is necessary and needs to be attained first. The manner of attaining *ma'rifat* is remaining engrossed in the remembrance of **Allâh** ﷻ. The various forms of ibâdah are for the purpose of remembering and thinking of Him. Different forms of ibâdah have been stipulated so that the heart does not lose enthusiasm, by being engaged in

---

[1] Musnad Abû Ya'lâ (455), Musnad Firdaws (1320)
[2] Shu'abul Imân (5536)

only one form of ibâdah. If one action of worship is done all the time, then one will become accustomed to it, and due to it being a habit, its effect on the heart will not be complete. For this reason, it was necessary to stipulate different times, for the different forms of ibâdah. As for those who have reached the level of fanâ (annihilation), there is no need for order and stipulation, since on reaching this level, only one ibâdah remains i.e. one is engaged in His Remembrance ﷻ all the time. However, this status cannot be attained by every person. For this reason, it is of utmost importance that you specify times for your acts of ibâdah e.g. from this time to that time, this particular ibâdah will be performed; at night another type of ibâdah will be done; during the day another type, and so forth.

However, if you are engaged in learning and teaching, or you are the ruler of a certain place, and are engaged in administering the affairs of the public, then it is more virtuous to remain engaged in these actions the entire day than any other form of optional acts of worship. The reason is that through the blessings of knowledge, one attains awe and respect for Divine Laws, and the benefit given to people by teaching or protecting their interests, is actual dîn.

## THE IBÂDAH OF A BREADWINNER, SCHOLAR AND RULER

For a breadwinner to work and earn halâl income, in order to fill the bellies of his children and dependents, is more virtuous than other bodily forms of optional ibâdah. However, even at such times, one should not become unmindful of <u>dh</u>ikr. Just as a lover of a beautiful woman is always engrossed in the thoughts of his beloved, even though his limbs are engaged in some other necessary occupation, similarly keep your heart engaged in the thoughts of **Allâh** ﷻ, even though your limbs are engaged in other activities. Sheikh Abul <u>H</u>asan Khirqâni ﷺ used to earn by manual labour. He would say, "We have been granted three things i.e. hands, tongue and heart. The hand is for earning a living, the tongue is for speaking, explaining and teaching people, and the heart is solely for **Allâh** ﷻ." We will suffice on this with regards to outwards actions. Insha-**Allâh**, this will be sufficient for those who desire to practice.

# SECTION TWO

## PURIFYING THE HEART FROM EVIL CHARACTER

**Allâh** ﷺ states, "Successful indeed is he who has purified his heart." *Rasulullâh* ﷺ said, "Purity is half of îmân (faith)."[1]

Perfection of îmân is based on purifying the heart from those qualities disliked by **Allâh** ﷺ, and then adorning it with those qualities beloved to Him ﷺ. Thus purification is half of îmân. How can one begin purifying himself, when he does not even know what is impure? Thus, one has to first know what the evil qualities are, from which he has to purify his heart. There are many. However, they all stem from ten basic evils.

## FIRST PRINCIPLE

## OVEREATING AND GREED FOR FOOD[2]

Overeating and filling ones belly is a quality which causes great harm to ones religion. It is a root of many other evils. Through this habit, the desires of the private parts increase. When this desire increases, the desire for wealth is formed, since other desires cannot be fulfilled without money. From this stems the love for fame, since it is difficult to acquire wealth without having some status. When the desire for wealth and fame is created, a host of other evils like pride, show, jealousy, hatred and enmity, etc. take form. The root of all these is the stomach. For this reason, *Rasulullâh* ﷺ has greatly stressed the virtue of hunger. *Rasulullâh* ﷺ said, "No person fills any utensil worse than his stomach. A few morsels which will straighten ones back are sufficient. If one has to eat more, than one

---

[1] Muslim (223), Sunan of Dârimî (679), Ahmad (5/342)
[2] ***Refer to Note in Foreword before reading this section***

portion has to be for food, one portion for water, and one portion for air."[1]

## THE BENEFITS OF EATING LESS

The benefits of hunger are innumerable. We will suffice on mentioning a few basic benefits referred to as principles. Attaining success in the Hereafter is based on these principles:

1. Purification of the heart and profound understanding of the dîn. Eating to a full stomach creates foolishness and blinds the heart. Divine recognition cannot be attained without purifying and illuminating the heart. These are attained by hunger.

2. Softness of the heart. A person will thus gain the enjoyment of duâ, and the heart will be affected by dhikr and ibâdah. Softness, duâ, fear and humility will be created. These are the keys to attaining *ma'rifat* (Divine Recognition).

3. Humbling the *nafs* and elimination of pride and disobedience. Nothing humbles the *nafs* like hunger. When the enemy is destroyed and the door of negligence is closed, one's attention turns to **Allâh** ﷻ, and the doors of felicity are opened. It is for this reason that when the world was presented to *Rasulullâh* ﷺ, he did not accept it. "I desire to remain hungry for one day, and I desire to eat to my fill for one day. When I am hungry I will be patient and humble myself. When I am satiated I will be grateful."[2]

4. A person should taste some of the difficulties of the Hereafter in this world, so that he can warn and frighten the *nafs* of its difficulties. It is apparent that a person cannot punish his *nafs* with anything more severe than hunger, as there is no need for one to make any preparation for this. Other benefits are also related to it. One will begin noticing the bounties of **Allâh** ﷻ continuously. This will lead to softness of the heart, and facilitate feeding of the needy. A satiated person is unaware of the pangs of hunger.

---

[1] Tirmidhi (2380), Ibn Hibbân (674), Hâkim (4/331), Ibn Mâjah (3349), etc.
[2] Tirmidhi (2347), Shu'abul Imân (1394, Ahmed (5/254)

5. Crushing of all desires which are the roots of sin, and control over the *nafs*, which only invites to evil. Zunnûn Misri ﷺ said, "Whenever I ate to satiation, I committed a sin, or intended to commit a sin." Hunger is sufficient to quell the evil desires of the private parts. Whoever eats to satiation cannot control his private parts. If taqwâ prevents him from fulfilling his desires (fornication, masturbation), he will be unable to control his eyes, since the eyes also fornicate, just as the private parts do. The cause of all these sins connected by the seven limbs is the strength attained by overeating. Aisha ﷺ said, "The first innovation, which surfaced after the demise of *Rasulullâh* ﷺ, was eating to satiation. Verily when the stomachs of people are filled to satiation, their souls draw them to the world."[1]

6. The body becomes lighter which facilitates tahajjud and ibâdah and sleep does not easily overcome one since overeating causes sleepiness, thus shortening one's life, since one is prevented from ibâdah at this time. Abu Sulaimân Dârânî ﷺ said, "Whoever eats to satiation, will be afflicted by six things:
a. Deprivation of the sweetness of ibâdah.
b. Difficulty in acquiring wisdom, foresight, intelligence, and the Noor of Recognition.
c. Deprivation of compassion for creation, as the one who eats to his fill considers others to be satiated also.
d. A heaviness develops in the stomach (that can lead to illness)
e. Increase in carnal desires
f. His condition will be such that when the believers will be proceeding to the masjid, he will be proceeding to the toilet."

7. Decrease in expenditure, being content with meagre worldly possessions, and giving preference to poverty. One who is content, will be saved from the lusts of his stomach, and will not be in need of abundant wealth. One will be thus relieved of many worldly concerns. When one desires to take a loan in order to fulfil the desires of his stomach, he will take a loan from his stomach i.e. he will keep it empty. When Ibrâhîm ibn

---

[1] Targhîb (3/712), Mîzânul-I'tidâl (3/335)

Adham ﷺ was told that a certain item was expensive, he would say, "Make it cheap by abstaining therefrom."[1]

## AMOUNT TO BE CONSUMED

Since eating to satiation has become a habit, it is difficult to leave it all at once. Therefore, gradually decrease your intake. Eat one morsel less daily. In a month you will eat one roti less, and it will not have any visible effect. Once one is used to eating less, then one should now look at the time, amount, and type of food one consumes. One should try and reach the highest level.

Highest level (Siddîqîn) - They suffice on that amount which if decreased, causes harm to one's life or intellect. This was the view of Sahl Tustari ﷺ. According to him, a salâh performed sitting due to hunger, is more virtuous than a salâh performed standing after having satiated oneself.

Intermediary level - To eat half *mudd* daily. This is one third of the stomach. This was the habit of Umar ﷺ and a group of Sahâbah ﷺ. Weekly, their food intake would not exceed one sâ' (3.2 kg) of barley.

Lowest level: To eat one *mudd* daily. If one eats more than this, he will be regarded as a slave of his stomach. Since people's natures and conditions are different, a specific amount cannot be stipulated for all. At times it is seen that some people can eat a whole kilo of grain, whereas others cannot manage even one handful. Remember the principle that only when you have true desire, then stretch your hands towards food; and stop before the desire is satiated. The sign of true desire is, that one has desire to eat whatever rotî or bread that is presented to him, even without any gravy. When one desires to eat a special type of bread or feels it difficult to eat rotî without any gravy, then know that one's desire is false. It shows that one's nature is so inclined towards enjoyments, just as one eats fruits after having eaten to satiation. It is obvious that this is not hunger, but enjoyment and pleasure.

---

[1] Târike-Dimishq of Ibn Asâkir (6/282)

# TIME INTERVAL BETWEEN MEALS

The highest level is to stay hungry for three days and thereafter eat on the fourth. Abu Bakr 🙥 would remain hungry for six days at a time. Ibrâhim ibn Adham 🙥 and Sufyân Thawri 🙥 would not eat for seven consecutive days. Some of our pious predecessors would not eat for forty days. Remember, whoever stays hungry for forty days, many amazing wonders and secrets from the unseen realm will be unveiled before him. To attain this rank all at once is difficult. Therefore, adopt the habit of hunger gradually.

The intermediate level is to stay hungry for two days and to eat on the third.

The lowest level is to eat once a day. Whoever eats twice a day will not have tasted hunger. He will thus be deprived of the virtue of hunger.

# QUALITY OF FOOD TO BE EATEN

The highest quality is bread made from wheat, together with some gravy. The lowest is barley bread, without gravy. To continuously eat gravy is reprehensible. Umar 🙥 advised his son, "At times eat bread and meat, at other times bread and ghee, sometimes bread and milk, sometimes bread and salt, and sometimes plain bread." This is for people who are used to eating gravy.

As for those who are traversing the path, never mind gravy, they abstain completely from fulfilling their desires. At times, some of them desired something for ten and even twenty years, but they abstained therefrom. *Rasulullâh* 🙷 said, "The worst of my nation are those whose bodies have been nurtured on delectable and luxurious foods; the desires of such people are only directed at different types of food and fashionable forms of dress. They speak in a pretentious and pompous way, but do nothing practical"

# SECOND PRINCIPLE

# EXCESSIVE AND FUTILE SPEECH

It is of paramount importance to control ones speech. While the actions of all the other limbs affect the heart, the tongue does so to a greater extent, because it vocalises what is present in the heart. The image that is engraved on the heart, and the thoughts that enter the heart – all these are expressed with the tongue. Therefore, its effect on the heart is much more noticeable.

If one speaks lies, a false image is created in the heart and thus the heart becomes warped. If one utters a word of futility, the heart becomes blackened, until a time when it is completely dead. It is for this reason that *Rasulullâh* ﷺ emphasized the importance of protecting the tongue. "Whoever guarantees me that which lies between his jaws and between his legs, I guarantee him *Jannah*."[1] Another hadîth sharîf states, "It is nothing but the speech of the tongue that will fling people onto their faces into Jahannam."[2]

*Rasulullâh* ﷺ said, "Whoever believes in **Allâh** ﷻ and the final day, should either speak good or keep quiet."[3] *Rasulullâh* ﷺ is also reported to have said, "Whoever's speech is abundant, his errors are abundant. Whose errors are abundant, his sins are many. Whose sins are many, he is more eligible for the fire."[4] For this reason, Abu Bakr ﵁ used to place a stone in his mouth, so that he would not speak without necessity.

---

[1] Bukhârî (6474), Tirmidhi(2408), Ibn Hibbân (5701), Hâkim (4/358)

[2] Tirmidhi (2616), Hâkim (2/412), Ibn Mâjah (3973) Tabraani, Musnadush Shahaab)

[3] Bukhârî (6018), Muslim(47), Ibn Hibbân (506), Hâkim (4/286)

[4] Tabrâni in Awsat (6537), Musnadush Shihâb (372)

Practicing on the following verse is sufficient to save oneself from sins of the tongue:

لاَّ خَيْرَ فِي كَثِيرٍ مِّن نَّجْوَاهُمْ إِلاَّ مَنْ أَمَرَ بِصَدَقَةٍ أَوْ مَعْرُوفٍ أَوْ إِصْلاَحٍ بَيْنَ النَّاسِ وَمَن يَفْعَلْ ذَلِكَ ابْتَغَاءَ مَرْضَاتِ اللَّهِ فَسَوْفَ نُؤْتِيهِ أَجْرًا عَظِيمًا

*"There is no goodness in most of their secret discussions, except he who commands others to give charity, to do righteousness, or to correct ties between people."*

This means that one should not speak unnecessarily, but should suffice on important and necessary matters only. There is salvation in this.

## DEFINITION OF FUTILE SPEECH

Anas ﷺ stated that a youngster was martyred during the battle of Uhud. After the battle, his body was found amongst other bodies. It was noted that a stone was tied around his stomach to alleviate the pangs of hunger. When his mother came to him, she wiped the sand off his face and said, "Glad tidings of *Jannah* upon you, O my son." *Rasulullâh* ﷺ remarked, "What do you know? Perhaps he spoke some futile speech." (Due to this, even though he attained the rank of martyrdom, there might be a decrease in his rank.)

Only such words should be spoken, which attract reward or repel harm. That speech in which there is neither reward nor removal of harm, is termed futile speech. Whoever suffices on necessary speech, his talking will decrease. A person should ponder that if he remembers **Allâh** ﷻ, instead of talking nonsense, he can attain a huge reward. How can an intelligent person give up such valuable capital, and collect clods of earth instead? If this is the situation in uttering words in non-sinful speech, if one utters words that are sinful e.g. backbiting, swearing, immoral speech, it is like leaving valuable capital, and choosing a blazing coal of fire instead.

Included in futile speech are story-telling and memoirs, discussing the condition of people, their habits and food. These are amongst the many things one will find people actively engaged in.

# HARMS OF THE TONGUE

There are twenty evils associated with the tongue. Since we cannot mention all of these in detail, we will suffice on mentioning five of these, which people openly indulge in, due to which their tongues have become accustomed to spiritual impurities.

## 1. Lies

*Rasulullâh* ﷺ said, "A person continues speaking lies until it becomes his second nature, and he is noted as a liar in the register of **Allâh** ﷻ."[1] In another hadith, *Rasulullâh* ﷺ said, "Woe be to the one who speaks lies in order to make people laugh! Woe be to him! Woe be to him!"[2]
Once *Rasulullâh* ﷺ was asked, "Can a believer fornicate? Can a believer steal?" *Rasulullâh* ﷺ replied, "It may happen." He ﷺ was then asked, "Can he lie?" *Rasulullâh* ﷺ replied, "No. Only those who do not believe in the signs of **Allâh** ﷻ will concoct stories."[3]

Lies are harâm (prohibited) in all cases. Once a woman said to her young son, "Come here, I want to give you something." *Rasulullâh* ﷺ said, "What will you give him if he comes?" She replied, "A date." *Rasulullâh* ﷺ said, "If you had no intention of doing so, then a lie would have been recorded against you."[4] Even in one's thoughts, one should abstain from falsehood, as this results in crookedness in the heart. Eventually, one will have false dreams. Secrets of the unseen world are not exposed to him in his sleep. Experience testifies to this.

Yes, permission has been granted to speak lies, when speaking the truth will lead to such harm that is worse than the sin of speaking lies. An example of this is that permission is given to eat carrion when one fears losing ones life. The hadith has granted concession for speaking lies on three occasions: A. In order to unite two brothers. B. Deception in the

---


[1] Bukhâri (6094), Muslim (2607), Ibn Hibbân (272)
[2] Hâkim (1/46), Abû Dâwûd (4990), Tirmidhi(2315)
[3] Ibn Asâkir in Tarîkhe Dimishq (27/241)
[4] Abû Dâwûd (4991), Ahmed (3/447)

battlefield. C. Speaking lies to your wife in order to please her.[1] The reason for the above is that the consequences of enmity and hatred amongst two brothers, are far worse than the harm of lying. Similarly, concealing secrets during battle is imperative, as thousands of lives will be lost if the enemy comes to know of them. In the like manner, some matters of the husband are worthy of being hidden. If the truth has to be spoken, this will inadvertently result in problems between husband and wife, the evil effects of which shall be worse than speaking lies. The permission granted to speak lies on such occasions, is like a person who is given a choice to act on one of two evils, and he chooses the lesser of the two.

In like manner, to speak lies in front of an oppressor, in order to prevent him from usurping your property or that of someone else, is permissible. If one is asked concerning the secret of another, or a sin committed, one is permitted to conceal it; as openly proclaiming one's sin is prohibited. A person is allowed to deny having more love for a co-wife to the other wife. Permission is allowed in these cases, as harm will be averted from one.

## LIES TO ACQUIRE WEALTH AND FAME

To speak lies in order to acquire wealth or honour, is not permissible under any circumstances, for should one's wealth or honour not increase, one will not suffer any harm. The worst scenario is that one will not aquire any further benefit. The lack of gaining further benefit, is not regarded as harm. Most people do not understand this fine point, and therefore speak lies, whereas it is absolutely prohibited. In reality, this will lead to the destruction of their religion, as they are unable to differentiate between that which is not necessary and that which is necessary. How sad is it that ignoramuses have regarded their thoughts and conjectures to be necessary, whereas the true, Shar'i necessities, are mentioned above. As long there is no compulsion and possibility of significant harm, it will not be permissible to consume carrion. Similarly, it will generally not be permissible to speak lies, except in cases of compulsion as recognised by the Sharîa'h.

---

[1] Abû Dâwûd (4921), Ahmed (6/404)

Even in such cases one should try to employ *tawriyah*[1] as far as possible, so that one does not become habituated to lying. Ibrâhîm Nakha'I ﷺ, when visited by anyone whilst engaged in some important work at his home, would say to his slave girl, "Tell him to look for me in the masjid."[2] Sha'bi ﷺ would draw a circle and would tell his slave girl, "Place your finger herein and say, "He is not here." " By this veiled reference, their objective would be attained, and in reality they would not be speaking lies. However, outwardly it was in the form of deception which is referred to as *tawriyah* or *ta'reed*. Such forms of *ta'reed* for simple objectives are permissible, as long as someone else's rights are not usurped.

## USAGE OF TAWRIYAH IN JEST

*Rasulullâh* ﷺ jokingly once said to an old woman, "An old woman will not enter paradise." On hearing this, she began crying. Outwardly she understood that no old woman will enter *Jannah*, whereas the meaning was that an old woman will not enter *Jannah* while she is old, but will be transformed into a young woman and thereafter entered into *Jannah*.[3]

A person asked *Rasulullâh* ﷺ for a camel. *Rasulullâh* ﷺ replied, "Wait, we will give you the offspring of a camel." The person enquired, "What will I do will an offspring of a camel?" *Rasulullâh* ﷺ then explained to him the meaning of this statement, "Even a full-size camel is the offspring of another camel."[4]

Once *Rasulullâh* ﷺ remarked to a woman, "There is whiteness in your husband's eyes."[5] It is obvious that there is whiteness in the eyes of every person. However, outwardly the statement seems to indicate some defect. The listener will thus become concerned, only to find out the true meaning thereafter, and be amused. Such forms of *ta'reed* used in order to delight the hearts of one's wife and children are permissible. Likewise, one should

---

[1] Tawriyah refers to uttering a statement which has two meaning, the first common meaning understood by the listener, and the second distant meaning meant by the speaker
[2] Wafayâtul A'yân (1/25)
[3] Shamâ'il (240), Tabrâni in Kabîr (5/357)
[4] Abû Dâwûd (4998), Tirmidhi (1991)
[5] Ibn Abid Dunya, Zubair ibn Bakkâr as stated by Allâmah Irâqî in Mughnî (3/129)

never say, "I am not hungry", when he is, but does not desire to eat. Rather one should say, "I will not eat now. Rather you eat."

## 2. Backbiting

**Allâh** ﷻ states, "None of you should backbite. Would you like to eat the flesh of your dead brother?" Backbiting is akin to eating one's dead brother's flesh.[1] Thus abstain therefrom. A hadith sharîf states, "Backbiting is worse than fornication."[2] In another hadith, *Rasulullâh* ﷺ states that on the night of mi'raj (ascension), he passed by a group of people who were scratching their faces with their nails. *Jibraîl* عليه السلام informed him ﷺ that they were those who used to backbite.[3]

Definition of backbiting: To speak ill of any Muslim in his absence, that if he comes to know of it, he will dislike it, even though this defect is found within him.[4] This is irrespective of whether the defect is found in his physical body, his intellect, his clothing, his actions, his speech, his lineage, his house, his animal or conveyance or any matter related to him, whether it be by tongue, hand or eye gestures or imitation. Once Aishâ ﷺ indicated with her hand that a certain woman was short. *Rasulullâh* ﷺ said, "You have defamed her." [5]

The worse form of backbiting is that of the ulamâ (scholars) and those who externally appear pious, as they backbite and still regard themselves as pious. Their backbiting takes on amazing forms. In a gathering, they will say, "All praise is due to **Allâh** ﷻ , who has saved us from going to the doors of the rulers and the wealthy. May **Allâh** ﷻ protect us from such shamelessness." The objective of these people is apparent. They desire to criticise those ulamâ who act in this way, and refer to them as shameless, whilst showing off their piety and nobility, whereas they are earning the sin of ostentation. Another example hereof is, "So-and-so is such a good

---

[1] A person feels that just as the deceased person does not feel any pain, the person who is backbited about will also feel no pain.

[2] Shua'bul Imân (6315), Tabrâni in Awsat (6586)

[3] Abû Dâwûd (4878), Ahmed (3/224)

[4] Muslim (2589), Ibn Hibbân (5758), Abû Dâwûd (4874), Tirmidhi (1934), etc.

[5] Shu'abul Imân (6307), Tabrâni in Kabîr (20/39)

person, if only he does not have the greed of the world, in which we ulamâ are involved." By pondering, the meaning of this is clear, that he wishes to highlight the other person's lack of patience, and by attributing greed to himself, he desires that the listener regards him to be humble. This is backbiting as well as ostentation. Even more surprising is that these people backbite, and still regard themselves to be pious and safe from backbiting.

At times someone exclaims, "SubhânAllâh! How surprising!" When people turn their attention to him, he says, "The thought of so-and-so person came to mind. May **Allâh** ﷻ shower Mercy on him and us, and grant us the ability to repent." It is apparent that these words were neither uttered out of compassion nor intended as a duâ, as the outward words portray. If duâ was the aim, then why did he not do so in the heart? Was there a need to utter "SubhânAllâh", thus turning people's attention to himself? And was there a need to highlight the sin? Is exposing a person's faults an act of compassion and beneficence? It is the habit of some people to say, "Do not backbite." However, internally they do not regard backbiting as reprehensible. The motive of their utterance is merely to show their piety and taqwâ. Similarly, in a gathering, backbiting occurs. A person, acting pious says, "Sir, to backbite is a sin. All of us listening will also be involved in the sin." He says this to the people, but his heart desires, "O, if only he will not practice on my advice, and continue backbiting." He then listens to this speech, and then feels that he has been absolved of the sin by prohibiting it. Remember that as long as one does not dislike speaking and listening to evil from the bottom of his heart, he will not be saved from the sin of backbiting, as the backbiter and the listeners are equal in sin. Just as verbal backbiting is prohibited, so too is backbiting with the heart. However, in some cases, permission for backbiting has been granted, which will now be mentioned:

a. An oppressed person may complain of the oppression meted out to him to any authority that has the power to remove the oppression. However, if one complains to those who are unable to remove the oppression, then this will be regarded as backbiting. A person spoke ill of Hajjâj ibn Yusuf in the gathering of one pious person. He remarked, "Verily **Allâh** ﷻ will take revenge on behalf of Hajjaj from those who oppressed him, just as He ﷻ will take revenge from Hajjaaj on behalf of those whom he oppressed."

b. If one wants to take assistance from someone to stop some evil, some matter contrary to the shariah, or some innovation, then it will be permissible to mention to him the name of the person involved.

c. In seeking a fatwa from a Mufti it is permissible to mention the person concerned. Hindah ﷂ mentioned to *Rasulullâh* ﷺ, "Abu Sufyân is a miserly person. He does not give me sufficient for myself and my children." Even though she cited his miserliness, *Rasulullâh* ﷺ did not reproach her. This was a complaint. However, remember that this form of backbiting will only be permissible when there is some form of benefit for oneself or another Muslim.

d. If a person intends to have some dealings with someone, or becomes aware of a marital matter related to him, and one is aware that there will be some harm when dealing with this person, then it will be permissible to highlight the harm, so that the person involved therein is saved therefrom. In like manner, it is permissible to expose the injustice of the accused in a court of law, so that the rightful owner is not deprived of his rights. One is only allowed to expose the injustice of a person, regarding whom there is fear of harm or loss, or upon whom the judgement or ruling hinges.

e. If a person is famously known by a certain name, which exposes some weaknesses within him, then by calling him such names one will not be guilty of backbiting (on condition that he does not mind such a name) e.g. A'mash (squint-eyed) and A'raj (paraplegic). If, however, he can be addressed by some other name it would be preferable to use that name, so that even the outward form of backbiting does not occur.

f. If any fault or sin is found so openly in any person, that if he has to be exposed, he does not feel displeased e.g. he is a hermaphrodite or eunuch. When this is being discussed, the thought does not even pass his mind that he is being addressed. This speech is not regarded as backbiting as well. However, if that person feels upset, then it is prohibited to say such things, since it is not permissible to even mention the sins of an evil-doer without a valid reason, if it will upset him (on condition that it is not perpetrated openly).

# PREVENTION

The remedy for preventing the *nafs* from backbiting, is to ponder over the harms and punishments mentioned for backbiting. A hadith sharîf states, "Backbiting has a more powerful and consuming effect on the actions of believers, than fire has on grass." i.e. by backbiting, ones actions are destroyed. Ponder, how sorrowful will a pious person feel on the day of judgement, when he will witness his good deeds which he performed with great sacrifice in the world, being transferred to the one whom he spoke ill of. It is far better for a believer to ponder over his own faults and weaknesses. When one has an opportunity, one should introspect. Whatever weaknesses he finds within himself, he should attempt to eradicate them. In this way, he will not have any free time to seek the faults of others. Realise that the harm caused to you, by your smallest sin, cannot be caused by the major sins of others. If you cannot find any fault within yourself, then this is in fact the worst of all faults, since no human is free from weaknesses. Regarding oneself as faultless is the greatest fault. Therefore, remedy this first, and thereafter attempt curing the other faults you have within yourself. If thereafter you happen to plunge in the sin of backbiting, then repent to **Allâh** in solitude, and ask the person concerned to forgive you for the wrong you had done to him. If you cannot meet him, then make duâ of forgiveness for him, and give charity on his behalf. Since you have oppressed your Muslim brother by backbiting, try to make amends as quickly as possible in whatever way possible.

## 3. Fighting and Arguing

*Rasulullâh* said, "Whoever abstains from arguing, whilst he is on the truth, a palace will be built for him in the highest level of *Jannah*. Whoever abstains from arguing whilst he is on the wrong, a palace will be built for him on the edge of *Jannah*."[1]

Definition of arguing: To object to the speech of others, by finding fault therein, either in the wording or its meaning. This generally occurs due to

---

[1] Abû Dâwûd (4800), Tirmidhî (1993)

one of two reasons. The objective is either to highlight ones greatness or excellence in speech, due to pride, or to silence the other person.

If what is being said is correct, then it is necessary to accept it; and if not, then remain silent. However, if there is some religious benefit, then it is not permissible to remain silent. Then too, one should bear in mind that one should advise with compassion and not harshness.

## 4. Joking

Any access of joking leads to an abundance of laughter, which suffocates the heart, creates enmity, and diminishes ones awe and dignity. *Rasulullâh* said, "Verily a man utters a statement by which he makes his companions laugh. Due to this, he is thrown further than Thurayya (a star)"[1] However, there is no harm in occasional light-heartedness, more so with ones wife and children, in order to cheer their hearts, as this was the practice of *Rasulullâh*.

However, even in this jesting, *Rasulullâh* would only speak the truth.[2] *Rasulullâh* jokingly once said to an old woman, "An old woman will not enter *Jannah*." On hearing this, she began crying. Outwardly she understood that no old woman will enter *Jannah*, whereas the meaning was that an old woman will not enter *Jannah* while she is old, but will be transformed into a young woman and thereafter entered into *Jannah*.[3]

Hazrat Ṣuhayb 's son Abu Umair had a bird, which died. *Rasulullâh* said, "O Abu Umair, what has happened to nughair?"[4]

Once, *Rasulullâh* said to Hazrat Ṣuhayb whilst he was eating dates, "Are you eating dates whereas your eye is sore?" He replied, "I only chew with the opposite side."[5]

---


[1] Ibn Hibbân (5716), Ahmed (2/402)
[2] Tirmidhî (1990), Ahmed (2/340)
[3] Shamâ'il (240), Tabrâni in Kabîr (5/357)
[4] Bukhârî (6129), Muslim (2150)
[5] Hâkim (3/399), Ibn Mâjah (3443)

*Rasulullâh* ﷺ even ran a race with Aishâ ﷺ in order to please her and make her happy.[1] There is no harm with such forms of joking, as long as it is not done habitually.


## 5. Flattery

You have noticed that the habit of most lecturers and worldly orientated Muslims, is to praise wealthy people and those of high status. They compose odes in their praise. There are six harms of flattery, four for the one who flatters, and two for the one who is addressed. As for the one who is flattering, the harms are:

a. he mentions such things that are contrary to reality, which are open lies and a major sin.

b. he expresses such love which he does not possess in his heart, thus he is guilty of hypocrisy and boasting.

c. he utters that which he has not established, based on mere conjecture e.g. he states, "Verily he is very pious, he is just." Once *Rasulullâh* ﷺ said, "If you have to praise anyone, then say, "I think that so-and-so is like this,"[2] since it is not permissible to regard assumptions as facts.

d. if an oppressor or open sinner is praised due to which he becomes pleased, then the one who praises will be committing a sin by pleasing him. *Rasulullâh* ﷺ said, "Verily **Allâh** ﷻ becomes angry when a sinner is praised."[3] (Baihaqi, Musnadul Firdaws)

<u>H</u>asan ﷺ said, "Whoever supplicates for long life for a sinner, he is pleased that **Allâh** ﷻ is disobeyed."[4] An oppressor and sinner should not be praised, but admonished in order for him to leave his oppression and sin. The harms for the one who is being praised are: i) It results in pride and vanity, both of which are destructive. It is for this reason that when a

---

[1] Abû Dâwûd (2578), Ibn Hibbân (4691), Ibn Mâjah (1979)
[2] Bukhârî (6061), Muslim (3000), Ibn Hibbân (5767)
[3] Shu'abul Imân (4543), Musnad Firdaws (1336)
[4] Shu'abul Imân (8986), Ibn Abid Dunyâ in As-Samt wa Adâbul Lisân (600)

person praised his companion before *Rasulullâh* ﷺ, *Rasulullâh* ﷺ said, "You have cut the neck of your companion."[1]

ii) He will hear his praises and become puffed up with pride, and this will result in laziness and negligence with regards to good deeds. A hadith sharîf states, "It is better for a person to slaughter his brother with a blunt knife, than to praise him in person." The reason is that by being killed, ones worldly life is destroyed, whereas the destructive ailments mentioned above result in the everlasting life of the Hereafter being destroyed. However, if a person is saved from these harms, then there is no harm in praising that person. In fact, at times, it is mustahab (commendable) and a means of attaining reward. *Rasulullâh* ﷺ said, "If the *imân* of Abu Bakr is weighed against the weight of all mankind (excluding the *Ambiyâ* ﷺ), his îmân will be weightier."[2] *Rasulullâh* ﷺ said, "O Umar! If I had not been sent, you would have been sent."[3] Similarly, *Rasulullâh* ﷺ praised many of the Sahâbah ﷺ , since he knew that this would increase their enthusiasm, and would not result in *ujub* (vanity) in them.

## CURE FOR PROTECTION OF PRIDE WHEN PRAISED

When one is praised, then he should think of the deficiencies in his actions, thoughts, and feelings. He should ponder over his end result. How will I leave this world? If in reality these qualities are within me, then at the time of death, will I still possess them? He should ponder over his spiritual ailments and weaknesses. He should understand, that if the one who praises him comes to know of his spiritual ailments and faults, then he would never praise him. Thus a believer should never become proud when praised. Actually, he should dislike it from the bottom of his heart. This is alluded to by *Rasulullâh* ﷺ saying, "Fill sand in the mouth of the one who praises."[4] When Ali ﷺ was praised, he would make the following dua, "

اَللّٰهُمَّ اغْفِرْ لِي مَا لَا يَعْلَمُونَ وَ لَا تُؤَاخِذْنِي بِمَا يَقُولُونَ وَ اجْعَلْنِي خَيْرًا مِمَّا يَظُنُّونَ

---

[1] Bukhârî (6061), Muslim (3000), Ibn Hibbân (5767)
[2] Ibn Adî in Kâmil (4/201), Tarîkhe Dimishq (30/126)
[3] Musnad Firdaws (5127), Tarîkhe Dimishq (44/114), Hâkim (3/85)
[4] Muslim (3002), Abû Dâwûd (4804), Tirmidhî (2393)

"*O* **Allâh**! Forgive me for those sins which they do not know, do not take me to task for that which they say, and make me better than what they think about me."

# THIRD PRINCIPLE

# ANGER

Anger is a flame of fire extracted from **Allâh** ﷻ's blazing fire. Learning to control one's anger is an important component of our *dîn* (religion). *Nabî* ﷺ has stated, "A strong person is not one who overcomes another in wrestling. A strong one is he who controls himself at the time of anger." [1] In another hadîth, *Rasulullâh* ﷺ stated, "Anger spoils îmân just as aloes spoils honey."[2] Anger is revolting. Outwardly, it causes one to hit others, swear them, and speak harshly to them, and inwardly it creates malice, jealousy, evil thoughts, happiness on the downfall of others, a desire to expose the faults of others, and to destroy their respect, and sadness when the other is happy. Every single one of these qualities is destructive.

## THE CURE FOR ANGER

The cure for anger is twofold:

1. To control it by spiritual exercises. This does not mean completely eliminating it, since this is not desired. In fact, if one does not possess this quality at all, then it will become compulsory to attain it, since it is a means by which one will engage in *jihad* with the disbelievers, cause one to prohibit wrongs, and leads one to attain many forms of righteousness. It is like a hunting dog. One needs to train it, so that it becomes obedient to one's intellect and the *sharî'ah*. It must thus rise when commanded to do so by the intellect and the sharî'ah, and must likewise control itself on their orders. This is just like how the dog is obedient to its master. When commanded to attack, it leaps forward, otherwise it sits quietly. This is possible when one strives. He has to learn to be forbearing and forgiving when any incident occurs that raises his anger.

2. Controlling the anger when it inflames by swallowing it. One cure is *i'lmî* (theoretical) and one is *a'malî (practical)*

---


[1] Bukhârî (6114) , Muslim (2609)
[2] Shu'abul-Imân (7941), Musnad Firdaws (4315)

The i'lmî cure is that one should realize that there is no reason for his anger, except that he dislikes something which occurs according to the wish of **Allâh** ﷻ, and not according to his wish. This is the limit of ignorance. Secondly, one should realize, "What right do I possess over the other person?" What are **Allâh** ﷻ's rights over me? How does **Allâh** ﷻ deal with you, and how do you want to treat this person? It is obvious that you are not the creator, sustainer, and owner of him. You have not granted him life. **Allâh** ﷻ has many, many rights over you. In every way, you have to be thankful and obedient to him. Despite this, day and night, you commit countless sins and wrongs. Despite His ﷻ Favours and Rights over you, He ﷻ tolerates you. If He ﷻ has to punish you for just one fault, what will be your condition? You possess no right over this person, but you lose complete control of yourself, on some matter which is contrary to your nature, and you are prepared to remove him from the surface of the earth. Is your obedience and pleasure more necessary than the worship and Law of **Allâh** ﷻ?

The *a'malî* (practical) cure is to recite *ta'awwuz* (اعُوذْ بِاللهِ مِنَ الشَّيْطَانِ الرَّجِيم) when overcome by anger, since anger is a satanic effect. When one seeks protection from shaytân's evil, then his effects will be repelled also. Together with this, change your posture. If you are standing, sit down. If seated, lie down. If one's anger is still not cooled, then perform *wudû* and place the cheek on the ground, so that your most honourable limb, the head, is placed on the lowest of places. The benefit of this is that your pride will break. This is the greatest cause of anger. By doing so, one realises that he is a lowly servant, and that pride is not appropriate for him. *Nabî* ﷺ said, "Verily a man attains with tolerance, the rank of one who stays awake at night in optional prayers and fasts during the day. At times, man is written to be a tyrant, whereas he only has rule over his family members."[1] In another hadîth, *Nabî* ﷺ is reported to have stated, "Whoever swallows his anger, whereas he has the power to vent it, **Allâh** ﷻ will fill his heart with safety and *îmân* on the Day of judgement."[2] *Nabî* ﷺ is also reported to have stated, "There is no gulp more beloved to

---

[1] Tabrânî in Awsat (6269), Abu Nua'ym in Hilyah (8/289)
[2] Tabrânî in Awsat (6023) and Kabîr (12/346)

**Allâh** than the gulp of anger, which a servant swallows. Whenever a servant swallows his anger, **Allâh** fills his heart with *îmân*."[1]

# FOURTH PRINCIPLE

# JEALOUSY

## THE REALITY OF JEALOUSY

The meaning of jealousy is to see someone else possessing a certain bounty, and you desire that the bounty be snatched away from him, or that some calamity afflicts him. Jealousy is *harâm* (prohibited). Zakariyyâ said, "**Allâh** states, "A jealous person is an enemy of My ()Bounty, one who is upset with My () Decree, and unhappy with My () Allotment which I have distributed among My ()Servants."[2] *Rasûlullâh* said, "Jealousy devours a person's good deeds just as fire devours dry wood." [3] It is however permissible to be jealous over such a person who uses the favours bestowed by **Allâh** in sin and for oppression e.g. a person is wealthy and he is squandering his wealth in alcohol or adultery. Desiring that such a person's wealth be snatched away is not a sin, since here the object is not that the wealth be snatched away from him, but one's desire is that this sin and wrong doing must come to an end. The sign of this is that if he renounces the evil, then you do not wish for the termination of the bounty. Remember, generally the cause for jealousy is pride, enmity or possessing a lowly and based character, since you are being miserly of **Allâh**'s Bounty on His Servant, without any reason.

**GHIBTAH**- Desiring something which another possesses, without having the desire that the bounty be snatched away from him, is referred to as ghibtah. This is permissible in the sharî'ah, since the object is not that the bounty be snatched away, but one hopes to attain for himself a like bounty. There is no harm in this.

---

[1] Ahmed (1/327)

[2] Shu'abul-Imân (6213)

[3] Abû Dâwûd (4903), Ibn Mâjah (4210)

**CURE-** Jealousy is a spiritual sickness. Its cure is *i'lmî* (theoretical) and *a'malî* (practical).

The *i'lmî* cure is that the jealous person should realize that his jealousy is harming none but himself. It is of no harm to the one over whom one is jealous, in fact it benefits him since he receives all the jealous person's good deeds. The jealous person causes harm to himself in his religious and worldly life. As for the harm in his religion, he destroys his good actions, and makes himself a target for **Allâh** ﷻ's anger, since he is displeased with **Allâh** ﷻ's Decree and he is being stingy with **Allâh** ﷻ's Bounties which He ﷻ has granted to His ﷻ Servants from His ﷻ Royal Treasury. With regards to harm in one's worldly life, the jealous person remains perpetually in sorrow and grief. He burns in this thought that how can so-and-so person become disgraced and poverty-stricken. The person upon whom you are jealous over, is your enemy. When you remain in grief and sorrow, your enemy becomes happier, since he knows that you want to cause him grief, but you yourself are in perpetual grief. Thus, his bounty becomes complete, and the jealous person remains in absolute loss. You should ponder, "By your jealousy, what harm befalls the other person?" It is obvious that no harm comes to him. In fact, he benefits, since all of your good deeds are transferred to his book of deeds. How strange! The jealous person wants that his adversary's worldly bounty be snatched away, whereas his bounty remains and together he receives the bounties of the Hereafter.

On the other hand, the jealous person earns for himself the punishment of the Hereafter, as well as difficulty in this worldly life, by losing his contentment and remaining continuously perplexed. This is similar to one who throws a stone at his enemy. However the stone falls onto his own eyes, blinding him. Even worse, shaytân, our enemy, becomes all the more pleased, since the jealous person neither gains the bounty nor happiness with the Divine Decree. If one was pleased with The Divine Decree, he would have received reward for this action. A very severe form of jealousy is to be jealous over some-one's knowledge or piety, desiring it to be destroyed. By loving knowledge and piety, one will be greatly rewarded.

As for the *a'malî* (practical) cure, remember that the demand of jealousy is to find faults in the other person and to be sorrowful and distressed day and night. Therefore, oppose the *nafs* and act contrary to its demands. Thus praise the concerned person, express happiness over his bounty, and humble yourself before him. After doing this for a few days, even with self-inflicted coercion, love will be created within you for him, and the jealousy will be removed. You will be saved from the sin and sorrow you were thus undergoing due to your jealousy.

Perhaps this doubt may cross your mind, that it is part of human nature for one to possess different feelings towards friends and enemies. It is not within your control to express that amount of happiness on seeing your rival in a suitable condition, as you would do on seeing your friend in a likewise condition. When this is not within your control, then how can you be held responsible for this? I therefore say that this is correct, and if these feelings remain till this level, then there is no sin. However, with regards to the matters which are volitional, one has to abstain from these two matters:

1. Do not make your jealousy apparent by your tongue, limbs and volitional actions. Act contrary to the demands of your *nafs* as has been mentioned above.
2. Dislike this feeling found within yourself of desiring that a certain bounty of **Allâh** ﷻ be snatched away from one of His ﷻ Servants. Realise that this feeling can cause great harm to your religious life.

If after you have practised on these two matters, these natural feelings still remain, i.e. that your friend be in a good condition and your rival be destroyed), then do not be concerned. Since you do not have the ability to completely remove these thoughts, there is no sin. Yes, it is necessary to detest such thoughts in your heart. The sign of this is that if you possess the ability to destroy the bounty which is possessed by the other person, then even though your desire will be to do so, you do not make any attempts to do so with your physical limbs. If you have the ability to assist him in increasing or sustaining the bounty, then you help him despite your aversion to it. If this is your condition, then understand that you have fulfilled **Allâh** ﷻ's Command which was within your control, and now you are free from sin. To remove natural and non-volitional thoughts are not within your control. Despite its existence, it is regarded as non-existent, since it is concealed within your volitional actions. Remember that one whose gaze has shifted from this world realizes that this life is temporary, and that all its bounties are soon going to terminate. If your rival is in comfort and ease, then for how long will this last? If due to his actions, he has to go to Hell, then of what benefit was the few days of enjoyment?    If he is an inhabitant of *Jannah*, then what comparison can there be between the bounties of *Jannah* and these ephemeral bounties? Thus being jealous and burning on seeing a rival in a happy condition, is completely futile and unproductive. The whole of creation has been created by **Allâh** ﷻ, and they all are the slaves of this Beloved Divine Being ﷻ. The bounties from the Beloved ﷻ should be exhibited on His ﷻ Slaves. Thus you should become overjoyed and pleased on witnessing the effects of your Beloved's Bounties on anyone, not sad and jealous.

# FIFTH PRINCIPLE

# STINGINESS AND LOVE FOR WEALTH

Stinginess is a very destructive disease. **Allâh** ﷻ states, "Those who are saved from the greed of their souls are the successful ones." In another verse, **Allâh** ﷻ declares, "And those who are stingy with that which **Allâh** ﷻ has bestowed them, due to His ﷻ Grace, should not think that it is better for them; in fact it is bad for them. Soon on the Day of Judgement, they will be yoked around their necks with that with which they were stingy." *Nabî* ﷺ is reported to have stated, "Abstain from stinginess, for verily it has destroyed those before you." [1]

It is not the quality of a believer to be stingy, thus leading himself to Hell. Stinginess is in reality due to love of wealth. Love of wealth turns the heart towards this world, due to which one's connection with **Allâh** ﷻ becomes weak. At the time of death, a stingy person looks at his beloved wealth with great sorrow, and he departs for his journey towards the Hereafter with a heavy heart. He is thus not pleased to meet his Creator ﷻ. A hadith sharîf states, "Whoever dislikes to meet **Allâh** ﷻ, **Allâh** ﷻ dislikes meeting him." As for one who does not possess money, then he will not

---

[1] Muslim (2578), Ibn Hibbân (5176), Nasaî in Kubrâ (11519)

be stingy. However, it is quite possible that he possesses love of wealth, and always desires becoming rich. Likewise, some wealthy people are generous, but they seek praise and fame through their generosity. Even though they cannot be termed as stingy, they can definitely be regarded as lovers of wealth. Thus together with the cure of stinginess, one has to be cured of the love of wealth. The love of wealth makes one unmindful of **Allâh** ﷻ's remembrance. Wealth is a great trial for a believer. *Rasûlullâh* ﷺ said, "When a person passes away, the angels ask, "What has he sent forward?" and the people ask, "What has he left behind?"[1] If he had spent his wealth in good causes, and had gathered sufficient provisions in the Hereafter, then at the time of death, he will be extremely pleased; since he will now receive the benefits of the wealth he had invested and sent forth. On the other hand, if he did not do so, he will be sorrowful and death will be difficult for him. *Nabî* ﷺ cursed the following person, "Destruction to the slave of wealth and clothing. Destruction and woe to him! When a thorn pricks him, he will not be able to remove it."[2] After receiving the curse of *Nabî* ﷺ, what will this person's condition be?"

Wealth is not evil in every aspect. *Nabî* ﷺ has stated, "How excellent is pure wealth for a pious person!"[3] How could wealth be condemned, when this world is a farm for the Hereafter, and a person is journeying towards **Allâh** ﷻ? The world is a phase from amongst the phases of his journey, and the physical body is his conveyance. It is not possible to traverse this journey without it. The body remains in existence with food and drink, which is attained by wealth. The person who understands the benefit of wealth, and realizes that it is a channel for attaining the fuel for his vehicle, will not become obsessed with it. He will only use how much is necessary. If he suffices on necessity, he will be successful. If a person has far more than necessary, then this will generally lead to his destruction, since a traveller keeps only so much of provisions as required by him. When his goods are excessive, then it becomes difficult for him to even travel and reach his destination. *Rasûlullâh* ﷺ said, "O Aishâ, if you wish to meet up with me, then be content with so much of the world as the provisions of a traveller. Do not take new things. Do not remove clothing until you do not

---

[1] Shu'abul-Imân (9992), Musnad Firdaws (1111)
[2] Bukhârî (2887), Ibn Mâjah (4136)
[3] Ibn Hibbân (3210), Ahmad (4/197)

patch it."[1] *Nabî* ﷺ made the following duâ, "*O* **Allâh** (ﷻ), make the provisions of the family of Muhammad (ﷺ) just about sufficient."[2]

Gathering wealth more than necessity is harmful due to three factors:
a) It leads a person to sin, since he now has the ability to fulfil it. When one has the ability to commit sin, it becomes difficult to abstain. When one does not possess money, it is obvious that he will not be able to do many sins.
b) If a wealthy person is a worshiper, as well as an abstinent person, and he spends his wealth in permissible avenues, then too, this harm will be realized, that his body will be nourished and habituated to enjoyments. Since money does not last forever, he will at many times be forced to seek assistance from others to sustain his habits. At times, he will be forced to stretch his arms before oppressors and tyrants, and flatter them so that his desires can be fulfilled till his last breath. Now qualities such as hypocrisy, lies, ostentation, enmity, hatred and jealousy will become perceptible. For this reason, *Rasûlullâh* ﷺ said, "The love of this world is the root of all sin."[3]
c) It makes one unmindful of the remembrance of **Allâh** ﷻ, which is the root of everlasting success. Disputes with farmers, reckoning with shareholders, debating ways to be wary of them, and preparation to invest one's wealth dominates the heart. Earning wealth, then looking after it, and then spending it, cause darkness of the heart, remove its lustre and divert one away from the remembrance of **Allâh** ﷻ. When one does not own more than necessary, then these thoughts and worries do not occur.

## SUFFICIENCY AND NECESSITY

Perhaps you desire to know the meaning of necessity, since every person, no matter how wealthy he may be, regards himself as possessing meagre amounts. Understand well, that there is no place for imaginary necessities. Man's real necessity is to fill his stomach and cover his body. If you abstain from beautiful apparel, then two dinars is sufficient for you annually, by

---

[1] Hâkim(4/312), Tirmidhî (1780)
[2] Bukharî (6460), Muslim (1055)
[3] Shu'abul-Imân (10019) (a mursal narration from Hasan ﷺ)

which you can prepare some thick clothing, which will protect you from the heat and cold.  As for food, if you abstain from luxurious foods and eating to satiation, then one *mud* (800 grams) is sufficient for your daily needs, which amounts to approximately 500 *ratls* yearly for grains. Using gravy sometimes, when the prices are low, will equal to about three dinars. Thus, you only need five dinars and 500 *ratls* grain yearly. This is if you are single. If you have the responsibility of a family, then estimate a likewise amount, for each person of the family. If you are a labourer, and you have earned sufficient for that day, then engage yourself in the worship of **Allâh** ﷻ. If you seek more, then you will be regarded to be a person of the world. If you are not earning, but are engaged in the acquisition of knowledge or *ibâdah*, and you acquire some land or property by which you will continuously receive this amount, then I have hope that you will not be regarded as a man of the world, especially in this era, when hearts have transformed, greed has overpowered people, and nobody cares to look towards the needs of the needy. Having this amount is far superior to begging. Buying properties and spending wealth on sand is impermissible when the object is seeking of this world, an increase in name and fame, or the desire to be a land-owner. In this instance, the object is the assistance of *dîn*, thus it will be excluded from the prohibition which *Nabî* ﷺ sounded, "Do not take property, then you will love the world."[1]

However, it is necessary to keep in mind, that peoples' natures and spirits are different. It is quite possible that some people will not be able to suffice on the amount mentioned. There is thus permission for them to double it, since there is no difficulty in *dîn*. However, the intention here must be, that we need extra so that we can remain engaged in **Allâh** ﷻ's worship with a contented heart, since there will be difficulty in having less and one will not be at ease in one's worship. The object should not be luxury or enjoyment. Whoever earns more than this is a person of the world. He possesses love of wealth, which can destroy his *dîn*. All extra wealth could then be spent on widows and the needy. Collecting more money than mentioned above can be for one of three reasons: 1) enjoying oneself and attaining pleasure 2) charity 3) assistance if some calamity occurs. All these intentions are incorrect. The first one distances one from

---

[1] Ibn Hibbân (710), Hâkim (4/322), Tirmidhî (2328)

**Allâh** ﷻ and makes one pre-occupied with the world. As for the second intention, then remember it is better not to possess wealth at all, than to spend in charity. As for the third intention, this is not taken into consideration. If poverty or any calamity is destined for someone, then it will not move away due to this wealth. Repel this evil thought with the thought that just as a calamity may afflict my wealth unexpectedly, a door of sustenance can also be opened up unexpectedly from whence one never imagined. A servant should never possess this evil thought that **Allâh** ﷻ will close his doors of sustenance and place him into poverty. He should maintain good thoughts regarding his Master ﷻ. Besides this, ponder over this point that the desire to remain wealthy and healthy your whole life, and never to be afflicted with some sorrow and difficulty, is not praiseworthy. It is not the work of an intelligent person to view a luxurious and easy life as better, since a servant attains lofty ranks through difficulties and worries. His heart is polished, his sins are forgiven and many other benefits are accrued, which cannot be otherwise easily achieved. It is for this very reason that the *Ambiyâ* ﷺ had to undergo the severest of trials. Then lighter difficulties were placed on those lower and so on. In short, according to the connection one has with **Allâh** ﷻ, so much of difficulties and worries he shall have to endure.

Remember that **Allâh** ﷻ is All Wise. None of His ﷻ Actions are devoid of wisdom. He ﷻ knows very well that which is beneficial for His ﷻ Servants. Thus choosing comfort for oneself and collecting money with this thought that it will save one from future calamities, is as though one is taking matters into his own hands, and giving preference to his choice over **Allâh** ﷻ's choice, which is completely incorrect. Besides this, think, 'What benefit is there in lamenting before death, and what will be the result of my concern of old age or illness?' You were neither created to worry about this, nor will your sustenance which has been apportioned to you increase or decrease by this concern. You are but a traveller to the Hereafter. You have been sent in this world to prepare goods for the Hereafter. Thus concern yourself with this. Do not concern yourself with the world, and how you will pass your life here.

The amount which I have mentioned is an approximate amount. According to people, conditions and difference in seasons, there may be an increase or decrease. The object here is that one should regard wealth as medication. A certain amount in moderation is beneficial, and an excess of it is destructive. An increase in it can lead to an increase in the sickness. Thus try to decrease your expenditure. If there is some difficulty in this, then this will remain for only a few days, since life is brief. Pass it anyhow. Remember also, that the enjoyment of food is in remaining hungry. The more you remain hungry in this world, the more you will enjoy the bounties of *Jannah*.

## THE LIMIT AND REALITY OF STINGINESS

It is necessary to know the definition of stinginess, because many people are left in a quandary, and do not know whether they are stingy or not. Understand that wherever the sharî'ah or ones self honour commands one to spend, and he does not spend in that avenue, then he is a stingy person. Thus if a person spends on his family members that amount which is fixed by the judge, and is not prepared to give even one more morsel, even though this harshness is not contrary to the sharî'ah , but since it is against the self honour of a person, it will be regarded as stinginess. Another example is of a person who returns bread or meat due to some slight fault in them, then even though this will be correct according to the sharî'ah, it will be regarded as stinginess, since it is contrary to one's self honour. If this is the case, then why has the sharî'ah regarded these actions as permissible? The answer to this is that the object of the sharî'ah in allowing these actions contrary to self honour to be correct, is to terminate fights between the general people, and to place such a light burden on the stingy person, which he can easily bear, keeping the worldly systems in place.

It is also necessary to fulfil those necessities which occur suddenly. A hadîth sharîf states, "That money by which a man can save his honour, is a means of charity for him."[1] For example, if a wealthy person knows that a certain poet will mock and deride him, but if he gives him a small amount of wealth he will keep his mouth closed, and even then he does not give, such a person will be regarded as stingy. The reason for this, is that he did

---

[1] Hâkim (2/50), Daraqutnî (3/28)

not use the means to protect his honour, and granted an opportunity to a foul-mouthed person to deride him.

It is apparent that wealth itself is not beloved, and is not one's objective. Therefore, no person eats or swallows it. However, since man's needs are fulfilled by it and benefits are attained, therefore wealth is desired. If a person now does not spend in those places in which there is benefit, then he has greatly erred. Realize that this person loves the money itself. He does not care for the benefit which is the purpose of wealth. At times, the love of wealth reaches such a stage that man cannot see his own benefit or loss. This is a very dangerous stage. This is referred to as compound ignorance. In such a case, bind yourself to the sharî'ah and your intellect. Wherever they both command you to spend, spend freely. This is with regards to stinginess. As for generosity, there is no limit. Once a person has left the domain of stinginess and spends, then he has entered the realm of generosity.

## THE CURE FOR STINGINESS

Its cure is *i'lmî* (theoretical) and *a'malî (*practical*)*. The *i'lmî* (theoretical) cure is to know the harms of stinginess - it creates destruction in the Hereafter, and dispraise in this world. One should realise that his wealth will not follow him. If it remains, it will only remain till the grave. Whatever wealth man is granted in this world has been given so that he can spend it to fulfil his necessities. If he now resembles an animal, and spends it to fulfil his bestial desires, then he will remain deprived of a very necessary bounty i.e. the enjoyments of the Hereafter. If he leaves his wealth for his children in this world, then it is as though he has granted comfort to his children, but he has gone forward empty-handed. Can there be any foolishness greater than this? If his children turn out to be pious and noble, will **Allâh** not take responsibility to fulfil their needs? Then what benefit is there in the hoarding of wealth? If, **Allâh** forbid, they turn out to be evil, then it is obvious that they will spend this wealth in **Allâh**'s disobedience. He will also be then taken to task, as he was a cause of the sin. As other people will enjoy his wealth, so will his punishment increase. By pondering over these matters as well as the result of stinginess, there is hope that Inshâ-Allâh, one will be saved from stinginess.As for the *a'malî (*practical*)* cure, one should force oneself to spend, until it becomes one's nature to do so.

Keep thinking that you will be lauded, and will attain some recompense. Once the desire to spend has been created, then remove these evil intentions, until your spending becomes solely for **Allâh** 's pleasure.

# SIXTH PRINCIPLE

# HAUGHTINESS AND LOVE FOR FAME

**Allâh**  states, "We have prepared that final abode for those who do not intend greatness in the land, nor corruption."

*Rasûlullâh*  said, "Two hungry wolves, left in a flock of goats, do not cause as much harm, as the love of wealth and position, causes to a person's religion."[1]

Know well, that haughtiness and love for name and fame is detrimental. Due to it, hypocrisy is created in the heart. In reality, those people who are obscure and unknown are in great comfort. They are dishevelled and clad in simple clothing. People do not seat them near themselves; neither do the wealthy permit them to enter their residences. If they desire to marry, no-one is prepared to give their daughter to them in marriage. They don tattered clothing and live with great humility. Amongst them are such people, that if they have to take an oath on any matter, **Allâh**  will definitely fulfil it. Remember that as soon as man is honoured and he desires to be positioned on locations of respect and to stroll ahead of people, then he will be destroyed. The servants of **Allâh**  conceal themselves. However, without desire and effort, if **Allâh**  makes some-one famous, then it is not appropriate for him to conceal himself. The *Ambiyâ* , *Khulafâ-e-râshidîn*  and many *Awliyâ*  acquired fame in this world, but none of them desired it. They were happy with whichever condition **Allâh**  placed them in. For this reason, neither did pride nor did love for fame develop within them. *Hubbe-jâh* (love for fame) refers to when a person aspires for fame and honour. Due to this, haughtiness is created. May **Allâh**  protect and save us!

---

[1] Ibn Hibbân (3228), Hâkim(3/420), Tirmidhî (2376)

# DIFFERENCE BETWEEN LOVE FOR WEALTH AND FAME

The meaning of *hubbe-jâh* is, that a person wants to possess control over the hearts of people. He desires that their hearts must become subservient to him; that they must praise him, run to fulfil his needs, and be even prepared to sacrifice their lives for him. Man possesses love for wealth for this reason, that it is a means for fulfilling one's needs. The desire for position and honour is the same i.e. that no need of a person remains unfulfilled. Thus, with regards to the object, these qualities originate in man so that he derives this benefit.

However, the desire for name and fame is more beloved than wealth. The reasons for this are:

1) By fame, one generally receives wealth, whereas one does not always gain recognition due to wealth. Fame cannot be stolen or usurped, which is always a fear when one possesses wealth. It is an accepted principle that when the honour and greatness of any person enters the heart of people, then they automatically begin praising him, and they try to draw the hearts of others towards him also. At times, they are successful in doing so. This then continues increasing. Thus, by acquiring name and fame, one becomes successful, without any strenuous effort and difficulty. This is contrary to wealth, in which a person needs to plan and make much effort to acquire. Then preserving and protecting it is difficult. For this reason, people have more love and desire for fame and popularity, compared to money, and it is for this reason that even poor people are entrapped in this disease.

2) Every person, by nature, loves to be honoured and to be great. He loves to be unparalleled and unique. However, this is a Divine Exclusivity and only worthy of **Allâh** ﷻ's Status, since only He ﷻ is unique. All of creation is like a shadow of the effulgence of His ﷻ Power. Thus it is as though a person entrapped in this disease of the love for name and fame desires to equate himself to **Allâh** ﷻ, and he becomes angered at the relationship which the shadow has with the sun. It is as though his carnal

self is calling out as Fir'awn did, أَنَا رَبُّكُمُ الْأَعْلَى ("I am the high Lord!").
The only difference is that Fir'awn stated it openly in front of people,
whereas other people conceal it in their hearts. Since none can ever attain
this quality of uniqueness, and it is highly impossible to successfully fulfil
this desire, man desires that, at least, he must attain complete control over
the whole creation - as he desires, so must it occur. Since it is unattainable
to gain control over the whole creation of **Allâh** ﷻ like the heavens, stars,
mountains, oceans and other huge creations, man lowers his expectation
and desires to attain at least control over the creation on land i.e. animals
should be subdued under him, and plants and minerals must labour in
obedience to him. He must also possess complete and perfect knowledge
over all heavenly objects and the huge earthly objects which he cannot
control physically. He also desires that the hearts of man becomes
subservient and obedient to him, having strong belief in his greatness and
honour, and must regard him to be a person possessing excellence. They
must fold their hands before him and honour him, and his fame must
spread to those lands where he could never reach physically.
لا حول و لا قوة الا بالله

## TRUE GRANDEUR

Man is going to die one day. After death, his fame and status will come to
an end. If one attains this temporary popularity and some name and
honour amongst the creation, then of what benefit is this? This is not
something of perfection and goodness. Perfection is attaining such things
which will not be reduced or destroyed by death. This is the *ma'rifat*
(recognition) of **Allâh** ﷻ. Even when a person who possessed *ma'rifat*
leaves this world, he continues ascending the countless stages of divine
recognition. Thus, cure this desire of love for name and fame, and remove
its love from the heart. Understand that even if the whole world has to
prostrate before you, then for how long will this last? Finally a day will
arrive, when neither you will remain in existence, nor will those who
prostrated before you. How amazing, that time is so stingy with you that
leave alone your country or province, you do not possess control of even
your own town? How can you ever be pleased to lose an everlasting
kingdom and honour and respect by **Allâh** ﷻ and His angels for some

lowly popularity by some foolish people, who can neither benefit, nor harm you, who do not control your life, death and resurrection, neither your sustenance, nor your life-span?

# PERMISSIBLE LEVEL OF JÂH[1]

Man requires status, according to necessity, just as he is requires wealth, so that he can be rescued from the oppression and excesses of people, and by which he can attain peace of mind, which will assist in him performing *ibâdat* comfortably. However, one should keep in mind that this *jâh*, according to necessity, should not lead to one doing acts of worship for show and ostentation, since these are impermissible. One should not don the form of a pious person and *sûfî* to give deceit to the people, because if one achieves some honour due to this, then he will be regarded as a deceiver in the Sight of **Allâh** ﷻ. Deception is prohibited. Anyhow, the desire for fame is very dangerous. Man is never satisfied and content on possessing a minute portion of it. He will continue desiring more. For this reason, a person's *dîn* is rarely safeguarded, except for one who is unknown and hidden from public fame.

## THE CAUSES OF LOVE FOR PRAISES

A major cause of the desire for name and fame is the desire for one's praises. Man derives pleasure when praised. The reason for this enjoyment is three:

1) Perfection is the quality of **Allâh** ﷻ. Every person desires that this quality be found within himself. Therefore, the *nafs* becomes pleased when praised, since it feels that the person praising is aware of my perfection. It is for this reason, that one does not become as pleased by the praises of a foolish and ignorant person, as he becomes by the praises of an intelligent and bright person.

2) Every person has the desire to control others. When one is praised, he discerns that he possesses control and has an effect in the heart of that person. Thus, the *nafs* derives pleasure from it. Thus, if an honourable person praises one, he becomes elated. If a beggar or poor person praises

---

[1] Jāh is Arabic for name, fame, and status.

him, then he is not pleased in the least bit, since possessing control of such a person's heart is not regarded to be any accomplishment or achievement. 3) This thought filters the mind that by means of these praises one will become famous, since people have now begin praising him. This will slowly spread until his fame will spread in the whole world. By praises, the *nafs* becomes bloated. Therefore, a person gains more pleasure when praised in a gathering, compared to when praised in private.

## THE CURE

Understand well that love of one's praises has destroyed people. Due to it, people become involved in show and a host of other vices and evils. Therefore, treat this sickness.

Ponder, what am I being praised over? If your wealth and status is being praised, then understand that these are not matters of accomplishment. Happiness should be for the true accomplishment i.e. attaining the recognition of **Allâh** ﷻ. One should actually cry over such imaginary accomplishments, and not laugh. If you are being praised over your piety and *zuhd* (abstinence), then there are two possibilities:
a) you are in reality pious and abstinent, and the praises are true.
b) false praises are being heaped on you merely to please you. If the praises are true, then the cure for this is to ponder whether these qualities are really present within myself, and whether **Allâh** ﷻ will accept it. If so, then one has cause to be overjoyed. Just the word of another person is not a sign of Acceptance and Divine Closeness. If the praises are false, then to be delighted is open foolishness. The example of this, is a person praising you saying that the fragrance of perfume is emerging from your stomach and intestines, whereas you are fully aware that it is gorged with excreta and impurities. If you are pleased with such misplaced praises, in fact clear lies, can there be any foolishness higher than this?

We have already mentioned above, the cure for love of popularity and fame. By practicing on it there is hope that the roots of the love of praises will be curtailed.

# SEVENTH PRINCIPLE

# LOVE OF THE WORLD

*Dunyâ* (the world) does not only refer to love for name and fame. Your *dunyâ* is the condition before your demise. The love of *dunyâ* is the root of all evils.

## REALITY OF THE LOVE OF *DUNYÂ*

All disputes, fights regarding worldly matters, and connection with the creation and existent things are referred to as love of the *dunyâ*. As for religious knowledge, divine recognition and noble actions whose fruits will be seen in the Hereafter, even though they are found in this world, they are excluded from the *dunyâ*, and love for them will not be regarded as love for this world. This is included in love for the Hereafter. **Allâh** ﷻ states, "Verily We have made that which is upon the earth an adornment for it, so that We may test them, to see who does the best of actions." i.e. **Allâh** ﷻ is testing us to see who will become enamoured with these commodities and destroy his life of the Hereafter, and who will regard it to be provisions for this journey of life, and use it to beautify his life of the Hereafter.

Besides wealth and status, man has adoration and feeling for the earth as well, which he will utilize for building and farming; love for plantations which he will use for medication and food; love for minerals by which he will attain wealth, jewellery and utensils; love for animals by which he can be transported and fed; and love for people, so that he can marry and have workers and servants. The love of all these things is referred to *hawâ* (desires) in the Qurân Karîm. **Allâh** ﷻ states, "As for the one who fears standing before his Sustainer and he prevents his *nafs* from its *hawâ* (desires), then *Jannah* is his abode."

# SELF INDULGENCE IS DESTRUCTIVE

Remember that the life of this world is mere play, amusement, beautification, competing with one another, and trying to increase one's wealth and children. All destructive, harmful sicknesses are created from these actions e.g. pride, malice, jealousy, ostentation, hypocrisy, boasting, competitiveness, love of the world and love for praise. When an enthusiasm is created within man to correct and beautify his worldly life, then he becomes engaged in ephemeral works like business, trade, farming, and manufacturing. Finally, he becomes completely unmindful of his origin and final abode, his internal and external is only focused towards the worldly attractions, the heart becomes occupied in love of this world, and the physical body in its amendment and development, whereas the world is a provision for the Hereafter. Its purpose is that the traveler to the Hereafter must easily complete his journey. However, foolish and idiotic people have made it their actual aim and objective, and they have fallen into its pre-occupations and its different attractions in such a manner that they have completely forgotten the future. The example of such people is like a person who sets out for Hajj. When reaching the main road, he becomes pre-occupied in feeding his horse grains and grass, and in fattening it. He falls behind his companions. In this condition, he remains alone in the jungle and the caravan leaves him behind. The object for which he set out i.e. hajj is not fulfilled. The end result is that the wild predatory animals of the jungle will tear his fat conveyance to pieces, and he will become a mere morsel for them.

Remember that this world is a farm for the Hereafter, and a pathway towards it. Your conveyance is your body made of sand, with which you are traversing towards the Hereafter. Therefore use food, drinks and other necessities according to need. Whilst engaged in your necessary goods for the journey, plant those seeds which you will be able to harvest in the Hereafter, where you can thereafter live forever in comfort. If you are entirely occupied in fattening and overseeing your conveyance i.e. your body, then your caravan will leave you behind, and you will not reach your destination.

# DIFFERENT TYPES OF TRAVELERS TO THE HEREAFTER

The example of the different groups traversing to the Hereafter, is that of people who had boarded a boat. It moved until it came to an island. The captain allowed the passengers to alight from the ship to fulfill their needs therein. He however warned them of dangers lurking there, and informed them that the ship would be departing after a very short time. The people descended and spread out. One group completed their necessary needs, and immediately returned. They did not feel it appropriate to waste time. On returning they found the ship to be empty. They thus chose the best place in the ship, according to their liking and settled there.

Some stood looking at the flowers, lights, amazing stones, and beautiful springs. They enjoyed listening to the singing of the birds. However, they quickly came to their senses, and returned to the ship. They found the place to be straitened. The spacious and beautiful places were already taken by the first group. Thus they sat in this restricted place, with a bit of discomfort.

A third group became enamored with the temporary beauty of this island. Their hearts refused to budge from the beautiful pearls and wonderful stones. They thus loaded them on their backs and carried them back to the ship. They found the ship to be filled. There was no place for them to sit, and no possibility of keeping this unnecessary weight. They were rendered dumfounded. On the one hand, they were not prepared to throw away these stones, and on the other hand there was no seating place. With great difficulty, they managed to squeeze into a tight place, carrying their heavy weight on their heads. Think for yourself what will happen? Their backs will ache, their necks will throb, and only their hearts will be able to elucidate with what difficulty they are passing their time.

The last group became so captivated and mesmerized by the entrancing splendor of the island, that they completely forgot the ship and their journey. They became pre-occupied with smelling the flowers and eating the fruits. Their minds did not even go towards their destination, as well as the danger of becoming a morsel of wild animals. When they eventually returned to the shore, they found that the ship had departed without them.

They stood at the shore looking at their companions with eyes of great sorrow. The carnivorous animals of the island attacked them, and tore their beautiful bodies to bits.

These are the different categories of people with relation to this world and the Hereafter. Ponder and see which category you fall into.

## REFLECTION

Whoever understands the reality of his *nafs*, has recognized **Allâh** , and knows the deceptive beauty of this world, and the everlasting life of the Hereafter, will comprehend that the eternal bounties of the Hereafter cannot be attained without the love of **Allâh** . Combining the love of **Allâh**  and the world is impossible, just as combining water and fire in one utensil is impossible. As long as man does not turn away from the world, cutting off short-lived relationships and being content with the world according to necessity, so that he could be engaged at all times in **Allâh** 's remembrance and in contemplation, the love for **Allâh**  will not be created. If this is your condition, and these secrets have opened up to you with the light of understanding, then there is no need for anybody to explain it to you. If not, then follow the sharî'ah and see how **Allâh**  has censured the world. Approximately one third of the Quran explains the evils of this captivating, yet destructive, world. **Allâh**  has stated, "As for him who transgresses and gives preference to this worldly life, then Hell is his abode."

*Rasûlullâh*  has stated, "Amazing is the condition of that person who regards the everlasting abode to be true, and yet he still strives for the house of deception."[1]

In another hadîth, he  said, "The world is accursed, all that which is within it is accursed except the remembrance of **Allâh** , that which leads to it, the scholar and the student of religious knowledge."[2]

---

[1] Musnadush Shihâb, Musannaf Ibn Abî Shaibah, Shu'abul-îmân
[2] Tirmidhi, Ibn Mâjah

*Nabî* ﷺ also said, "Whoever passes the morning in this condition, that the world is his greatest concern, then he has no value in the sight of **Allâh** ﷻ. **Allâh** ﷻ will bind his heart with four qualities: worry which will never end, pre-occupation from which one will never emerge, poverty which will never terminate, and hopes whose apex will never be reached."[1]

Abû Hurayrah ؓ narrates, "Once *Rasûlullâh* ﷺ said, "O Abû Hurayrah, should I show you the (reality of the) world?" I replied, "Yes." *Rasûlullâh* ﷺ took hold of my hand and proceeded to a rubbish dump. Lying there were skulls of people, excreta, tattered and torn clothing, as well as bones. *Nabî* ﷺ remarked, "O Abû Hurayrah, these skulls used to possess hopes, as you do. They were covetous just as you are. Today, they are bones without any skin. Soon they will become dust. This excreta is the different types of delicacies they used to consume. They cared not from where they earned them, whether it was *halâl* or *harâm*. Today this same food has been expelled from their stomachs. This food now gives off such a stench that people scurry away from it. These tattered rags were their adornments and clothing. Today, the wind is scattering it away. These bones were the bones of their conveyances upon which they used to travel around cities fighting and waging war. Whoever wants to cry over the world, let him do so."[2]

Once the reality of the world was exposed to Isa ﷺ. He saw her in the form of an old, ugly lady wearing different types of beautiful jewellery and clothing. He asked her, "How many people have you married?" she replied, "I cannot count them." He then asked, "Did they divorce you or did they die?" she said, "In fact I killed every one of them." Isâ ﷺ then remarked, "Woe to your remaining husbands! Why do they not take lesson from your past husbands?"

O Muslims! Be intelligent and take heed! The world is very disloyal. Abstain from it. Its magic is more effective than that of *Hârut* and *Mârut* (two angels who were sent to teach magic). If you have to eat barley bread with salt and wear clothing of inferior material, and live in this manner, then rather do so, and be concerned regarding your life in the Hereafter.

---

[1] Musnadul-Firdaws
[2] Ibn Abid-Dunyâ, mursal narration from Hasan ؓ

# DESIRE FOR THE WORLD WILL NEVER TERMINATE

Some people are deceived into thinking that no matter how involved they are in the world, their hearts are completely void and free of the world. Remember that this is a satanic whispering. *Nabī* ﷺ said, "The example of the person of this world is like one who walks on water. Is it possible for the one who walks on water not to wet his feet?" [1]

If you become a seeker of the world, and are always engaged in earning more than necessary, then definitely you will always be perplexed and worried. You will lose your religious bearings very easily. Remember that the seeking of the world never comes to an end. The desire for it continues rising. The example of the world is that of the salty water of the ocean. The more one drinks, the more thirsty will one become. If being totally absorbed in that which you will have to leave someday does not cause you grief, then what else will happen? The world is like a snake. It is soft to the touch, but it possesses a poisonous and destructive poison in its mouth. Departing from this disloyal place is certain. Being pleased on attaining it and sorrowful when losing a portion of it is foolishness. To regard the world and its adornments to be a cause of attaining satisfaction of the heart, is extreme foolishness. How can one have contentment in such a place where one will not reside forever?

## THIS WORLD IS A GUEST HOUSE

This world has been likened to a house prepared and beautified by a host for his guests. When they enter, he places in front of them a tray filled with flowers, fragrances, and perfumes. It is obvious that the object of the host is that his guests must smell the beautiful fragrances, and then pass it to the next people so that they could also benefit. His desire is not that one guest must now take possession of them. If a person is unaware of the etiquettes of the gathering, and takes the plate to be his, placing it under his arm and going away, then all the people in the gathering will laugh at his foolishness and mock him. Eventually, the owner will forcefully snatch

---

[1] Shuabul Imân

away from him the tray, and place it before another. You can well imagine the sorrow of this person.

In like manner, this world is a guest house of **Allâh** ﷻ for those travelling to the Hereafter, not for those residing here forever. **Allâh** ﷻ wants the travelers to the Hereafter to benefit according to necessity, just as one derives benefit from a loaned item and fulfils his need. Thereafter, he happily hands it over to the next person, and reaches his destination. Keeping the heart attached to loaned things will lead you to be extremely sad, and embarrassed at the time of departure from this world.

# EIGHTH PRINCIPLE

# PRIDE AND ARROGANCE

**Allâh** ﷻ has stated, "How evil is the abode of the proud people."

*Nabî* ﷺ said, "**Allâh** ﷻ has stated, "Grandeur is My (ﷻ) lower covering, and Greatness is My (ﷻ) top cover. Whoever tries to snatch them from Me (ﷻ), I (ﷻ) will destroy him."[1]

### EFFECTS AND REALITY OF PRIDE

*Rasûlullâh* ﷺ said, "The person who possesses one atom's weight of pride will not enter *Jannah*."

Blessed are those who, despite possessing wealth and honour, humble themselves, and meet people with humility and submissiveness. There are great ranks for them. Their honour is increased in this world and the Hereafter.Pride means that a person regards himself superior to others in certain qualities of perfection. The result thereof, is that his *nafs* bloats up. Thereafter, its effects become apparent e.g. whilst walking, one wants to walk ahead; one desires to be seated in a place of honour; one looks at others with disdain and scorn; one becomes angry if he is not greeted first; one becomes upset if he is not respected, or his needs are not fulfilled; if

---

[1] Muslim, Abû Dâwud

one is advised or taught something he frowns and becomes displeased; one is not prepared to accept the truth after knowing it to be so; one looks at the general people as one looks at donkeys; etc. (May **Allâh** ﷻ save us!)

Pride is such an extremely evil action, that one who possesses an atoms weight of it will not enter *Jannah*. It holds within it three grave evils:

1) Greatness and Loftiness is an exclusive quality of **Allâh** ﷻ. It is only appropriate for His Being ﷻ. How can man, who is so utterly weak that never mind anyone else, he does not even have control over his own self, ever be so bold as to partner **Allâh** ﷻ in this quality? Since a proud person desires to equate himself with **Allâh** ﷻ, despite his weakness and lowliness, and is contesting with **Allâh** ﷻ in this quality of perfection, he will be regarded as the most vile and most foolish person.

2) Due to pride, one rejects the truth. This leads to the door of success and felicity being closed. A proud person looks at the creation of **Allâh** ﷻ with contempt and derision. This is abhorred by **Allâh** ﷻ.

Dhun Nûn Misri ﷺ said, "**Allâh** ﷻ has concealed three things within three: He has concealed His Pleasure in His Obedience, thus do not regard any good action as small, perhaps His Pleasure lies therein; He has concealed His Anger in His Disobedience, thus do not regard any act of disobedience to be insignificant, whether major or minor, perhaps **Allâh** ﷻ's anger is in it; and He ﷻ has concealed His ﷻ Friendship amongst His ﷻ Servants, thus never despise anyone of them, perhaps he is a friend of **Allâh** ﷻ."

3) It does not allow a person to attain noble characteristics and qualities. A proud person is deprived of humility, he cannot like for others what he likes for himself, he is unable to abstain from arrogance, jealousy and anger, he cannot show softness in advising, and he cannot break free from showiness. In short, in the intoxication of his greatness and feeling of superiority, and regarding himself to be independent of advice due to his false thoughts about himself, he is completely deprived of correcting his evil *nafs*.

# THE CURE FOR PRIDE

A person should hasten to cure himself from this evil quality. If an effort is not made, there remains no hope for it to be cured in the future by itself. Man should firstly realize his reality and origin. First he was an impure drop of sperm, and finally he will become a dead corpse and the food of worms and insects. At the present moment, which is referred to as life, he is carrying stools and filth in his stomach. **Allâh** states, "Definitely a portion of time has passed over man when he was not a thing which was even mentioned." After non-existence, **Allâh** made him into sand, thereafter a drop of sperm, then a clot of blood, and then a piece of flesh which possessed no ability to see and hear, and which did not have any life or strength. **Allâh** then gave all these bounties, but then too man is perpetually deficient. Sicknesses and ailments afflict him, he is always hungry and thirsty, and upon a little bit of difficulty, he sits down defeated. He tries to learn something, but cannot do so; he intends to forget something, but it continues coming to his mind; he desires something, but this is harmful for him; he dislikes something but that is beneficial for him. At any moment, his life, intellect, or health can be snatched away. A limb of his can be destroyed. Finally he has to face death. He will be placed into a dark and narrow hole. He has to face reckoning for his actions. Then eventually will be the Decision of **Allâh** whether he will be granted everlasting bliss in Heaven or everlasting doom in Hell. If man is from the denizens of Hell, then a swine is better than him. How can it be possible that such a lowly and useless servant ever think himself to be equal to such a Great and Powerful King ? How can pride and arrogance be appropriate and proper for one who has to wash his excreta twice a day with his own hands, and for one who carries this load throughout his life?

Generally, pride is created by one of four factors: 1) knowledge 2) piety 3) family lineage 4) money and beauty. Since the cure for each one of them is different, we will mention in detail each one in detail.

# 1. KNOWLEDGE

Verily few ulemâ are void of pride, since nothing holds virtue like knowledge. After attaining knowledge, two thoughts are created:
a) Nobody is equal to us in the sight of **Allâh** ﷻ.
b) It is compulsory on the people to honour and respect us. If someone does not adopt humbleness before them, they become surprised.
The first type is a religious pride and the second is a worldly pride. Such an âlim is worthy of being called a *jâhil* (ignoramus), since the demand of knowledge was that man understand his evil *nafs,* gain recognition of the Grandeur of **Allâh** ﷻ, and realize that consideration will be given according to one's final action. No one knows how he will leave this world. A person who regards himself to be worthy of honour and respect, it is as though he is unaware of his origin, and he possesses no fear of having an evil end. This is a major sin. If an ignorant person commits a sin due to his ignorance, he can still be excused. However, since an âlim sins purposely, he will not be regarded as excused. All are aware that the crime of a person who is aware of the law, is more severe than the one who is unaware of the law. How amazing is it that despite being learned, one is still so ignorant; and worse still, one is unaware that he is ignorant, which is referred to as ignorance compounded.

Remember that the knowledge from which pride is created, is worse than ignorance; since the more true knowledge one attains, the more his apprehension and fear increases. Abû Darda ﷺ said, "Whoever increases in knowledge, increases in humility." **Allâh** ﷻ commanded *Nabî* ﷺ to be humble with the believers. In one hadîth, *Nabî* ﷺ said, "Such people will appear who will read the Qur'ân, but it will not transcend their throats. They will state, "We read the Qur'ân. Who is more learned and knowledgeable than us?" Then *Nabî* ﷺ turned away and said, "*O Ummah,* they will be from amongst you, they are the fuel of Hell."[1]

Study the life of the pious predecessors to see how particularly they kept a watch on themselves. Once, Hudhaifah ﷺ lead the people in salâh. After

---

[1] Bazzâr (1323), Abu Ya'lâ (6698)

*salâm*, he said, "Seek another imâm besides me, or perform salâh individually. This thought came to my mind that I am the most virtuous amongst you."[1] (That is why I was made imâm)

Remember, no matter how great a scholar is, it is not necessary that he leaves this world with îmân; and no matter how ignorant a person may be, there is no conviction that his end will be evil. If an âlim can understand this much, then how can he possess pride? Is it not compulsory for him to practice on his knowledge? A hadîth sharîf states, "An âlim will be brought on the Day of Judgement. He will be flung into the Fire. His intestines will be exposed. He will move around holding them just as a donkey walks around a mill. The denizens of Hell will surround him and ask, "What has happened to you?" He will reply, "I used to command righteousness, but I did not do it myself; and I used to prohibit evil, but would perpetrate it myself."[2] (May **Allâh** save us from this!)

Ponder! **Allâh** likened a great scholar like Bal'am Baûrâ, to a dog whose tongue hangs out all the time. **Allâh** likens the Jewish scholars to donkeys carrying loads of books. The reason for this, is that they fell prey to their sensual desires; they possessed pride and thought highly of themselves; and advised others but were unmindful of themselves.

Ponder over these incidents and ahâdîth, pride will slowly leave one. If one does not find pride departing, then understand it to be the result of remaining preoccupied in teaching and studying unnecessary knowledge e.g. logic, philosophy and the art of debating, or it is due to the filth of your internal self, due to which the medication is not benefitting, but actually causing more harm. Thus, make an effort to lessen its ill effects.

## 2) ABSTINENCE AND ACTS OF WORSHIP

Very few worshippers are devoid of pride. The foolishness of some has reached such a level, that they attribute the difficulties encountered by people to their status. For example, if someone causes harm to them, they

---

[1] Baihaqî in Kubrâ (3/127), Musannaf Abdur Razzâq (1/489)
[2] Bukhârî (3267), Muslim (2989)

angrily blurt out, "Watch how **Allâh** ﷻ will punish him! He has oppressed us. Soon he will encounter such a punishment which he will never forget." Thereafter, if according to Divine Decree, he has to fall ill, or pass away, they then prove their claim and utter, "Did you see the result of causing harm to **Allâh** ﷻ's poor servants?" Someone should ask this foolish person, "The disbelievers caused untold difficulty to the *Ambiyâ* ﷺ. None of them ever desired to take revenge. The result of this, was that many of these same disbelievers eventually accepted îmân, and they were blessed with success in this world and the Hereafter. If the Messengers ﷺ took immediate revenge and wished that their enemies die, then how would people attain guidance? Can any worshipper surpass a *Nabî* ﷺ? *Astaghfirulllâh!* A worshipper should humble himself before every person.

## THE CURE FOR PRIDE DUE TO ONE'S PIETY

If for example, one looks towards a sinful âlim, then too one should humble oneself before him, due to his knowledge. He should not bring to mind the scholar's sin, since knowledge in itself is greatly virtuous. If one sees an ignorant and sinful person, then he should ponder, "Perhaps his internal condition is far superior to mine. He may possess such a wonderful quality, which will conceal all his outward wrongs. I may possess such an evil quality, due to which all my outward actions are destroyed. **Allâh** ﷻ looks at hearts. None besides Him ﷻ knows the condition of the hearts of man. Then how can I be proud?" Besides this, pride itself is an internal sickness. Thus it is clear that your condition is worse, since you possess pride. The other person whose sin is open is free from pride.

A sinful person from the *Banî Isrâ'il* once sat next to a pious man with this intention in mind that **Allâh** ﷻ may shower His ﷻ Mercy on him due to the blessings of this pious man. The worshipper on seeing him exclaimed, "How can a sinner of this magnitude sit by me?" He said to him, "Go away from here." **Allâh** ﷻ sent revelation to the Messenger ﷺ of the time saying, "Tell both of them to restart their actions. I have forgiven the sinner and I have destroyed the good actions of the worshipper."

Once an extremely disrespectful person tramped the neck of one worshipper from the *Banî Isrâ'îl*, whilst he was in sajdah. The worshipper angrily retorted, "Get off me. By **Allâh** ﷻ, **Allâh** ﷻ will never forgive you." **Allâh** ﷻ inspired him, "*O you who take an oath in My Name, in actual fact it is you whom* **Allâh** ﷻ *will not forgive (since you are making My servant despair of My Mercy and Forgiveness).*"[1]

Atâ Sulamî ◌, despite being extremely pious, used to say whenever the winds became severe or lightning struck, "All of this is afflicting the people due to me. If Atâ has to pass away, then the people will be safe."[2]

See! Despite their sincerity and abundance of worship, how much humility and fear of **Allâh** ﷻ they possessed. In today's times, the condition is such that one performs a few actions of worship, and then is boastful over it. He acts as though he is doing **Allâh** ﷻ a favour. He wishes to establish his rule and control over everyone, even though there is a fear that his acts of worship were tainted with show and insincerity, the result of this being disastrous.

## 3) LINEAGE AND FAMILY STATUS

The cure for this, is that one should ponder over his lineage. His father was once an impure sperm, and his grandfather was once soil. What can be more despicable than a drop of sperm, and what can be lower than soil? The one who is proud over his lineage, is actually proud over the good characteristics and qualities of others. If his ancestors could speak, they would say to him, "What qualities do you possess? Who are you? You are nothing but a worm from the urine of those who possessed beautiful qualities." Thus see yourself in your origins i.e. the impure sperm and urine drop, not in the praiseworthy acts of your ancestors.

Then, if one is proud of his ancestors who were people devoted to the world, then this is foolishness to the limit. Perhaps they have become coals of the fire of Hell, desiring that they should have been swine and dogs, so that they could be saved from the problems in which they find themselves.

---

[1] Musanaf Abdur Razzaq (11/183), Hilyah (4/205)
[2] Hilyah (6/221)

Thus they are in such horrifying circumstances, whilst their descendants are boasting over their ancestry.

If one is proud due to being in the lineage of pious ancestors, then this is also foolishness and idiocy. Whatever honour and respect they received, was due to their piety and humility. When they themselves were not proud over their religiousness, then how can their unworthy descendants be proud and assume airs over the honour and respect they enjoyed? The condition of their pious predecessors was such that they feared an evil end. They desired, "If only I was a blade of grass, so that some animal could chew me!" "If only I was a bird, so that I could be eaten by some human or animal!" Those who were possessors of knowledge and action, dashed far away from pride; whilst you, who are void of both these qualities, are proud and boastful of your lineage.

## 4) WEALTH AND BEAUTY

Some people are proud due to beauty or wealth. Pride based on these qualities is idiocy. Wealth is so ephemeral that if a thief has to approach, all can be snatched away in a matter of seconds. Beauty also is temporary. One month of fever and sickness can cause all one's beauty to fade. If some pimples have to emerge, the whole form of the face will change. How can one be proud over this? If a person of beauty has to ponder over his internal filth, then it will be utterly impossible for him to possess pride over his outward beauty. Such beauty which has to be always seen to, is not worthy of pride. If one does not bath at least weekly, then witness the color and odor emitting from that body. The body is stuffed with impurities like saliva, dirt, urine and stool. Then how can a waste dump and a lump of impurities ever possess airs and pride over a bit of external beauty?

# NINTH PRINCIPLE

# UJUB (SELF ADMIRATION)

**Allâh** ﷻ has stated, "Do not regard yourself as pure. He ﷻ knows best who is the most pious." Regarding oneself and one's own actions as good is the quality of the disbelievers. A hadith sharîf states, "Three qualities are destructive: greed which is pursued, desires which are acted upon, and a man who is pleased with himself." [1]

Abdullâh ibn Masûd ؓ said, "Destruction is in two matters: becoming despondent and self admiration." Destruction is found in these two because a person who is despondent does not seek success due to his loss of hope; and a vain person also does not seek success because he feels that he has already attained it."

Once Aishah ؓ was asked, "When will a person be regarded as evil?" She replied, "When he thinks that he is good."

A man once looked towards Bishr ibn Mansûr ؓ while he was engaged in lengthy salâh and other acts of devotion. When he had terminated, he remarked, "Do not be deceived by these actions which you saw me performing. Iblîs worshipped **Allâh** ﷻ and performed salâh for thousands of years, but then we are all aware of his final condition."
In short, it is not the quality of a believer to regard his acts of worship as worthy. Firstly, he does not know whether it is accepted or not. Secondly, one does not know what one's final moments in this world will be, and all actions will be accepted only if he left this world with *îmân.*

## DIFFERENCE BETWEEN PRIDE AND VANITY

Vanity and self admiration is a branch of pride. The difference is that in pride, one regards himself superior to others, whereas in vanity one does

---

[1] Musnadush Shihâb (325), Musannaf Abdur Razzaq (403/11),Shu'abul Imân (731)

not look down on others. He regards himself as perfect and accomplished, and he regards **Allâh** 's Favours upon him as a right which he is deserving of, i.e. he does not regard it as the Grace and Kindness of **Allâh** , and he does not fear that it can be snatched away. This is referred to as vanity and self admiration.

If the matter reaches the extreme, that one regards himself as having some status and position in the Sight of **Allâh** , then this is referred to as nâz or idlâl. The sign of this is, that a person is surprised when his dûâs are not accepted, and when his enemies are not punished and destroyed.

Remember, to be pleased over one's acts of worship, and to regard oneself as an accepted servant of **Allâh**  and worthy of position, is the height of foolishness. However, if one is pleased on the Bounties of **Allâh**  manifested upon himself, whether it be some knowledge, action, or any other bounty, whilst fearing that it could be snatched away, and he is pleased since he realizes that it has come from **Allâh** , then this is not vanity. A vain person is he who does not fear the termination of the bounty, and he does not attribute it to **Allâh** , regarding it to be his right.

Vanity and self admiration is absolute ignorance. Its cure is knowledge. If one is vain due to strength, wealth, beauty, or any other matter which is not within his control, then he should reflect: What did he do to attain this resulting in his pride? He should actually be surprised with the Being  who granted him these bounties, despite being completely undeserving and unworthy of it. He should also realize that these bounties in a short while can be snatched away by a slight sickness or weakness. If vanity occurs due to knowledge, practice, abstinence, piety, worship and sacrifices, in short, all volitional actions, then one should ponder how he achieved these perfections and excellences. If **Allâh**  did not bestow him with intellect, strength in his limbs, brains, senses, hands and feet as well as the intention to carry out these actions, then how would he have attained any of these excellences? **Allâh**  decreed that there must be no barrier, or else one would become helpless and unable to accomplish anything.

It is an accepted fact that **Allâh** ﷻ has granted man choice and will, by which he can perform evil as well as good deeds. However, this choice and intention is also granted by **Allâh** ﷻ. Then the preparation of all the means and granting success to one in his efforts, is from **Allâh** ﷻ. In short, from the beginning till the end, all lies in the control of **Allâh** ﷻ. Then how can one boast and be vain in such a condition? If the keys of the treasury are in the hands of the king, and after opening it, he allows you to take as much as you desire in your lap, and then you begin boasting that you have attained so much wealth, it is obvious that you will be regarded as foolish. The reason for this is that although you gathered the wealth in your lap, the treasury belongs to the state. The keys are in the hands of the king. It is his favour that he handed you the keys and allowed you to open it and enter. How can it ever be correct for you then to boast and be vainglorious over your action?

Astonishing indeed is the condition of even intelligent and learned people who, on occasions become ignorant, and are proud over their knowledge and intellect. If they happen to see an ignorant person in affluence, they are amazed and utter, "We are learned and intelligent, but are deprived of wealth and these foolish ones and ignoramuses are rolling in wealth." Ask such a person, "Why were you granted knowledge and understanding, whilst the ignorant person was deprived of these bounties? These are Divine Bounties. Are you making this bounty the cause for being worthy of another bounty? In fact, if you had to have both wealth and intelligence, and the ignorant person was deprived of both, then this would have been a cause of greater surprise, since one received everything and the other received nothing. If the king gives one person a horse and another a slave, then can the first person say, "How can you give so-and-so a slave, whereas he possesses no horse, and how can you deprive me when I possess a slave?" He is thus making one gift the cause of his being worthy of receiving another gift. This is utter foolishness and ignorance.

Intelligence demands that one remains grateful to **Allâh** ﷻ for His ﷻ bounties, and he should understand that it is **Allâh** ﷻ's great favour that He ﷻ has bestowed so much of His ﷻ Kindness upon us initially, whereas we were undeserving. He should realize that he has been granted the bounty of knowledge and intelligence, in front of which wealth has no reality. Thereafter **Allâh** ﷻ even granted one the favour of worshipping Him ﷻ and thanking Him ﷻ, whereas others are deprived of this; and this deprivation was not due to some previous sin or the recompense of some weakness. When one continuously ponders over this, then Divine Fear will be created. One will realize that if the Being ﷻ who granted me His ﷻ Bounties, without me being deserving of them, snatches them away without any cause or sin, then what right do I have to complain? What will I do if these bounties upon me are only temporary and deceiving, and will eventually lead to punishment and harm to my life? **Allâh** ﷻ states, "We opened upon them the doors of everything. When they became pleased with that which they were given, We seized them suddenly (in punishment)."

If these thoughts are kept in the mind, then fear will never separate from you, and you will not become exultant over any bounty. In this way you will be easily saved from vanity and self-admiration.

# TENTH PRINCIPLE

# RIYÂ (OSTENTATION AND SHOW)

**Allâh** ﷻ has stated, "Destruction be to those worshippers who are unmindful of their salâh, who perform actions for show." It is binding upon every Muslim to create sincerity in his actions, and to abstain from show and ostentation in his virtuous actions; since these are minor forms of *shirk* (polytheism).

*Nabî* ﷺ has stated, "The thing which I fear upon you the most, is minor *shirk*." The Sahâbah ﷺ enquired, "What is that?" *Nabî* ﷺ replied, "Ostentation." **Allâh** ﷻ will say on the Day of Judgement when He ﷻ is recompensing His ﷻ Servants for their actions, "Go to those for whom you used to show off your acts of worship. See if you will find any recompense from them."[1]

---

[1] Shu'abul Imân (6412), Ahmad (5/428)

In a lengthy hadith, mention is made of the Day of Judgement, when a warrior, a scholar and a philanthropist will be brought before **Allâh** ﷻ. When they will make apparent the good works they had engaged in, they will be informed, "You lie. You wanted that people must say that he is a great warrior, a great scholar or a generous person. You had attained these praises in the world." Then these three will be flung in the Fire.[1]

*Nabî* ﷺ said, "**Allâh** ﷻ will not accept any action, in which there is an atom's weight of show."[2]

Îsâ عليه السلام said, "If any one of you fasts, then he should oil his head and beard, and keep his lips moist, so that people do not know that he is fasting. When he spends in charity with his right hand, then he should conceal it from even his left hand. When he performs salâh, then he should lower the cover of his door (so that none can see him)."[3] For this reason, Umar ﷺ said to a man who was lowering his head, "*O* possessor of the neck, raise your neck. Humility is not in the (lowering of the) neck, but it is in the heart."

## REALITY OF *RIYÂ*

*Riyâ* refers to desiring status and honour in the hearts of people, due to one's acts of worship, and other noble actions. This is completely contrary to the object of worship, since its objective is the Pleasure of **Allâh** ﷻ. Since now there is another objective i.e. one desires the Pleasure of **Allâh** ﷻ as well as attainment of status, *riyâ* is referred to as a minor *shirk*.

## DIFFERENT FORMS OF *RIYÂ*

*Riyâ* is done by one of the following six:
1) Body- A few examples of this are:
- Making apparent weakness and tiredness, so that people will realize that one is fasting and he stayed awake in worship during the night.
- Feigning grief, so that others think that you are very concerned about the matters of *dîn*.

---

[1] Subject matter of a hadith in Muslim (1905) and Tirmidhi (2382)
[2] This is not a hadith, but statement of Yusuf ibn Asbât in Hilyah (8/240) (Ithâf)
[3] Shu'abul Imân (6498), Musannaf Abdur-Razzâq (4/313)

- Staying in a shabby state, so that people will think that one is so engrossed in *dîn* that he has no time to care for himself.
- Lowering ones voice, so that people will understand that one has become weak due to intense striving.

2) Appearance and form - A few examples of this are:
Shaving the moustache, lowering the head whilst walking, slowness in movement, keeping the effect of sajdah (prostration) on the face, closing the eyes so that people think that one is in some spiritual state, or he is witnessing some supernatural matter, or he is completely engrossed in thought.

3) Clothing - A few examples of this are:
Wearing woolen or rough clothing, raising it to half shin, shortening the sleeves, and leaving one's clothing in an unkempt and dirty state, so that people think that one is so absorbed and engaged, that he finds no time for these matters.

Donning patched clothing, and performing *salâh* on a special mat, so that one is thought of as being a great *sufî*, whereas he is completely ignorant of the reality of *tasawwuf*.
Wearing a tight-sleeved *kurtâ* or *jubbâ* or lengthening one's sleeves so that people think of one as a great scholar.
Placing a scarf over one's turban or wearing leather socks so that people realize one's high level of piety that he abstains from even the dust of the road.

Amongst them are two groups of people:

A) Some are those who seek rank and place in the hearts of the pious and religious-minded. For this reason, they always don old clothing. If they are made to wear such clothing which is new and beautiful, sanctioned by the shariah, and which the pious predecessors had worn, then they feel like they are being slaughtered alive. The reason for this is that their aim will not be fulfilled. When people witness them donning such apparel, they will lack honour for them, as they used to have when they adorned themselves with tattered and antiquated clothing. They fear that people will say, "His abstinence and disinclination of the world has decreased."

B) Others are such that they seek prominence amongst the rulers and wealthy ones. They pre-suppose that should they don tattered or patched clothing, then these people will look down upon them, and will in fact despise sitting near them. If on the other hand, they wear clothes of pride, then people will not regard them to be *sufis* and pious. Thus they have chosen a new path. They dye their expensive, fine clothing with expensive pigments. The price of their clothing is like that of the wealthy, while in form and color like the clothing of the pious. If they are given old and tattered clothing to wear, they become extremely upset, since this can cause them to descend from the eyes of the wealthy. Similarly, if they are given some expensive garments like fine cotton clothing, etc., which are permissible in the shariah, then this is severer than death, since they will not be regarded as *sufis* and *zâhids*. This shows that their clothing is only worn for show. (May **Allâh** protect us!)

4) Speech - A few examples of this are:
You may have witnessed some worldly orientated lecturers, who beautify their speech and rhyme their wordings, imitating the pious predecessors in speech, together with softening their voices and feigning sorrow, whilst being completely void of sincerity and truthfulness, so that they can be regarded as an exemplar of the pious elders. He thus simulates grief in public, but disobeys **Allâh** in solitude.

Some people claim to have memorized many ahâdith, met many *mashâikh*, and hasten to pass rulings on certain ahâdith (that some are weak, some are strong) so that they are regarded as well grounded in knowledge.

Others utter 'âh' or other words of sorrow, when sins are discussed. They show their hatred for matters contrary to the shariah, whereas there is not a trace of sorrow or dislike in their hearts. Their only object is that people must regard them as extremely pious and followers of the shariah.

5) Action - A few examples of this are:
Lengthening one's *qiyâm* (standing posture in *salâh*), beautifying one's *rukû* and *sajdah*, lowering one's head, not turning to anyone, closing one's

eyelids, so that people regard one as very pious and a great worshipper, whereas **Allâh** ﷻ knows very well that he is completely void and empty of these qualities. The sign of this is, that when one performs *salâh* in solitude, he performs it with great haste. If he becomes aware that he is being watched, then immediately he begins performing his *salâh* with great tranquility and dignity, in a slow manner, so that the onlooker is made to believe that there is great concentration and serenity in his *salâh*. This is a clear sign of show and ostentation.

6) Having many students and *murîds* (disciples), and making mention of *mashâikh* in great amount, so that people realize that he has met great, great *mashâikh*. Some are such that they desire to be visited by kings, leaders and scholars. They formulate plans for this to occur. This is done so that they become famous and people say, "So-and-so is a very great *buzurg*. Influential people go to him. All the kings and scholars regard it an honour to humble themselves before him."
All of these are examples of *riyâ* in religious matters. *Riyâ* is completely prohibited, and a major sin. May **Allâh** ﷻ protect us!

There are two reasons why *riyâ* is prohibited:
1) A person deceives others, just so that they can regard him to be sincere, and an obedient servant to **Allâh** ﷻ. Deception is completely prohibited. If a person has to hand over some money to a group of people as a loan, but he does it in such a manner that others feel he is giving a gift, then this will be a sin, since there is deception involved. Even worse is the case where a person feigns something, and then desires to create this thought in the heart of people that he is pious and worthy of honour, and in this manner, capture the hearts of people. Why will such a deceiver and fraudster not be termed as a wrongdoer (*fâsiq*) then?

2) Ostentation and show is actually a mockery of **Allâh** ﷻ. An example of this, is of a man who stands before the king, as a servant and worker. However, the purpose and aim of his is not to serve the king nor to humble himself before him, but it is to actually see one of the king's other servants or to ogle at one of his slave girls. It is apparent that he will be regarded to be a very disrespectful and insolent person. Similarly, when one does not have the aim of pleasing **Allâh** ﷻ, rather to please His ﷻ

Servants, then he has firmly believed that **Allâh** 🕮's Servants have more power than Him 🕮 to benefit and bestow goodness. The grandeur and respect of people in his heart is so much, that it leads him to beautify his actions for them. For this reason, *riyâ* is referred to as *shirke-asgar* (minor shirk).

The sin of this action will increase in accordance to one's incorrect intention. Some people only desire status and position in the eyes of people. Others desire that they be regarded as pious; so that people will keep their trusts by them, make them trustees of certain endowments, or the wealth of orphans, so that they could utilize some of that wealth for their personal needs. This group is more evil than the first group. Yet others desire that women and children must be drawn close to them, so that they can engage in sexual or homosexual acts with them, or they can receive a great amount of wealth from them, which they can squander in alcohol and other futile games. It is obvious that this group of people is worse than the first two, since one has made the worship of **Allâh** 🕮 a means to sin and to disobey Him 🕮. (May **Allâh** 🕮 protect us from this!)

**Difference in *riyâ* according to the different forms of worship**

In those acts of worship in which one does for ostentation, there are different ranks. Some sins are more severe than others:
1) *Riyâ* in one's *îmân* (belief)- an example of this is a hypocrite who outwardly shows himself to be a believer, but is void of *îmân* in his heart. Another example is that of a *mulhid* (deviate), and one who regards prohibited actions to be permissible. They outwardly portray themselves to be Muslim, whereas the reality of *îmân* has left them. The sin of this form of show is extremely grave. **Allâh** 🕮 has declared that the hypocrites will be in the lowest levels of Hell fire.

2) *Riyâ* in one's acts of worship e.g. one performs *salâh*, or gives *zakâh* in front of people. If he was alone, he would not have performed these actions. Thus, these acts of worship were only to show people. However, only **Allâh** 🕮 is aware of the conditions of our heart, and with what intention it is being performed. Even though this level is lower than the

first, it is a very severe sin, and is referred to as *shirke-asghar* (minor form of polytheism).

3) *Riyâ* in one's acts of voluntary worship, and not in the obligatory duties (*farâidh*) e.g. if people are present, then one performs extra *nawâfil*, he performs his fardh*h* with more care and concentration, when the day of *Arafah* or *Ashurâ* arrives, then he fasts, and when the time comes to give *zakâh*, one takes out his superior and best quality goods. However, when he is alone or on journey, then he does not perform his *salâh* correctly, he performs no extra *nawâfil salâh* nor fasts. Fardh*h* *salâhs* are performed with extreme speed; *zakâh* is discharged from one's inferior wealth, just to remove the responsibility from one's head. This form of *riyâ* is lower in severity than the other two forms, but is also prohibited and sufficient to destroy one's *dîn*.

Remember that according to differences in one's intention of *riyâ*, there will be a difference in the severity of sin. For example, one form is that one's object of *ibâdah* is only show e.g. one performs *salâh* without *wudhu* just to show people, or he fasts outwardly, but eats in solitude. The severity of this sin is great. Another form is when one's object is *ibâdah*, but is merged with show. This is of three types:

1) One's object is ibâdah. The proof of this is that if one is in solitude, then too he would have done that action. However, since others are observing him, his enthusiasm increases, and the action is not burdensome on him. In this instance, there is hope that **Allâh** ﷻ will accept this action, and reward him. However, he may be punished for the intention of show, or his reward may be lessened.

2) The main object is show, even though the intention of worship is present to a very limited extent. One's condition is such that the amount of worship he can perform in public, he can never do in solitude. This form of worship is not worthy of acceptance, because even though one has some inkling and intention of worship, it is so minimal, that it is of no real significance. This will be regarded as clear show and there is fear of severe punishment for such acts of worship.

3) The intention of worship and show is equal e.g. just as obedience to **Allâh** ﷻ is intended, so too is the intention to show off to people. Since the good and evil are found to an equal level, it is possible that there will be neither reward nor sin. However, since **Allâh** ﷻ has declared, "I am the most independent of all partners," it is not surprising if the harm overpowers the good, and the act of worship is nullified. **Allâh** ﷻ only knows how this person will be dealt with finally, but outwardly it seems that this condition is not void of sin.

## HIDDEN FORMS OF RIYÂ

Riyâ is of different categories. At times it is apparent, at times it is hidden, and at times, it is more concealed than the crawling of an ant. An example of apparent riyâ is, when a person will not even perform an action of worship if others are not present. An example of a hidden form is when one always performs tahajjud, but his enthusiasm increases when visitors stay by him. This is also a form of riyâ, but is more concealed than the first type. An even more obscure form is, when one's desire does not even increase, but during or after the act of worship, if someone comes to know of his actions of worship, a type of happiness is created in the heart.

This shows that riyâ is veiled deep in the heart, just as fire is veiled within a piece of coal. For this reason, one becomes pleased when others are made aware of it. An even more obscure form is, when one does not even become pleased when others find out, but his desire is that others must honour him, greet him first, and shake his hand. He is astonished at those who try to harm him; who do not deal with him favourably in business and who do not honour him. This is also riyâ. From these thoughts and desires, we see that he feels deserving of favour from people due to his acts of worship. He desires honour and respect from them, despite his action being concealed from them. Only the siddiqîn (the truthful) are void of these hidden sicknesses. All of these forms are sin, and there is a fear that one's actions can be destroyed.

On the other hand, if a person becomes pleased due to one of the following reasons, then there is no harm:

* A person hides his good and evil from people, but **Allâh** ﷻ has exposed his good, and concealed his evil. He is thus pleased how **Allâh** ﷻ has dealt with him by only exposing the good and concealing the evil.
* He is happy thinking that just as **Allâh** ﷻ has dealt with him in this world, he will deal with him likewise in the Hereafter.
* He is happy because he knows that those who saw him will try to do likewise, and they will be encouraged.

The proof of this is, that one becomes just as pleased when the worship of another person is exposed; as he is when his actions are exposed. The object of desire and courage being created in others will be found whether people look at your acts of worship or others. So if this is the actual object of one's joy, then it will be equal for oneself and for others.

Since *riyâ* is completely concealed from our gazes, and due to its destructive effects on the internal, the pious elders were very wary. They thus concealed their acts of worship from the gazes of people. Alî ﷺ has stated, "Verily **Allâh** ﷻ will address the wealthy on the Day of Judgement, "Did we not grant you opulence? Would people not make salâm to your first? Were your needs not fulfilled quickly, in comparison to others? Since you have taken the full reward of your deeds in the world, there is no reward for you here."

O Muslims! If you desire to be safe from this, then regard the (presence of) people by you as (the presence of) animals and little children. Their presence and absence must be equal. Their knowledge and ignorance of your actions must not be regarded. Be content that **Allâh** ﷻ is fully aware. Worship only for His ﷻ Pleasure, since only He ﷻ can reward, and Only He ﷻ is Appreciative. Besides Him ﷻ , there is none else in this world and the Hereafter who can give anything. If you do actions sincerely for him, then you will definitely benefit, otherwise at the time of extreme need you will be empty handed.

## ANSWERING A QUESTION

Perhaps this thought crosses your mind, that to abstain from this hidden riyâ is impossible. Yes, it is quite possible to avoid the external form of *riyâ*. In that case, one will then not know whether his act of worship is correct or nullified. Therefore we will explain this point at this juncture.

Note that the thought of show is found at one of three times:

1) At the commencement of an act of worship - if a person from the beginning till the end performed salâh to show people, and to be called a person punctual in salâh, then this salâh will be void, since there was no intention for salâh at all. A person offers salaah at all times, but he reads it at the start of the time to show off to others; then outwardly it appears that the compulsion of the salâh has been discharged, but he will not receive the reward for performing salâh early and one will receive a separate sin for including an incorrect intention in an act of worship.

2) During an act of worship – the second case is where riyâ is found during an act of worship, or in perfection of any act of obedience e.g. whilst performing salâh, one remembers something that he had forgotten, or some event occurs nearby that creates the desire to break the salâh and proceed there. If he was performing salâh in solitude, and there was no one present, then he would have definitely broken his salâh. However, since some person is present, he completes the salâh due to shame that this person will remark, "He has broken his salâh for such a trivial and useless matter." Then, too, the salâh will be void, since it is necessary to possess correct intention in acts of worship, from beginning to end. Now in the middle, when due to riyâ, the intention is not found; the act of worship is ruined.

Another example is while a person is engaged in salâh, he perceives others looking at him, so he becomes so overjoyed since people are aware of his act of worship, so much so that his actual intention of worship becomes overpowered, and he performs one whole rukn (posture) with this feeling, then there is the strong likelihood that his salâh will also be void. Even though his intention (of worship) has not terminated, it has become so imperceptible, that its existence and non-existence are equal. Yes, if a person perceives only a slight amount of happiness, which does not overpower his intention - which is the Pleasure of **Allâh** ﷻ and obeying the Command of **Allâh** ﷻ - then the salâh will be correct. However, one will receive sin for intending riyâ.

3) After the act of worship – the third case is when riyâ is found after completing the act of worship e.g. one becomes pleased when others come to know of one's ibâdah, or a person himself makes it apparent, exhibiting pride. This has no effect on the correctness or incorrectness of the action, since the action was complete at the time of riyâ. However, one will attain the sin of this happiness, and exhibiting of one's action. Whenever the desire develops to mention one's act of worship, either openly or by indication, then this points to the fact that riyâ was concealed in his heart.

## CURE OF RIYÂ BY GAZING AT ITS SOURCE

Riyâ is an extremely destructive sickness. The cure for it should be done thoughtfully. Riyâ is generally caused by one of the following: a) desire and love of praise  b) fear of reproach  c) desire for wealth and worldly goods.

The first cause is the desire and love of praise. Examples of this are 1) a person goes forward in battle so that he can be called brave. 2) a person makes apparent his acts of worship so that he can be labeled as pious. The cure for this is the cure for the love of fame, as has been mentioned under the sixth principle. A person must realize that fame and honour is a fictitious and whimsical excellence, which has no reality. All those who are praising one, as well as all their praises, will all come to naught when a person leaves this world. They will be of no benefit. True excellence and perfection is that which will remain with a person after death i.e. Divine Recognition, which will never terminate.

Besides this, especially for riyâ, one should keep in mind the following thought – which is beneficial for this sickness – that these very actions of bravery, ibâdat, etc., which are being done for praises, will be the cause of my disgrace and embarrassment on the Day of Judgment, when I will be referred to as, "O sinner", "O deceiver". This disgrace will be enough to prevent a person from riyâ. However, together with this disgrace, punishment will also be meted out, one's acts of worship will be destroyed, and the scales of evil deeds can at times tilt with these actions, after being equal to the noble deeds, leading to one's destruction.

How illogical is it for one to purchase the Anger of **Allâh** ﷻ and disgrace on the plains of Qiyâmah, just to attain the pleasure of people and the temporary praises in this world? Added to this is that **Allâh** 🌸 can cause the one whose pleasure we seek in this world to become infuriated with us, if He 🌸 so pleases. Instead of praises, they will begin condemning us. This is because the hearts and tongues are all within His 🌸 Control. How can one give preference to imaginary and possible praises, over **Allâh** 🌸's Pleasure which is the actual success?

The second cause, is fear of people's reproach and criticism. One should entrench the thought in his mind, that the people's condemnation cannot cause him any harm if he is praiseworthy in **Allâh** 🌸's sight. Then why should he fear this? More so, it is definite that if one displeases **Allâh** 🌸 due to the fear of some imagined displeasure and criticism, then this will lead to disgrace and embarrassment in this world also. If people become aware of this internal riyâ, they will despise him. **Allâh** 🌸 can easily expose his internal condition, so that his hypocrisy can be ascertained. Subsequently, the people will also despise him after **Allâh** 🌸 has despised him. If however, one possesses sincerity, turns his heart away from them, and solely turns his gaze towards **Allâh** 🌸, **Allâh** 🌸 will expose his sincerity to the people, and they will in turn love him.

The third cause is, desire and greed for wealth and worldly goods. A person should realize that the thing which he seeks is imaginary. When doing an action for show, one will be deprived of Divine Pleasure, and that is certain. Who will ever prefer placing **Allâh** 🌸's Anger above himself, maintaining an imaginary benefit in front? Since **Allâh** 🌸 is the Controller of hearts, the worldly benefit which you desire by ibâdah will not be attained. In fact, due to greed, you will have to face disgrace and humiliation in front of the creation. Due to their favours on you, you will have to lower yourself before them. If however, you are devoid of greed, then **Allâh** 🌸 will take responsibility to fulfill all your needs. The everlasting and enjoyable bounties you will receive in the Hereafter, due to your sincerity, is separate.
In short, if you keep these definite and true factors in mind, then no trace of riyâ will remain, and **Allâh** 🌸 will grant you the quality of ikhlâs (sincerity).

# THE BENEFITS OF CONCEALING ACTS OF WORSHIP

Perhaps you may say, "The dislike of riyâ has been created in my heart. However, what is the cure for the thoughts of riyâ which suddenly engulf me, when people come to know of my acts of worship?"
The actual cure for this, is that you should conceal your acts of worship. You should cloak these acts of obedience, just as you cloak your sins and weaknesses. In this is safety. Once a companion of Abû Hafs Haddâd ﷺ condemned the world and those who incline towards it. Abû Hafs Haddâd ﷺ said to him, "You have made apparent that which you were supposed to conceal. Therefore, do not sit with us in our gathering anymore."

Remember that concealing of one's ibâdah is difficult in the beginning. Once it becomes a person's nature, then he will perceive the enjoyment of ibâdah in solitude. Whenever one feels happiness when people come to know of one's ibâdah, then immediately remember that which has been mentioned before, that the weak creation cannot benefit me in the least bit. Therefore, my pleasure with such unconstructive matters is futile, and to be a target of **Allâh** ﷻ's Displeasure is a very serious matter. When this thought is ingrained, then the feeling of happiness will change into displeasure. This will in turn lead a person to ikhlâs (sincerity) which is the object.

## NON-VOLITIONAL HAPPINESS IS NOT HARMFUL

Then too, if the feeling of pleasure remains in the heart, then you are not liable for this, since this is a natural feeling. It is not within one's control. One will not be taken to task for that which is not within one's control. In short, your effort is that you do not purposely make apparent your acts of worship, and you do not publicize it. If the people themselves come to find out, and you feel a sense of pleasure, then make an effort to remove it by changing this thought into a form of displeasure, so that this happiness does not cause any effect on any action of yours. Thereafter, do not concern yourself whatsoever with any feelings that remain, since they are not within your control.

# EXPOSING ACTS OF IBÂDAH IS AT TIMES BENEFICIAL

Exposing one's act of worship to encourage people, and so that they follow likewise, is permissible, as long as one's intentions are pure and sincere. If the *nafs* wants to entrap a person by this means, or there is a fear of one's hidden desires being inflated, then one should never dare to expose his acts of worship. It is then better to conceal one's acts of ibâdah. The sign of sincerity is that, if people have to follow some contemporary, then this person should become pleased. Therefore, take stock of the heart, checking its desires. If one's desire is that his ibâdah be a cause of creating desire in others, and that he must be a leader, followed by the people, then this is riyâ, desire for fame, and love of name. It is obvious that in this case, one becomes void of sincerity.

Similarly, concealing one's sins and acts of disobedience is permissible, on condition that one's intention is that people must not call him a fâsiq (sinner), and not that they regard him as pious.

There is no harm if one is pleased and happy when one's sins are concealed from people, and one feels grief when they are exposed. This happiness can be due to the fact that 1) this is in conformity to the command of **Allâh** ﷻ as He ﷻ loves that one conceals his sins, and dislikes a person exposing them, 2) one dislikes that he be censured and criticized, causing him pain, since feeling pain when censured is not prohibited, but part of man's nature 3) **Allâh** ﷻ has concealed his faults. Thus to be pleased when one's sins are kept hidden is not prohibited, due to any of these reasons. However, to be pleased on one's acts of worship because one will be praised and they will regard him as a great worshipper and pious, is definitely prohibited. This is because it is like taking a reward for one's ibâdah performed, which is not correct.

This can be understood in another manner. Generally, a person feels ashamed when his sins become exposed. Since shame and riyâ (show) are two separate entities, it is not prohibited to conceal one's sins and to be pleased thereby; contrary to acts of worship. The only reason a person becomes pleased when acts of worship become known, is due to the imagined benefit of some recompense, or some other lowly worldly benefit. There can be no other reasonable reason. However, it is not appropriate to abandon acts of worship and obedience, due to the fear of riyâ. Continue with acts of worship, and if riyâ occurs, then make an effort to remove it. However, in those acts which are related to the creation e.g. being an imam of salâh, taking the post of a judge, giving lectures, etc. if there is overwhelming fear of riyâ, that the *nafs* will definitely take wrong benefit, and one will not be possess sincerity in any way, then definitely, one should refrain from these posts. This was the way of the salaf (pious predecessors) and in this, there is greater goodness. As for salâh, fasting, charity, etc. it is not permissible to abstain from them for fear of riyâ.

However, if you possess no sincerity at all, and from the beginning to the end, you have no intention whatsoever to please **Allâh** ﷻ and to worship Him ﷻ, your only intention is to show off to people who are just as weak as you are, then it will not be permissible to perform that action. If you are in the habit of performing any noble action, and co-incidentally other people gather there, then do not leave out the action, but continue according to your normal habit, and as far as possible, try to remove the thoughts of riyâ, if they afflict you.

# CONCLUSION

## NOBLE CHARACTER AND THE DECEPTION OF THE *NAFS*

The evil qualities, from which the *nafs* needs to be purified, are many. However, their roots are the ten which we have just mentioned above, in great detail. Each of these qualities is linked to one another. As long as one is not cured from every single one of them, he will not possess control of his *nafs*. By reforming one quality and being unmindful of the other is not beneficial. A person who is suffering from ten illnesses will not be regarded as healthy, until he is cured from all ten illnesses. A person can only be referred to as handsome when all his limbs are perfect. Similarly, a person will only be internally beautiful when all his inner qualities are worthy of praise and commendable. Nabi ﷺ said, "A muslim is he whose character is perfect. The most virtuous believer is he whose character is the best."[1] Nabi ﷺ was sent in this world to perfect noble character.

There are many views of the great scholars regarding the definition, the reality, and the fruits of noble character. Here briefly, we will mention its reality.

### THE ESSENCE AND EFFECTS OF GOOD CHARACTER

The word خُلق (with a pesh) and خَلق (with a zabar) are two different words. Khalq refers to the outward form, and khulq refers to the internal form. Man is composed of a body, which can be perceived by the eyes, and of a soul and *nafs*, which can be perceived by insight (the eyes of the heart). This structure cannot be seen with the outward eyes. **Allâh** ﷺ has created both of these compositions in people differently: some are beautiful internally and externally, and some are ugly. Some are beautiful internally but ugly externally, and vice versa. However, the internal is more important than the external. For this reason, **Allâh** ﷺ has attributed the internal to His ﷺ Own Being, whereas He ﷺ has attributed the body to

---

[1] Tabrâni- This hadith is not mentioned in the original Arabic kitâb.

sand. **Allâh** ﷻ states, وَنَفَخْتُ فِيهِ مِن رُّوحِي. In this verse, He ﷻ has attributed the ruh to Himself ﷻ. In another verse, He ﷻ states, قُلِ الرُّوحُ مِنْ أَمْرِ رَبِّي Here the soul is characterized with the quality of being a Divine Command. On the other hand, **Allâh** ﷻ states regarding the physical body إِنِّي خَالِقٌ بَشَرًا مِن طِينٍ.

At this juncture, ruh and *nafs* refer to one and the same thing i.e. the faculty in man that perceives and recognizes things through the inspiration of **Allah** ﷻ, according to the vested ability within each person. It has been established that man's internal condition is more worthy of concern. As long as there is no beauty in his internal being, he cannot be referred to as a person of good character. Just as the physical body has components like the eyes, ears, mouth and cheeks, similarly the internal structure of man also possesses components. These are the faculty of knowledge, the faculty of anger, the faculty of desire and the faculty of justice.

When these four faculties reach a state of equilibrium, then one's character will be regarded as noble. The example of immoderation in these faculties, can be understood by immoderation in the external features. If a person's leg is only half a metre, but his hand is three times the size; or if one hand is half a metre and the other hand is a metre long, then this person cannot be labeled handsome. In like manner, if one's faculty of anger is below the level of moderation, or if the faculty of desire is above the normal limit, then this person cannot be referred to as one possessing noble character. Hereunder, we will mention the beauty and moderation of these four faculties:

Faculty of knowledge: The moderate level and beauty of this faculty is, when it enables one to differentiate between truth and falsehood in speech, between truth and falsehood in beliefs, and between good and evil in actions. When this ability has been attained, the fruits of *hikmat* (wisdom) will be acquired, which is the root of all virtues. **Allâh** ﷻ states, "And he who has been granted *hikmat* (wisdom), then he has been granted an abundance of goodness. Only the intelligent take lesson."

Faculty of desire and anger: The moderate level and beauty of these faculties is, when they remain constrained under the laws of shariah and wisdom. They should remain obedient as a trained hunting dog, that wherever it is commanded, it attacks; and whenever it is commanded to stop, it immediately stops, and sits in its place.

Faculty of justice: The moderate level and beauty of this faculty is, when it controls the faculty of anger and desire, keeping them confined to the indication of the shariah and one's intellect. The intellect is thus an advisor. The faculty of justice is immediately subservient to its advisor, and tries to implement the ruling of the intellect, on the faculty of anger and desire. They are like the obedient dog or horse, which obeys its master's commands.

When these four faculties are in equilibrium, then this person will be the possessor of noble character and be worthy of praise. From here, all the noble traits and qualities will arise.

When the faculty of anger is in moderation, then it is referred to as *shujâ'at* (bravery), a quality loved by **Allâh** ﷻ. If this faculty is in excess, then it is referred to as boldness. If this quality is deficient, then it is referred to as cowardice. When in moderation, the following qualities arise: kindness, manliness, courage, forbearance, steadfastness, control of anger, far-sightedness, and dignity. If this faculty is in excess, then the qualities of shortsightedness, bragging, shrewdness, uncontrolled anger, pride, and vanity arise. If this quality is deficient, then the qualities of cowardliness, disgrace, lowliness, wickedness, shamelessness, inability to protect one's family's honour and an inferiority complex are created.

When the faculty of desire is in moderation, then it is referred to as *iffat* (chastity). If there is an excess of this quality, then this is referred to as gluttony, and carnal desire. Deficiency of this quality is referred to impotency or uselessness. From chastity, the following qualities arise: generosity, shame, patient, contentment, piety, assisting one another, purity of the heart and lack of greed. An excess of this quality leads to greed, gluttony, wastage, stinginess, show, flattery, jealousy, joy on other's difficulties, degrading oneself in front of the wealthy and looking with the eyes of contempt at the poor.

When the faculty of intellect is in moderation, then sound administration, beautiful thinking, correct opinion, understanding of the finer points of actions, and the hidden illnesses of the soul are found. An excess of this quality leads to trickery, deception, cunningness, and depravity. Deficiency of this quality leads to foolishness, weak-mindedness, inexperience, and being the victim of deception.

In short, when all of these qualities are in moderation, then only can one be referred to as the possessor of noble qualities. An excess or deficiency in any of them will be disliked. خير الامور أوسطها "The best of matters are those which are in moderation." For this reason, **Allâh** ﷻ states, "And do not tie your hands to your neck (i.e. do not be stingy), and do not open it completely (do not be extravagant)." In another place, **Allâh** ﷻ states regarding His ﷻ special servants, "And when they spend, they do not waste, and they are not stingy, and they remain between the two."

## CORRECTION OF EVIL CHARACTER BY FORCE

These evil characteristics can be cured by striving and by spiritual exercises. If any of these evil qualities are within one, he has to impose on his *nafs* e.g. if he has the quality of stinginess, then he must impose on himself to spend, no matter how much he dislikes it, until eventually the quality of spending becomes a habit. If one is used to spending extravagantly, then he must force himself to abstain from imagined generosity and stop spending, until he attains the habit of spending less.

When his condition is corrected, then he will have the quality in moderation, which is beloved by **Allâh** ﷻ. Understand however, that the person who compels himself to spend is not generous, and the person who humbles himself forcefully, whilst it is a strain on himself, is as yet void of humility. These qualities will be regarded to be within a person, when they arise spontaneously, without any coercion. However, this coercion and force on the *nafs* is the path to attaining this quality. When a person continuously does an action, even by force, then this eventually becomes a habit and second nature.

# DIFFERENT STAGES OF GOOD CHARACTER

Just as there are differences in outward beauty – some are more beautiful than others - similarly people are diverse with regards to their inward beauty. The being who possessed the most beautiful character was undoubtedly *Rasulullâh* ﷺ, regarding whom **Allâh** ﷻ declared, "Verily, you possess great character." According to the closeness one possesses with the character of *Nabî* ﷺ, will he be regarded as the possessor of noble-character. Salvation is not dependent on perfect beauty. However, the inclination to beauty should be dominant. A person of perfect beauty will be beloved and desired, whereas an extremely ugly and bad-natured person, will be seen with the eyes of hatred and dislike. Between these two states, are countless stages of beauty and ugliness.

Just as those who are closer to perfect beauty are more successful in this world compared to those closer to ugliness, similarly the success of the Hereafter will be different according to the amount of inner beauty a person possesses.

## DIAGNOSIS OF CHARACTER SHOULD BE ESTABLISHED BY A SINCERE FRIEND

Many times man falls into error and deception, regarding the condition of his *nafs*. Even a person of evil character regards himself to be a man of noble character and manners. At times, a person becomes angry, and he thinks that his anger is for **Allâh** ﷻ. A person makes apparent his acts of worship, and he deceives his *nafs* saying that he has done this so that he could be followed, and so that others are inclined to this action. A person becomes a great worshipper, abstains from sins, turns away from this world, becomes particular on salâh and fasting, but his intention is only for show. However, the *nafs* will not allow him to make apparent this weakness. In short, the evil *nafs* deceives a person very greatly, and in order to remain in this condition, it portrays the vice to be virtue. Therefore it is appropriate that you enquire from a sincere friend about your condition. What is his opinion of you? Other people can judge your evil qualities and characteristics. The person who always deals with you, will easily be able to judge, as there will be many occasions when your character will be tested.

If your friend has your interests at heart, then without any formalities, he will inform you of your evil qualities. Thereafter, engage yourself in correcting this evil. If a few qualities are evil, then make effort first on the one which is dominant, and the one whose result will be critical. Regard the cure for this sickness to be precedent. I feel that the most dominant weakness found in people, from which very few are saved, is love of the world. All sins and evil qualities ensue in its wake. It is the root of all evils. Thus regard its cure to be most vital.

The cure for it, is to sit in solitude and ponder over the reason why you are focusing so much attention towards the world and away from the Hereafter. If in solitude you ponder, then you will understand that there is no other reason besides ignorance and neglect. Even if you are given a life of a thousand years and you receive kingdom of the whole world, then too, what will be the result? Finally, everything will be annihilated. A day is soon to come when neither you, nor your kingdom will remain. But, simltaneoulsy, you will lose that kingdom which will never come to an end, the kingdom of the Hereafter. If a person cannot understand the meaning of living forever, then think of the whole world being filled with grains. Every million years, a bird comes and takes only one grain. Eventually, a time will come when these grains will come to an end, since these grains are finite, whereas the Hereafter will never come to an end. Then why do you turn your attention to this temporary and fleeting kingdom, and why does your *nafs* prefer to be independent and inattentive towards the everlasting kingdom.

Then ponder over the difficulties you bear in undertaking journeys, either for business or for attaining of some position. After all of this effort, attaining wealth or the position is supposed and not definite. It is possible that death will come to one first. At times, one attains his high position, but he does not enjoy the ease, comfort and peace of mind, which he desired from this post. However, one regards these difficulties as trivial, since in his mind he regards this year or two, as little compared to the remaining portion of his life. He feels that by this journey, he will attain comfort for the remainder of his life. However, one's whole life compared to the Hereafter, is far less than one year compared to the rest of your life.

In fact, there can be no comparison. Therefore, if you spend your life in this world trying to attain the everlasting life of the Hereafter, and you bear the difficulties of a few days here for the eternal and perpetual enjoyments there, then what difficulty is there?

## DECEPTION OF THE *NAFS*

The *nafs* deceives a person and makes him negligent. It says to him, "**Allâh** ﷻ is Karîm (Most Kind) and Most Forgiving. He ﷻ will forgive all sins, and enter us into *Jannah*." I ask you, "Why do you not contemplate in the same way when it comes to your business and farms?" Is there a different **Allâh** ﷻ in this world, and a different one in the Hereafter? When the Creator ﷻ and Sustainer ﷻ is One ﷻ, then why do you not sit in your house having trust in **Allâh** ﷻ that since He ﷻ is Razzâq (The Provider) and Qâdir (All-Powerful), He ﷻ will fill our stomachs without any effort on our side? Why do you not have hope that He ﷻ will direct you to a hidden treasure in a dream, by which you will become wealthy without any exertion? Sadly, the answer to all this, is that it is necessary to seek livelihood because coming across a hidden treasure is coincidental; such a thing occurs very rarely; though it is within the Power of **Allâh** ﷻ, it does not happen generally.

Think of the same with regards to the Hereafter. Hoping for forgiveness, while possessing evil character and actions, is like hoping for a hidden treasure in a desolate place. Such forgiveness is also most rare. **Allâh** ﷻ has cautioned man regarding this, "And there is not for man, except that which he strives" and "Have We made those who believe and do good actions, like those who cause mischief in the land?" **Allâh** ﷻ has not made it necessary to choose means in the matters of the world, in fact He ﷻ has made us disinclined towards it by stating, "And there is not any creature on the earth, except that **Allâh** ﷻ has taken responsibility to provide it with sustenance."

It is a matter of amazement that you do not place your trust in Him ﷻ when it comes to earning the world, whereas you destroy your dîn and life of the Hereafter by hoping for forgiveness due to your evil actions and false hopes. Remember well, that this is a shaitâni whispering, which has destroyed people, and made them lazy due to which they have stopped actions of worship and obedience. May **Allâh** ﷻ save us!

## MANNER OF ATTAINING CONVICTION IN THE UNSEEN

You may say that you have seen the results of worldly efforts, and day and night you are experiencing its results, whereas you have not witnessed the matters of the Hereafter, due to which you have desire to earn the world, and you are disinclined from the Hereafter. If somebody has not seen something, then he cannot be truly convinced in his heart. Also it is accepted that every person gives preference to cash over credit, thus all efforts can be exhausted earning this world. As for dîn, let alone the optional duties (*nawâfil*), it is difficult to even fulfill the compulsory duties (*farâidh*). The answer to this is, that if **Allâh** ﷻ grants light to the eyes of your heart, and you become the possessor of insight, then you will see the results of religious matters, just as you are able to see the results of worldly matters.

If you have not attained this insight, then ponder over the statements of the *Ambiyâ* عليهم السلام and the *awliyâ* رحمهم الله. In this honourable and huge group, you will not find one of them, who were not convinced of the reality of the everlasting pleasures and everlasting punishment of the Hereafter. It is obvious that the eternal and perpetual felicity of the Hereafter cannot be attained without turning ones attention towards **Allâh** ﷻ. As long as you do not turn your attention away from the world, you will not be able to turn your attention to **Allâh** ﷻ.

When you ponder over the above mentioned matters, then you will acquire true belief in the Hereafter, and you will attain tranquility in your heart regarding the unseen matters. It is binding on the person who is blind, to hold onto and follow the person whose sight is perfect, since he is able to see all the pitfalls, and he can see the road which will take you to your destination. If you become sick, and you possess no knowledge of medicine, then will you regard it as necessary to obey the instructions of the doctor or not? This will apply to a greater extent when all the doctors are unanimous on a certain matter. Now, there is no scope for you to harbour any doubt. Keep the same point in mind with regards to your beliefs. The *Ambiyâ* عليهم السلام, the *awliyâ* رحمهم الله and the people of insight are spiritual doctors. They all are unanimous on the fact that the Hereafter is definite, wherein one will definitely receive the recompense of his good and evil actions, of this temporary and brief life. Thus there is no place for any doubt.

## THE REALITY OF MAN'S SOUL

Yes, there is a group of people who have not understood the reality of the ruh (soul). Their gaze is confined to the bodily soul by which man possesses the quality of movement i.e. those vapors which arise from the heart and spreads in all the vessels of the body. They have regarded this to be the soul, whereas this is found in animals also. Then what difference is there between man and animals?

Understand well that the soul is attributed to **Allâh** ﷻ. **Allâh** ﷻ states, "Say (*O Nabî* ﷺ), the rûh is from the command of my Sustainer." This is the soul we are referring to. Since the shortsighted doctors and astronomers cannot understand the reality of this divine soul, they are in deception and they deny the Hereafter, remaining as atheists. They feel that when the soul emerges from the body, the movements of the body come to an end. The body disintegrates, and now it can neither perceive pain, nor pleasure. Woe to the thinking of these shallow-minded people! Firstly, the opinion of these few people, opposed to such a huge group, is not even worthy of consideration. If you accept their view, then I ask you, "Do you regard their view to be definite, or do you feel that there is a possibility of error?"

If you feel that there is a possibility of error, then you should rather accept the first view, as there is more precaution in it. It is obvious that the demand of precaution is that you prepare, and have concern for the Hereafter. If, for example, you are hungry and food is placed in front of you, then a small child informs you that there is poison mixed in the food, or a snake has spat its poison in it, then it is obvious that you will bear the pangs of hunger, and leave the food. You will say to yourself, "Even though there is no certitude that there is poison therein, then too there is definitely a possibility. Therefore, it is better to remain hungry than to eat this doubtful food, because if I eat it, there is a chance that I can die. In the event I don't eat it, I will be saved from death. I will only have to bear some pangs of hunger, which I can easily do. If I do not enjoy the food, at least my life will remain. If there is life, I have everything."

A poet, despite possessing a low level of intellect, has so beautifully mentioned

زعم المنجم و الطبيب كلاهما  لا تحشر الاموات قلت إليكما

إن صح قولكما فلست بخاسر أو صح قولي فالخسار عليكما

*"The astronomer and doctor both said to me*
*"The dead will not be resurrected." I said to them, "Go away from me!"*
*If your statement is correct, I will not be in any loss,*
*and if my statement is correct, then loss will only be upon you!"*

What he meant is, that if their belief is correct, then he will not be in any loss, except that his actions will be in vain. However, if his belief is correct, then they will be in great loss, as they have not sent forward any preparations, whereas he is prepared. In short, there is only benefit if one, whilst living in this world, makes effort in his spiritual matters, and begins storing up a treasure of good actions.

## INCURABLE STAGE OF THE LOVE OF THIS WORLD

If you say, "I believe the view of the ignorant astronomer and the irreligious doctor to be completely correct, without any doubt of falsehood. All the *Ambiyâ* ﷺ and the *awliyâ* ﷺ are in deception. There is no such thing as the Hereafter, reward or punishment." If, **Allâh** forbid, you possess such a thought, then your sickness is terminal, since the rot in your temperament, and the weakness of your intellect has become glaringly open. Then too, you regard this as intelligent that you regard a thought, which is not backed by proof, to be definite and obvious. In this case, what hope can there be for your cure and remedy? We do not even want to waste our time explaining to such people.

## THE FINAL REMEDY FOR THE LOVE OF THIS WORLD

However, in passing, we will just mention that if you love the world, and are desirous of comfort and ease here, then too it is necessary for you, as we say, to curtail your connection with this transitory abode, since the enjoyment and comfort attained by freedom, cannot be attained by being entrapped. If you have become enslaved and bound by your *nafs*, and you are entangled in fulfillment of desires and in having numerous acquaintances, then remember you will have to bear every type of disgrace and embarrassment. You will be forced to stretch your hands in front of the creation who are weak like you, and you will be compelled to flatter them.

All the acquaintances of this world and complications associated thereby are so revolting, that many disbelievers, who do not even believe in the Hereafter, have given up the world, and have gone into seclusion by becoming monks and yogis. They too, have understood that the world is not a place where a person should place his heart, since we all have to leave this transitory abode one day. Whatever contact or love one possesses in the world soon terminates. Either we leave them, or they leave us. It is obvious that the result of this separation is nothing but sorrow and grief. When the disbelievers who do not even believe in the Hereafter find comfort by cutting their association in the world, then how can a person who claims to be a Muslim ever find comfort in worldly connections and relationships?

Finally, if a person does not look towards the difficulties and the briefness of this world, and logically he cannot understand the reduction of connections to be beneficial, then he is a foolish person, regarding whom **Allâh** ﷻ states, "(O Muhammad ﷺ), leave them, they will eat and enjoy themselves, and long hopes will place them in negligence, soon they will come to know."

Alhamdulillâh, the second section has come to an end. May **Allâh** ﷻ grant us all the ability to practice on whatever has been mentioned and may He make it a means of guidance!

آمين بجاه سيد المرسلين ﷺ و آخر دعوانا ان الحمد لله رب العالمين

و الصلوة و السلام علي رسوله و صفيه محمد و آله و أصحابه أجمعين

# SECTION THREE

# NOBLE CHARACTER

# FIRST PRINCIPLE

# TAWBAH

## PLEASURE OF ALLÂH ﷻ WHEN A SERVANT SEEKS FORGIVENESS

**Allâh** ﷻ states, "Verily **Allâh** ﷻ loves those who seek repentance abundantly." In another verse, **Allâh** ﷻ states, "*O* Muslims, all of you turn in repentance to **Allâh** ﷻ so that you may be successful." *Nabî* ﷺ said, "A person who seeks repentance is like one who has not committed a sin."[1] In another hadith, *Rasulullâh* ﷺ said, "**Allâh** ﷻ becomes happier with the repentance of His ﷻ Servant than a man who reaches a barren and terrifying land. He has with him his conveyance, upon which is his food and drink. He rests his head down and falls asleep. When he awakens, he finds that his conveyance has slipped away and left him. He searches for it, until eventually hunger and thirst overcome him. He then says, "I will return to the place where I was. Then I will sleep until I die. He places his head on his forearm so that he may pass away. When his eyes open, he sees his conveyance standing by him, together with his provisions and drinks. **Allâh** ﷻ becomes happier when His ﷻ believing servant seeks forgiveness than this man with his conveyance."[2]

---

[1] Ibn Mâjah (4250), Tabrânî in Kabîr (10/150)
[2] Bukhârî (6308), Muslim (2744)

# REALITY OF TAWBAH

The meaning of tawbâh is to return to **Allâh** ﷻ from afar, to close proximity. It has a beginning stage and an ending stage.

The beginning stage is *imân* i.e. the light of *ma'rifat* (recognition of **Allâh** ﷻ) spreads in the heart to such an extent that it becomes completely clear to someone that sins are poisonous and destructive. The fire of fear and sorrow is then ignited, due to which true desire is created to make amends for one's wrongdoing, and to be mindful in the future. At the present moment, he abandons the sin. As for the future, he makes a strong intention to stay away from that action. As for the past, he makes amends wherever possible. When this occurs, then one has reached the perfection of tawbah, which is also the ending stage.

## TAWBAH IS COMPULSORY ON ALL

After understanding the meaning and reality of tawbah, it will become apparent to you that tawbah is binding on every person, in every condition. **Allâh** ﷻ addresses all the believers in this verse, "And repent, all of you, to **Allâh** (ﷻ), so that you may be successful."

The reality of tawbah is to realize that sins are poisonous and destructive, and to make a firm intention to abstain from it. This realization is a portion of *imân*. Then how can it not be binding on every believer?

As for its compulsion on every person, understand that every person is composed of four types of qualities:

1) Animalistic qualities- This breeds fulfilment of desires, greed and open sinning.

2) Beastly qualities – This breeds anger, jealousy and hatred.

3) Satanic qualities – This breeds deception and treachery.

4) Godly qualities – This breeds pride, boastfulness, love for praise, love of name and fame, leadership and position.

These qualities are deeply ingrained in man. The only way he can attain freedom from the darkness of these evil qualities, is by the light of *imân*, which is derived from the shariah and one's intellect. These qualities appear on their respective times, and effect man. The first quality which comes into man is the animalistic quality in childhood. Greed and desire dominates one. When one reaches adolescence, then the beastly qualities overpower him. He now becomes jealous of others, has enmity for others, and becomes angry. If anything contrary to his temperament occurs, he loses control of himself. He will yell and shout. If he sets eyes on someone in a good condition, he will burn with rage, and will ponder how to snatch away that bounty. In short, he becomes similar to a wild beast.

Then in the prime of youth when one's faculties are at its peak, these animalistic and beastly qualities goad one to fulfill one's desires, and to give vent to one's anger. At this time, the satanic qualities have dominated one. When one desires something, these qualities try to achieve it by deception and trickery. When one becomes upset with any person, then this deception and treachery lays forth its strategy. In short, at this age, the satanic qualities assist and help the animalistic and beastly qualities to fulfill their habits. Man becomes a devil incarnate. When man sees success and his desires being fulfilled, then pride and arrogance are created. Man desires that every person must aid him. They all must become subservient to him. Every person must acknowledge his greatness and perfection. Every person must regard him to be intelligent and worthy of respect. A person now feels that there is none like him.

## THE HEART IS THE BATTLEFIELD

When these four qualities appear in man (the armies of shaytân), then the intellect comes forth, which is lit by the lamp of *imân*, and which can grant a person the ability to differentiate from good and evil (the army of **Allâh** ). If this light does not appear, then it is very difficult to attain salvation from the darkness of these aforementioned qualities. This intellect reaches perfection at the age of forty. It begins at the age of puberty. All the armies of shaytân have already reached the heart before the age of maturity and overpowered it. The *nafs* has become accustomed to it, and allows it to fulfill its desires, until the light in the intellect stops it. Then a battle ensues between these two forces in the heart. Each one tries to defeat the other. If the intellect and the light of *imân* are weak, then they will not have enough strength to overcome the armies of shaytân. Thus the armies of shaytân will remain firm in their place, as they had been previously. Shaytân will now possess safe control over the kingdom of the heart.

This battle is thus bound in man's disposition. The qualities found in the father, will definitely be found in the son. For this reason the incident of *Adam* الﺴﻼم عليه is mentioned to teach us that these qualities are ingrained within us, which can never be changed. Thus, no person is independent of tawbah.

## NO PERSON IS FREE FROM FAULT

No person is free from sin. Either his limbs or his heart is engaged in sin. If not, then no person is void of one of evil traits, from which the heart must be purified. These things take a person away from **Allâh** ﷻ. Eradicate this distance from **Allâh** ﷻ with tawbah.

If we accept that there is a person of angelic qualities and who is extremely cultured, and there is no quality of his which needs reformation, then too there will be some time when he will become unmindful of **Allâh** ﷻ. **Allâh** ﷻ has commanded, "When you forget, then immediately remember your Sustainer (ﷻ)." Thus returning to Him ﷻ by remembrance is tawbah, since negligence takes one away from **Allâh** ﷻ.

If we have to accept, that there is a person who is at all times completely absorbed in the remembrance of **Allâh** ﷻ, that his heart is not unmindful for even a second – even though this level is nearly impossible – then too one is in need of tawbah, because no matter what level he reaches, this will be defective with regards to the stage above it. It is necessary for every person to emerge from the deficient stage and to progress to the higher, and more perfect stage. When he reaches the next stage, then too, he will have to repent from the stage on which he was previously, as it was deficient with regards to the stage above it. No matter how much one progresses, he will be compelled to make tawbah, as the stages to **Allâh** ﷻ are infinite. For this reason, *Rasulullâh* ﷺ said, "I seek forgiveness from **Allâh** ﷻ seventy times daily."[1]

---

[1] Bukhâri (6307), Muslim (2702)

The tawbah of the general masses is from open sins, the tawbah of the *sâlihîn* is from internal sins and evil character, the tawbah of the *muttaqîn* is from doubtful matters, the tawbah of the lovers is from unmindfulness from **Allâh** 's remembrance, the tawbah of the *ârifîn* (those who have recognized Him ) is from their being on a rank, above which there are higher stages; and since there is no ending to the stages in closeness to **Allâh** , the tawbah of the *ârif* has no limit.

## TAWBAH, WITH ALL ITS REQUISITES WILL BE ACCEPTED

When all the conditions of tawbâh are fulfilled, there is no doubt that it will be accepted. The meaning of acceptance is that the heart attains the ability to accept the manifestation of the Luminance of Divine Recognition. Man's heart is like a mirror. The grime of desires and lusts prevent it from witnessing this manifestation. Sins add to its blackness. However, good actions, due to its inherent luminance, polish the mirror of the heart and remove its blackness. For this reason, *Rasulullâh* said, "Follow an evil action with a good one, it will obliterate it."[1]

The relationship of tawbah to the heart is of soap to clothing. If soap is used correctly, it will definitely remove the stains found on the clothing. Similarly, if the heart turns to **Allâh** with sincerity, then it is not possible that the purity of the heart, and the ability to perceive the manifestation of divine recognition, will not be created. Some *buzurgs* after making tawbah would be uncertain of their repentance being accepted. The reason for this was, that there were doubtful whether they had fulfilled the conditions of tawbah.

An example of this, is a person who has taken a laxative. Now he has doubt whether his stomach will work, not because of any doubt in laxatives, but because he is not sure whether he had taken this medication according to the correct method. Did he take the correct amount or not? Was the laxative suitable to the season and time? If he is sure about all these matters, then he will not possess any doubt that his stomach will

---

[1] Tirmidhi (1987), Ahmad (5/153)

start working, and that all the putrid and rotten matter will be expelled. Similarly, if one is convinced that he has fulfilled the conditions of tawbah, then there is no need to have any doubt in its acceptance.

When it has been established that tawbah is binding on every person, and every person is in need of this treatment, then it is not correct to be unmindful in this matter, since unmindfulness and following of one's desires are such destructive sicknesses, due to which man persists in sin and disobedience of **Allâh** . When a minor sin is done repeatedly, it becomes a major sin. When one leaves this persistence, then only will one attain salvation from internal sicknesses. This sickness of unmindfulness and following of desires, is far greater than bodily sicknesses like fever, colds, sores, etc. due to the following reasons:

1) A person can see his bodily sicknesses, whereas this sickness cannot be seen.  An example of this, is a person who has white spots of leprosy on his face. He possesses no mirror by which he can himself witness the sickness. This sickness is thus more dangerous, as it is possible that he will not even believe another person who informs him. This sickness will thus increase day by day.

2) Man has not seen the result of this sickness. Due to this, man sits in comfort, and without concern, having hope in **Allâh** 's Mercy, without giving any attention to this sickness. This is contrary to bodily sicknesses, the consequences of which are clearly observed. Therefore, in this condition, man does not possess such hope and trust in **Allâh** , but makes an exhaustive effort for treatment, whereas it is obvious that the Creator  of all sicknesses and health, whether bodily or spiritually, whether outwardly or inwardly is the same Being  i.e. **Allâh** .

3) Lack of spiritual doctors. This is something which is extremely lamentable and sorrowful, since the doctors of these spiritual sicknesses are the scholars and the intellectuals. They too however, have become sick. When they are not concerned about their own treatment, then how can they treat others? It is obvious that the most destructive disease, is the love of wealth and this world. In this era of great trials, it is the scholars who are most entrapped in this sickness. It is for this reason, that they do not

possess the courage to prevent others from the love of the world. In fact out of fear for disgrace, they do not even make apparent that the love of the world is evil, and that from all the spiritual diseases, this is such a destructive one, from which it is difficult to escape. It is for this reason that the sickness has become incurable. When an epidemic or plague breaks out, no one is aware of the treatment, and the doctors themselves are suffering from the same sickness, then how can safety from this sickness be envisaged?

The worst calamity is, that the general people, on observing these scholars have now inclined to the world even more. There is no way to turn these masses towards medication and cure, since these are the scholars who are being followed. The general person regards them as his guide and leader. When he sees them entrapped in the love of this world, then he feels this to be a good trait, and follows them headlong. When this occurs, then what hope is there of reform? How lamentable that those who were sent as doctors in this world have, instead of providing the treatment, actually increased the sickness.

Those who have come as reformers, have become the mischief makers. Those who have been placed as guides, are themselves astray, and desire to lead others likewise. It is as though they have placed a barrier at the mouth of a spring which exudes sweet water, thus not drinking themselves, and not allowing others to drink as well. *O!* If only the world would be rid of such people, and this barrier be removed from the mouth of the spring! If they themselves are unworthy, let them be so, but why are they closing the spring for others? They should move aside, so that at least others could satiate, and quench their thirst.

In short, the remedy for this sickness is to ponder over the reason why one persists in sin. The reason can be one of the following five:

a) The stipulated punishment is not handed out immediately. A person does not give so much importance to that which does not take place in the present.

The remedy for this is to realize and ponder, that whatever is to occur in the future, is very close. How can that thing be far-off when it is definitely to occur? This is more so for death, whose coming is certain. Its time is not stipulated. This can never be referred to as far-off. Today can be our final day, this month may be our final month, and this year may be the final year. To be oblivious of this is idiocy. Think how you bear great hardships and journey to far-off lands, to earn your sustenance, due to fear of future poverty. Do you have so much of concern for the perpetual life of the Hereafter, as you have for the transitory and brief life of this world?

b) The *nafs* is entrapped in fulfilling its desires and aspirations at present. It is unable to extricate itself from them.

The remedy for this is to ponder that if a Christian doctor has to say, "Drinking cold water is harmful for you. It may lead to your demise.", then what will be the effect of his advice on you? Even though it may be the most delectable thing to you, you will leave it, whereas this is the statement of an ordinary person, and that too, a disbeliever. There are so many possibilities, that he could be saying something which is completely false. Then how can you even delay in breaking those desires, which have been declared to be harmful by **Allâh** ﷻ? Are the statements of **Allâh** ﷻ and *Rasulullâh* ﷺ not even equal in your eyes to the statement of a non-believing doctor? Is dying due to a bodily sickness more painful than burning in the eternal fire of the Hereafter? Think also, that if leaving all your enjoyments and desires for a few days is so difficult on you, then how much more difficult will remaining in the fire and being deprived of *Jannah* and its bounties be on you?

c) The *nafs* has made you lazy and causes you to procrastinate, "Why the hurry? I will repent tomorrow." In this way, a person's life passes, and he is not granted the ability to repent.

The remedy for this, is to ponder that no one knows when he will leave this world. How can one believe, that he will live until such a time that he can repent? Most of the shrieking of the people in the fire of Hell will be regarding their procrastination. They procrastinated until a sickness suddenly overtook them, leading to their demise. A person only procrastinates, because he is unable to control and leave the fulfillment of his desires immediately. If he is waiting for a day in which it will be easy for him to fight his desires, then he should remember that such a day will never arrive. When he deems it difficult to fight his desires today, then tomorrow when these desires have become stronger and more engrained, then how will he be able to prevent himself? An easy example is, that you have been commanded to uproot a tree. You say to yourself, "I will do it next year." However you know that the roots of the tree are growing deeper day by day, whilst you are growing weaker day by day. When you are not going to uproot it today, then how will you be able to do so the following year? This is complete ignorance.

d) The *nafs* has placed hopes on **Allâh** ﷻ's Forgiveness and Kindness. It says to man, "**Allâh** ﷻ will not be concerned about our sins. He ﷻ is the Most Forgiving, Most Merciful. He ﷻ will forgive all our sins" Remember that this is the height of foolishness, which shaytân has presented in the form of religiousness, whereas *Rasulullâh* ﷺ has stated, "An intelligent person is he, who takes a stock of his *nafs*, and practices for that which is after death; whereas a foolish person is he who follows his base desires and then places hope in **Allâh** ﷻ."[1]

e) A person has doubt in the occurrence and matters of Qiyâmah (**Allâh** ﷻ save us!). The remedy for this has been mentioned at the concluding section of the evil qualities. Refer to it and practice accordingly.

## PERSISTENCE ON MINOR SINS

Tawbah from all sins are necessary and binding. However, tawbah from major sins are more important. You have already learnt that persistence on minor sins, causes the sin to become major. In actual fact, when minor sins are continuously done, they create more darkness in the heart compared to a person who has done a major sin once. The example of minor sins done continuously is of small drops of water which continuously trickle on a rock, and the example of a major sin is like a deluge of water which falls suddenly on the rock. It is apparent that the drop, despite being regarded as petty, will eventually cause a hole in the rock, contrary to the deluge,

---

[1] Hâkim (1/57), Tirmidhî (2459), Ibn Mâjah (4260)

which even if it falls on thousands of stones once, will not cause the effect done gradually by the small drops. Thus minor sins done continuously, over a period of time, is far more devastating than a major sin done just once.

The reasons for this are:

1) A person regards a minor sin as trivial, and he does not attach much importance to it. He does not grieve after committing it, contrary to a major sin, which due to knowing of its gravity, there is hope that a person will make effort to abstain from it. Someone has mentioned, "The sin which will not be forgiven is the one which a person felt trivial and said, "If only all which I did, was like this one!"

2) At times a person becomes happy when committing these sins, and even regards it to be a bounty. Many times you will hear a person saying, "Did you see how I swore him? Did you see how I disgraced him? Did you see how I deceived him in this transaction?" This has a great effect in blackening the heart.

3) A person regards the sin as minor, due to **Allâh** concealing him. He thinks that this is because of the status he enjoys with **Allâh**. He does not know that he is despised. **Allâh** is granting him respite, so that he may indulge in more sins, and eventually be caught suddenly, taken to the lowest depths of Hell.

4) Due to a sin being minor, a person openly perpetrates, it or a person openly boasts about the sin after committing it. *Rasulullâh* has said, "All people will be forgiven except those who openly sinned."[1]

5) If any scholar or *sufi* does a minor sin, then the effect is worse, since the general people will notice it, and become bold and audacious in perpetrating it. In this way, this action will remain alive. At times, even after this person's demise, the sin will continue to be perpetrated. The sin of all those who followed this guide, will fall onto him. It is obvious that

---

[1] Bukhâri (6069), Muslim (2990)

the sins which remain perpetually are far worse, than those which come to an end. Here the sin remains because it was taught to be trivial. Fortunate is he who's dies sins terminate at death. It has been narrated that a scholar of the Bani Isrâîl sought forgiveness for his sins and innovations. **Allâh** sent revelation to the *Nabî* of that time, "If the sin was between Me () and him, I () would have forgiven him. However, what will happen to all those servants of Mine () he led astray, and caused them to enter the fire?"[1]

In short, it is necessary for every person to seek forgiveness for his every sin. Tawbah will only be done, when there is the fear of **Allâh** , which is created by His  recognition. Therefore we will now mention the virtue of fear, its reality, and the manner of acquiring it.

# SECOND PRINCIPLE

# FEAR

The fear of **Allâh**  is one method of gaining desire for good actions and abstaining from all sins. **Allâh**  has promised guidance, mercy, knowledge and His  Pleasure for those imbibed with this quality. **Allâh**  states, "Guidance and mercy for those who fear their Sustainer." "Only the people of knowledge truly fear **Allâh** ." and "Verily **Allâh**  is pleased with them, and they are pleased with Him (). This is for those who fear their Sustainer."

*Nabî*  said, "The root of wisdom is the fear of **Allâh** ."[2] In another hadith, *Rasulullâh*  said, "Whosoever fears **Allâh** , **Allâh**  will make everything else afraid of him. Whoever fears those besides **Allâh** , **Allâh**  will make him afraid of everything."[3] In a Hadith-e-Qudsî, **Allâh**  states, "By My Honour () and My Grandeur (), I () will not combine two fears on My () servant, nor will I () gather safety

---

[1] Musannaf Ibn Abî Shaibah (8/251)
[2] Shua'bul Îmân (730), Musnadul Firdaws (3258)
[3] Musnadush Shihâb (429), Musnadul Firdaws (5539)

twice on him. If he is unafraid of Me (ﷻ) in the world, I (ﷻ) will make him frightened on the Day of Judgement. If he fears Me (ﷻ) in the world, I (ﷻ) will grant him safety on the Day of Judgement."[1]

## THE REALITY OF FEAR AND METHOD OF ACQUISITION

The meaning of fear, is the pain and burn in the heart due to the anticipation of something disliked in the future. As long as a person does not possess recognition of **Allâh** ﷻ's qualities of Might and Grandeur, fear will not be created. When this thought becomes firmly embedded in the heart that **Allâh** ﷻ has complete control over every minute and large thing, that in one second, He ﷻ can do as He ﷻ pleases, and none will be able to object, then this quality of fear will be created.

Thus if one wishes to create this quality of fear, then let him look towards the Might and Independence of **Allâh** ﷻ. He should contemplate that *Jannah* has been created, and its occupants have been predetermined. Similarly, *Jahannum* has been created, and its inhabitants have been pre-ordained. The final result of every person has been written in such a book, which can never be altered or changed. There is none to stop this ruling which has been determined before time was even created. So, *O nafs!* you do not know what decision has been passed regarding you. What will your final result be? It is possible that you will be entered into *Jannah*. However, it is also possible that the everlasting fire of Hell, has been ordained for you.

Remember well, that only the person who is void of true Divine Recognition, will be unafraid of his hidden and final condition. It is thus appropriate to read and study the lives of those who possessed recognition of **Allâh** ﷻ i.e the *Ambiyâ* عليهم السلام, the *awliyâ* ﷺ , and the people with deep insight.

Despite these personalities possessing such closeness to **Allâh** ﷻ, they possessed great fear. *Rasulullâh* ﷺ said, "Whenever *Jibraîl* عليه السلام came to me,

---

[1] Shua'bul Îmân (759), Ibn Hibbân (640)

he would be trembling, due of the fear of the Fire."[1] It has been narrated, that when Iblis was banished from *Jannah*, then *Jibraîl* ﷺ and *Mikâîl* ﷺ began crying. **Allâh** ﷻ asked them, "Why are you crying?" They relied, "O! our Sustainer (ﷻ), we are afraid of Your (ﷻ) Decision." **Allâh** ﷻ said, "Remain like this. Do not be unafraid of My (ﷻ)Decisions. None are unafraid of the planning of **Allâh** ﷻ except the disbelieving people." [2]

A boiling sound (like that of a pot boiling on a stove) emanating from the heart of Ibrâhîm ﷺ could be heard from the distance of a mile. Dawûd ﷺ cried continuously for forty days, until eventually grass began growing due to his tears. Abu Bakr ﷺ addressed a bird saying, "O bird, if only I was like you, and I was not created as a human being." Abu Dharr ﷺ said, "If only I was a tree that would be cut." Aishâh ﷺ said, "If only I was non-existent."

In short, whoever possessed recognition of **Allâh** ﷻ and understood His ﷻ Independence, they would never be unafraid. Being unmindful and unafraid is the path of the oblivious rulers, whose gaze is not on their end, and who have not turned their attention to preparing for the Hereafter. These heedless ones are like small children, who do not fear poisonous snakes. However if someone explains to the child its danger, he will understand. When this unintelligent child sees his father fearing the snake and running away, he begins doing the same, even if he does not understand the reality of the snake. The unmindful and heedless Muslims should thus study the life stories of the special devotees of **Allâh** ﷻ, and the spiritual doctors, and take lesson from it.

## TOO MUCH FEAR IS HARMFUL

Fear is actually a whip which drives a person towards everlasting success. As long as it remains a driving force towards righteousness, it is approved. However, it should not be so excessive, that it leads one to despondency, eventually causing him to renounce all good. Such excessive fear that creates despondency is disliked in the Shariah, since a hadith states, "*Imân* is suspended between fear and hope." Thus together with fear, hope is also

---

[1] Kitâbul Azmat (page 789, vol.2)
[2] Kitâbul Azmat (page 814, vol.3)

necessary. However, a sinful Muslim should keep the quality of fear dominant. When he becomes obedient, then both these qualities should be balanced. Once Umar Fârûq ﷺ stated, "If an announcement is sounded, 'All will enter *Jannah* except one person,' then I fear that I would be that person. If an announcement is made, 'All will enter Hell except one person,' then I have hope that I would be that person."[1]

During one's youth and sound health, fear should be the dominating quality, since during this era of overpowering desires, there is a need for the whip of fear to break carnal desires and mould it so that one reaches his destination. When a person reaches old age or becomes sick, then hope should be dominant, since a person cannot really fulfil his desires at this age, and if fear overcomes him, then even the little he is doing will terminate. *Nabî* ﷺ is reported to have stated, "None of you should die, except whilst maintaining good hopes in **Allâh** ﷺ."[2]

## THE DIFFERENCE BETWEEN HOPE AND FALSE HOPE

It is obvious that a person will only harbour good hopes in **Allâh** ﷺ, when he possesses good actions. If a person cares for his land, places seeds in the ground, and then waters it, only then will he cherish hope on the Grace of **Allâh** ﷺ, and hope to harvest his plantations. If he does not even plant seeds, and then too desires crops, then this will not be regarded as having hope, but will be regarded as possessing false hopes and desires, which is a satanic deception. **Allâh** ﷺ states in the Qurân Sharif, "Verily those who believe, and those who migrate and strive in the path of **Allâh** ﷺ, they have hope in the Mercy of **Allâh** ﷺ." From here we learn, that one can entertain hopes after making effort. Just as a farmer after making full effort, waits to see if his crop has been protected from any natural calamity, then only does he hope to receive seventy seeds from just one ear of corn, similarly a Muslim after making great effort and sacrifice in **Allâh**ﷺ's obedience, has hope that if **Allâh** ﷺ accepts my actions due to

---

[1] Abu Nuaym in Hilyah (53/1)
[2] Muslim (2877), Abû Dawûd (3113)

His Grace ﷻ, then he will attain seven hundred rewards, and even more, from every good action.

In short, due to fear of punishment, one should abstain from all sins and disobedience of **Allâh** ﷻ. Due to having hope in Divine Mercy, desire for good actions should be created. Fear will be regarded as correct, when it stops a person from sin, and does not give him the audacity to transgress. If this is not attained, then this is not fear, but just thoughts and imagination which have no value. It resembles the softness of a woman, which bears no fruits. When fear becomes complete, it creates disinclination from this world (referred to as zuhd). It is thus appropriate that we discuss zuhd here.

# THIRD PRINCIPLE

# ZUHD

**Allâh** ﷻ states, "(O *Nabî* ﷺ) do not stretch your eyes towards those beauties of the world which We have granted some groups amongst them, so that We may test them thereby. And the sustenance of your Sustainer is far better and everlasting." Regarding Qârûn, **Allâh** ﷻ states, "Qârûn came out to his people after adorning himself. Those who intended the worldly life said, 'If only we were granted the same as that which Qârûn was given, verily he is a very fortunate person.' Those who were granted knowledge said, 'Woe to you! The reward of **Allâh** ﷻ is far greater for those who believe and do good actions.'" From this incident we learn that zuhd is the product of knowledge.

*Nabî* ﷺ said: "He who wakes up in the morning while his major concern is the dunya, Allah ﷻ shall scatter his affairs, create disarray in his worldly plans, place poverty in front of his eyes, and he will only get that much of this world that was written down for him; and he who wakes up in the morning while his major concern is the Hereafter, Allah ﷻ shall take care of his worries, shall make his worldly matters go right, shall place riches in his heart, and the world shall come to him in abundance."[1]

In the Qurân Sharif, **Allâh** ﷻ states, "Whomsoever **Allâh** ﷻ wishes to guide, He expands his breast for Islam." When *Nabî* ﷺ was asked the meaning of the breast expanding, he ﷺ replied, "When light enters the heart, the chest opens and expands." *Nabî* ﷺ was then asked, "Are there any signs of this?" *Nabî* ﷺ said, "Yes, turning away from the house of deception, turning towards the everlasting abode, and preparing for death before it approaches."[2] *Rasulullâh* ﷺ said, "Be bashful of **Allâh** ﷻ, fulfilling the right of bashfulness." The Sahâbah ﷺ said, "We feel bashful." *Rasulullâh* ﷺ then said, "You build those houses in which you do not live, and you gather that which you do not eat."[3]

*Rasulullâh* ﷺ said, "Whoever adopts zuhd (disinclination from this world), **Allâh** ﷻ will insert wisdom into his heart, and make his tongue articulate it. **Allâh** ﷻ will teach him the sicknesses of the world, and its cure, and **Allâh** ﷻ will take him from the world safely to the house of safety (*Jannah*)."[4] In another hadith, *Rasulullâh* ﷺ has mentioned, "A servant cannot perfectly attain the reality of îmân until his concealment is more beloved to him than being exposed; and until possessing less is more beloved to him than possessing an abundance of things."

Another hadith states, "When **Allâh** ﷻ intends good for a servant, He ﷻ creates disinclination in him for the world, creates a desire within him for the Hereafter, and exposes to him his faults."[5]
*Nabî* ﷺ said, "Be disinclined towards the world, **Allâh** ﷻ will love you. Be disinclined with that which people possess, people will love you."[6]

---

[1] Tirmidhi (2465), Ibn Mâjah (4105)

[2] Shua'bul Imân(10068), Hâkim(4/311), Musannaf Ibn Abî Shaibah (8/126)

[3] Shua'bul Imân(10078), Tabrâni in Kabîr (25/172),

[4] Shua'bul Imân(10049), Musnadul Firdaws (6215)

[5] Shua'bul Imân(10053), Musnadul Firdaws (935)

[6] Hâkim(4/311), Ibn Mâjah (4102)

*Nabî* ﷺ said, "Whoever wishes that **Allâh** ﷻ grants him knowledge without learning, and guidance without misguidance, then let him be disinclined from this world."[1]

## THE REALITY OF ZUHD AND ITS FRUITS

The reality of zuhd is turning the heart away from the world gladly, despite possessing the ability to acquire it. The root of zuhd is the knowledge and radiance which **Allâh** ﷻ places in the heart of His ﷻ Servant, until the chest expands, and it becomes clear that the Hereafter is far superior and everlasting, and that the relationship of the world in comparison to the Hereafter is less than the relationship between a rag and a gem.

The result of zuhd is that one will be content with necessities. The zâhid will suffice on that amount which a traveller keeps as provisions for his journey. Necessities in this world are a house, clothing and some commodities in the house. There are different stages of zuhd in each of these things which we will now discuss with a bit of detail:

**FOOD**: With regards to food, there are three things to consider :
1) time
2) quantity
3) type

1) As for time, the highest level of zuhd is to suffice on one meal a day i.e. if hunger is appeased in the morning, then one should not keep anything for the evening. The middle level is where one stores food for about a month to forty days. The lowest level is when one stores for a year. If he exceeds this, then he has emerged from possessing any amount of zuhd. However, if one does not have any source of income and he does not take wealth from anyone, then if he stores food for more than a year, this will not be contrary to zuhd. Dâwûd Tâi ﷺ owned twenty gold coins. He kept

---

[1] Shua'bul Imân(10098), Hilyah (6/312)

them and sufficed on them for twenty years. Neither did this destroy his status of zuhd, nor his rank in the Hereafter.

2)As for quantity, the highest level of zuhd is to consume half ratl (200 grams), the moderate level is to consume one ratl (400 grams), and the lowest level is to consume one mudd (800 grams). More than this is contrary to the status of zuhd.[1]

3)As for the type, the highest level is to eat that food which will grant strength, even if it be the chaff of grain. The middle level is to consume barley bread, and the lowest level is to eat bread made from wheat, which has not been sifted. If the wheat is sifted, then this is not zuhd, but luxurious living.

As for gravy, the highest level of zuhd is to consume vinegar, vegetables and salt, the middle level is to consume oil, and the lowest level is to consume meat, on condition that it is eaten only once or twice a week. If one has a habit of eating more meat than this, then he cannot be termed a zâhid. Ayeshâ ﷦ says, "Forty days used to pass, and no lamp, nor fire was lit in the house of *Rasulullâh* ﷺ."[2] Another narration states, "*Rasulullâh* ﷺ did not eat wheat bread to satiation for three days, from the time he entered Madinâh Munawwarah."[3]

**CLOTHING:** The highest level of zuhd is to have sufficient clothing to cover the private parts, and to protect one from heat and cold. The lowest level is to possess a kurtâ, a trouser and a scarf of an inferior material. If one has to wash it, he must not possess another. If a person owns two kurtâs, he is not a zâhid. Abu Burdah ﷦ said, "Aishâ ﷦ took out and showed me a thick lungî and a châdar (upper covering). She then said, "*Rasulullâh* ﷺ passed away in these two."[4] Once, *Rasulullâh* ﷺ wore a pair of new shoes. Its beauty delighted him. He ﷺ then fell in sajdah and said, "Their beauty has captivated me. I humbled myself before my Creator, out

---

[1] **Refer to *NOTE* in Foreword**
[2] Hâkim (4/126)
[3] Bukhâri (5416), Muslim (2970)
[4] Bukhâri (5818), Muslim (2080)

of fear that He must not dislike me." *Nabî* then went outside taking these shoes. He then gave them to the first poor person he met."[1] Twelve patches were counted on the kurta of Umar, some of them leather.[2] Alî said, "Verily **Allâh** has commanded that the leaders of guidance must be according to the person of the lowest status, so that the rich can follow him, and so that he does not despise the poor due to his poverty."

**HOUSE:** The highest level is to pass one's life in a room in a masjid or khanqah, just like the ahle-suffah. The lowest level is that a person seeks for himself a specific room, either owning it or taking it on rental, on condition that its size does not exceed necessity, it should not be built high, and the house should not be coated or plastered. Living in houses which are plastered or coated expels one from the ranks of zuhd.

Abdullah Ibn Umar said, "*Rasulullâh* passed by us, whilst we were plastering our hut with lime. He said, "Verily the matter (of death) is faster than this."[3] The meaning of this is what is the necessity of making your house so firm for this fleeting life? When death will come, the house will remain here, of no benefit to you. Nûh had built a hut from dry straw. People said to him, "Why don't you build a house?" He replied, "This too is excessive for one who is going to die." [4] *Rasulullâh* said, "Whoever builds more than that which is sufficient for him, will be burdened to carry it on the Day of Judgement." [5]
*Rasulullâh* said, "Every building will be a calamity on its owner on the Day of Judgement, except that which protects one from heat and cold."[6]

**COMMODITIES**: The highest level is that of Isâ. He possessed nothing but a comb, and a drinking utensil. Once, he saw a person combing his hair with his fingers. He thus threw the comb away. At

---


[1] Al Mughni (1/164)

[2] Hilyah of Abu Nuaym (1/52), Zuhd of Ibn Mubârak (964)

[3] Ibn Hibbân (2997), Abû Dâwûd (5235), Tirmidgî (2335)

[4] Shuabul Imân (10266), Tarikhe Dimishq (62/280)

[5] Tabrâni in Kabîr (10/151)

[6] Abu Dawûd (5237)

another time, he saw a person drinking water cupping his hands. He then threw away his drinking cup. The intermediate level is when a person keeps an inexpensive utensil, which is of necessity, and that too, not more than one. As far as is possible, try to fulfil many necessities with one utensil. Umar ﷺ said to Umair ibn Sa'd ﷺ, the governor of Hims, "What worldly possessions do you own?" he replied, " I own a staff, with which I lean upon, and I use it to kill snakes if I come across them. I have a bag in which I carry my food. I possess a dish from which I eat, and I use it to wash my head and my clothing. I own a utensil in which I carry my drinking water and water for istinjâ. Whatever other needs I have in the world, I fulfil it with these four utensils." Umar ﷺ said, "You have spoken the truth."[1]

Hasan ﷺ said, "I met seventy of the best of people. They possessed nothing but their clothing. None of them would place a cloth between himself and the ground."[2]

The bedding upon which *Rasulullâh* ﷺ slept was a pillow made of leather, filled with leaves of the palm tree, and a thick covering.

This in short is the condition of some of the zâhids, which we have mentioned as an example. If one is deprived of attaining these ranks, then at least he should feel sorrow of this deprivation, so that the love for zuhd and the desire to attain it remains within the heart. Try as far as possible to sit in the company of these zâhids, compared to sitting with those who enjoy luxurious lives. As far as possible, try to become similar to the zâhids, and attempt to attain their high ranks.

## STAGES OF ZUHD

Zuhd has different stages:
1) Even though a person is inclined to the world, he forcefully tries to make himself disinclined, and he vehemently prevents himself from attaining the world. This is not actually zuhd (disinclination), but tazahhud

---

[1] Hilyah of Abu Nuaym (1/247), Târikhe Dimashq (46/489)
[2] Hilyah of Abu Nuaym (2/146), Musannaf Ibn Abi Shaibah (8/259)

(compelling oneself to disincline), and this is the commencing stages of zuhd.

2) A person possesses an aversion to the world, and he is completely disinclined from it. He understands that it is not possible to combine possession of this world, and the bounties of the Hereafter. Therefore, to attain the enjoyments of the Hereafter, he is prepared to forsake the world, just as a person is prepared to forsake a few rands, to procure a valuable gem. In fact, a person happily hands over his money and takes the gem. Similarly, a zâhid happily forsakes the goods of this world, and attains the bounties of the Hereafter.

3) The third stage is, when one does not incline towards the world, nor does he possess aversion for it. In fact, possession and non-possession of it is equal in his sight. Money according to him is like water, and the Treasures of **Allâh** are like the ocean. Neither does his heart turn towards it with desire, nor with disdain. This is the highest stage, since a person who dislikes something is pre-occupied with it, akin to one who likes it. Turning towards something shows one regard for that thing. Once, some people in the presence of Rabiyâ Adawiyyah spoke ill of the world. She remarked, "If you did not possess value for this world, you would not have criticized it (i.e. because the honour and grandeur of the world is in your hearts, you spoke ill of it. Does any person censure a thing of no value and despicable?)"

Remember that when the grandeur of the world leaves the heart, then a person becomes void of love or hatred of that thing. Once a hundred thousand silver coins were given to Aishâh. She did not detest it, but took it and distributed all to the poor on the same day. Her servant said to her, "If only you bought meat for one silver coin, by which you could break your fast!" She remarked, "If you had reminded me, I would have done so." This level is referred to as ghinâ, which is higher than zuhd. However, the ignorant *sufi*s fall into deception here as they regard themselves to be on this level. They feel that since their hearts have no connection with the world, abundance of worldly possessions will not be harmful to them. This is a satanic ruse. Only when tested will the reality be known. The sign of this, is that you can notice no difference in effect on him when his money is stolen or somebody else's money is stolen. If there is a different effect, then this shows that he is still pre-occupied with this wealth.

## PERFECTION OF ZUHD

The perfection of zuhd, is to have zuhd in zuhd i.e. after obtaining zuhd, one should not even feel he has accomplished something great. If a person abstains from the world, and then feels he has executed an impressive action, then this shows that he regards the world as great.

According to people of insight, the world is of no value at all, less than even the value which a great king gives to one cent. Understand this by means of the following example. A person wishes to enter the royal palace. At the door is a dog, preventing him from entering. The person throws a piece of bread to the dog so that it engages in eating, and he can reach the royal court. Similarly, shaytân is the dog of **Allâh** ﷻ, who is preventing the sâlik from reaching **Allâh** ﷻ. The whole world has less significance than a piece of bread. The sâlik throws this world in front of himself, so that the road to his objective is cleared. To attain this honour of being in the royal court, the bread which is thrown is of no value in the sight of the person, nor does he understand it to be something worthy of mention and thought. In fact, there is some compatibility between a king and the piece of bread, as both are going to terminate one day.

When a transitory thing which is of no honour, is exchanged for something else which is also transitory; then realize that there is no comparison whatsoever with this world and the Hereafter. If there are millions in this world, then too one day, they will cease to exist. If one has to thus hand over the world to shaytân, so that one may attain the everlasting bounties of the Hereafter, and the perpetual rulership of a permanent kingdom, then to even think about it and discuss it is superfluous.

## THE CAUSES LEADING TO ZUHD

The reason which leads a person to adopt zuhd is one of three:

a) Fear of the fire of Hell. This is referred to as the zuhd of the khâifîn (those who fear). This is the lowest level.

b) Desire for the bounties of the Hereafter. This is referred to as the zuhd of the râjiyin (those who possess hope). This level is higher than the first one, since worship due to hope is better than worship due to fear, as hope creates love, and you are already familiar with the virtues of love.

c) The highest level is to turn away from everything besides **Allâh** 🕮, and regarding all besides **Allâh** 🕮 as completely insignificant. This is true zuhd, referred to as the zuhd of the *ârifîn* (those who have recognized **Allâh** 🕮), since in the previous two, there is some form of transaction. A person leaves something despicable so that, in the first instance, he is saved from a calamitous disaster; and in the second instance, he attains something far more valuable.

## THE OBJECTS FROM WHICH ONE SHOULD ADOPT ZUHD

Perfection is to turn away from all of that which is besides **Allâh** 🕮, whether it refers to this world, or the Hereafter. A slightly lower level is to turn away from the things of this world only, not the Hereafter. Money, honour and luxuries are all included in this category. The lowest level is when a person turns away from wealth, but not status and honour. This is a weak form of zuhd, since jâh (name and status) is more appealing than wealth. Abstinence from it is essential to a greater extent.

## DIFFERENCE BETWEEN ZUHD AND FAQR (POVERTY)

Zuhd refers to the state when one disinclines from the world happily, despite possessing the ability to acquire it. However, if the world turns away from one, and he hankers after it, then this is referred to as faqr (poverty). Faqr is not on the same level as zuhd. However, a poor person has virtue over a wealthy person, since he is fervently being deprived of the enjoyments of the world. He is thus more virtuous than one who has being granted the world and its enjoyments, until he develops a liking for it, is content with it, and his heart dislikes turning away from it. At the time of death, he will undergo great sorrow and experience pain on its separation.

The world will be regarded by him to be his paradise, and the Hereafter a jail. This is contrary to a poor person, who has not tasted the enjoyments of this world, since the world has been forcefully denied to him. Therefore, at the time of death, his heart will not be attached here. He will in fact regard the world to be a place of difficulty and poverty, and the Hereafter as a place of freedom and happiness.

There is no doubt however, that poverty is also a great bounty of **Allâh** ﷻ, and a very powerful means to attaining everlasting success. *Rasulullâh* ﷺ said, "Verily **Allâh** ﷻ protects His ﷻ believing Servants from the world when He ﷻ loves them, just as you prevent your sick ones from eating and drinking."[1] *Rasulullâh* ﷺ also said, "The poor people of my ummah will enter *Jannah* five hundred years before the wealthy."[2] Another narration states, "When you see a poor person approaching, then say, "Marhabâ (welcome) to those who possess the signs of the pious."[3]

Once Mûsâ عليه السلام asked, "*O My Sustainer, who is most beloved to you, so that I may love them for Your (ﷻ) sake?*" **Allâh** ﷻ replied, "Every poor person."
Remember that if a poor person is content with his lot, and he is not greedy for more, then his status is close to that of zuhd. *Nabî* ﷺ said, "Blessed be to the one who has been guided to Islam, his livelihood is sufficient, and he is content with it."[4] *Nabî* ﷺ also said, "The most beloved one to **Allâh** ﷻ, is a poor content person."[5]

**Allâh** ﷻ sent revelation to Ismâîl عليه السلام, "Seek Me (ﷻ) by those whose hearts are broken." He عليه السلام said, "Who are they?" **Allâh** ﷻ replied, "The truthful poor ones."

---

[1] Hâkim (4/208), Tirmidhi (2036), Ahmad (5/427)
[2] Tirmidhi (2353), Ahmad (2/451)
[3] Musnadul Firdaus (4469)
[4] Muslim (1054), Tirmidhi (2349), Hâkim (1/34),
[5] Ibn Mâjah (4121)

In short, the reward of a poor person is enormous, when he adopts contentment and sabr (patience). To be pleased with poverty, and to possess sabr (patience) in this condition, is the beginning point of zuhd. Therefore, we will now discuss sabr.

# FOURTH PRINCIPLE

## SABR

**Allâh** ﷻ has granted such favours for those who possess the quality of sabr, which He ﷻ has not granted to anyone else. **Allâh** ﷻ says, "And adopt sabr. Verily **Allâh** ﷻ is with those who adopt sabr." In another verse, He ﷻ states, "And upon them (those who adopt sabr), are special Blessings from their Lord and a general Mercy. And they are the rightly-guided ones." "Verily those who adopt sabr, will be granted their rewards without any limit." In the Qurân, **Allâh** ﷻ has mentioned the quality of sabr in over 70 places.

*Rasulullâh* ﷺ said, "Sabr is half of îmân."[1] Sabr has been referred to as a treasury from the treasures of *Jannah*. Whoever is blessed with this quality, is a very fortunate person. His rank surpasses one who fasts during the day, and stands awake in optional worship at night.

### SABR IS A SPECIALITY OF MAN

The actual meaning of sabr is to remain steadfast on the laws of **Allâh** ﷻ, opposing the desires of the carnal self. This quality is only found in man. Man possesses two opposing qualities. One is a Divine Army i.e. the army of angels, intellect and the shariah, which desires to control man and guide him in the right direction. The second is a shaytâni army i.e. the army of anger, fulfilment of carnal desires and all that leads towards these two qualities.

---

[1] Shua'bul Imân (9265), Musnadush- Shihâb (158)

The aim of this army is to control man, and to render him a follower of his desires. Once man reaches maturity, he has to differentiate between these two groups, and combat this shaytânî army. If his intellect prevails, keeping him steadfast on the religion of Islam, and the divine law brought by *Nabî* ﷺ, then one has attained the rank of sabr. Animals only possess the quality of fulfilment of desires. They are void of intellect. On the other hand, angels have been created with the ability to gain closeness to **Allâh** ﷻ. They are void of anger and sexual desires, thus they are engaged day and night, in the glorification and praises of **Allâh** ﷻ. Thus sabr cannot be found in any of these two. Since two opposing forces are found within man – carnal desires on one side; and intellect plus the ability to understand right from wrong, and a sound nature on the other side – he has to overpower the one, by means of the other. This is referred to as sabr; thus, sabr is a special quality only found within man.

When both these opposing forces come to the fore, then man should use his intellect, and ponder over the result, so that he will keep his religion in front, and thus acquire the rank of sabr. The example of this is of a sick person who has been given a bitter medicine. The person who is a slave of taste, will not desire to consume it, whilst the intellect will desire to forcefully drink it, so that cure can be attained quickly. If one's intellect dominates, then one will patiently bear the bitterness of the medication. Likewise, in religious matters, if the intellect and one's sound nature dominate, then one will be prepared to bear the difficulties of spiritual exercisers and a bit of striving.

*Imân* refers to knowledge and practice. Practice is also of two types: some actions have to be observed, and some have to be abstained from. In character and habits as well, one has to imbibe noble traits and rid himself of evil traits. This cannot be attained without sabr. For this reason, *Rasulullâh* ﷺ referred to sabr as half of *imân*. Sabr is brought in opposition to anger and carnal lusts. Since fasting assists greatly in breaking carnal passions, it has been referred to as half of sabr.[1]

---

[1] Tirmidhi (3519), Ibn Mâjah (1745), Darimî (680)

# DIFFERENT LEVELS OF SABR

Sabr is of three levels:

The highest level is to completely destroy the matter of desire, so that it does not possess the power to oppose one. This will be reached by continuously engaging in sabr, and striving for a lengthy period. Regarding such people **Allâh** ﷻ says, "Verily those who say, "Our Master is **Allâh**, then they are steadfast….. (when departing from this world, they will be conferred the following glad tidings,) "*O content nafs*, return to your Lord (ﷻ), whilst you are pleased with Him (ﷻ), and He (ﷻ) is Pleased with you."

The lowest level is when one's carnal desire overcomes him, and the heart is handed to the forces of shaytân. Regarding such people, **Allâh** ﷻ has declared, "However, My decision has been passed that I will definitely fill Hell with jinn and man." (**Allâh** ﷻ save us!)

There are two signs of such a person:

1) He says, "I desire to repent, but it is difficult for me." This person has reached a state of despondency. He will be destroyed.

2) The desire for repentance does not even remain. He says, "**Allâh** ﷻ is Most Merciful, Most Kind. He ﷻ is not in need of my repentance. If He ﷻ sends me to *Jannah*, then such a vast place like *Jannah* will not become narrow, and there will be no decrease in **Allâh** ﷻ's All-encompassing Mercy." This unfortunate person has become a slave to his passions. He uses his intellect, only to try to prove his wrong-doings. His example is of a Muslim person who has been captured by the disbelievers. At times, they force him to feed and look after the swine, and at times they make him look after and carry alcohol, on his back and neck to their homes. If he does not regard this condition to be dishonour, then how will he ever be able to free himself from this condition? What will be the condition of the beloved son of a king, who is captured and forced to serve a lowly and ignominious slave?

This is the condition of a heedless Muslim, who has given preference to this lowly world, over the closeness of **Allâh** ﷻ, and who has become a prisoner of his sensual desires, that he does not even possess any desire and enthusiasm for repentance and focusing towards **Allâh** ﷻ. (May **Allâh** ﷻ protect us from this lowly condition!)

The intermediate level is when the two armies continue their combat. At times, one overcomes the other and vice versa. Neither is there a decisive victory, nor is there complete loss on either side. These are the people regarding whom **Allâh** ﷻ has stated, "And the others are those who have acknowledged their sins. They have combined noble actions and evil ones. There is hope that **Allâh** ﷻ will turn His ﷻ Attention towards them."

The sign of this is, that one is able to abstain from weak desires, but is unable to stay away from those desires which are strong. He is thus overpowered by them. When this occurs, he is overcome with remorse and sorrow. He is always concerned as to how he could manage to keep his *nafs* under control, and this is better for him. This is referred to as 'jihâd-e-akbar' (the greater test). A person must judge himself to see how much of success he has attained. If one remains overshadowed, and his intellect is not prepared to dominate, then he is equal to an animal, in fact he is even worse, since animals do not possess intellect. Despite man possessing intellect, he whiles away his time in fulfilling his carnal passions like animals. However, if he manages to overcome the *nafs*, then he is successful.

## SABR REQUIRED IN ALL CONDITIONS

Man is in need of sabr throughout his life, and in every condition. In this world, man passes through one of two conditions: 1) according to his desires 2) contrary to his desires. If conditions are in conformity to his desires e.g. health, safety, wealth, honour, and an abundance of progeny, then too, man is greatly in need of sabr. If he does not control himself in this condition, he will exceed the bounds, fall freely into luxury and pursuing of carnal desires, and will fail to remember his beginning and end. For this reason, the Sahâbah ﷺ said, "When we were tested with difficulty, we adopted sabr; then we were tested with ease, we could not adopt sabr."[1]

1) The meaning of sabr in ease, is that one's heart does not incline to the chattels of the world, and he realizes that whatever he has been granted from the Royal Treasuries, is but a trust from **Allâh** ﷻ, which will soon be returned. As long as he possesses it, he will have to be grateful for it, and he must not immerse himself in heedlessness and luxury.

2) Conditions contrary to one's desires are of four types:

a) Actions of obedience – the *nafs* dislikes and flees from certain actions due to laziness e.g. salâh; or due to stinginess e.g. zakâh; and sometimes due to a combination of both e.g. hajj and jihad. One has to place force on his *nafs* to fulfil these actions, no matter how difficult they may be. After a bit of struggle, the *nafs* will become subservient. Thereafter, one has been commanded to adopt three types of sabr:

1) To have sincerity of intention before commencing the action, removing traces of show, and to save oneself from the tricks of the *nafs* and shaytân.

2) Not to portray laziness during the action, so that the *Sunnah*s and etiquettes are fulfilled properly; and to keep the heart focussed during salâh, not allowing any stray thoughts to disturb one.

3) To refrain from making a show of the action after completion, just for praises or fame.
This is sabr which is severe on the *nafs*.

b) Sins – *Rasulullâh* ﷺ said, "The true warrior is he who opposes his desires, and the true emigrant is he who migrates from evil."[2]
This form of sabr is more gruelling, especially on those sins which one is accustomed to, and in which one attains pleasure. Here two armies attack one's dîn i.e. the army of shaytân and the army of habit. Added to it, if

---

[1] Statement of Abdur Rahmân ibn Auf ﷺ as quoted in Mukhtârah (921)
[2] Hâkim (1/10), Ahmad (6/21)

there is minimal cost in it, and it is easy to commit this sin, then only those who are siddique (truthful) will be able to save themselves. An example of this sin is the sin of the tongue e.g. backbiting, lies, fighting, self-praise, etc. Great amount of sabr is needed to repel these desires.

c) Those actions not within one's control, however one has the ability to repel it and redress it. For example, if someone causes harm to another, verbally or physically, and he has the ability to retaliate, but he controls himself. At times, this sabr is compulsory, and at times, it is commendable.

A Sahâbi ﷺ said, "We would not regard a person's *imân* as complete, if he could not bear sabr on difficulties." **Allâh** ﷻ mentions that the quality of believers is that they bear patiently, difficulties caused by the disbelievers and they say, "Definitely, we will observe patience on the difficulties which you inflict on us."

d) Those actions which are completely out of one's control i.e. one cannot even repel it e.g. the demise of a close family member, loss of some money, sickness, loss of a limb and all other types of calamities. Adopting sabr on this occasion is of the highest level. *Rasulullâh* ﷺ said, that **Allâh** ﷻ states, "When I test My (ﷻ) Servant with some difficulty; and he exercises patience and does not complain of Me (ﷻ) to his visitors, I (ﷻ) will grant him flesh better than his flesh, and blood better than his blood. If I (ﷻ) cure him, I (ﷻ) will cure him in this condition, that he is free from sins. If I (ﷻ) take away his life, then I (ﷻ) will take him into My (ﷻ) Mercy."[1] In another hadith, *Rasulullâh* ﷺ is reported to have said that **Allâh** ﷻ has announced, "When I place a difficulty on My Servant in his body, wealth, or child; and he handles it with patience, then I feel ashamed to set up a scale for him on the Day of Judgement, or to spread out his book of deeds."[2]  In short, man is always in need of sabr. Sabr is half of îmân, the other half being shukr. Since it also is related to all one's actions, it is appropriate that mention of it be made next.

---

[1] Hâkim (1/348), Mâlik (2/940), Shuabul Imân (9473)
[2] Musnadush Shihâb (1462), Musnadul Firdaus (4459)

# FIFTH PRINCIPLE

# SHUKR

**Allâh** states, "If you will be grateful, I will definitely grant more to you." *Nabî* said, "The person who eats and is thankful, has the same status by **Allâh** of one who is fasting and bearing patience."[1] *Nabî* used to stand so long in acts of worship, that his blessed feet would become swollen. *Nabî* would also cry profusely in his tahajjud sâlâh. Once Aishâ asked, "What is causing you to cry when all your past and future errors have been forgiven?" *Rasulullâh* replied, "Should I not be a grateful servant?"[2]

Shukr occupies a very lofty status. It surpasses the quality of zuhd, sabr, and all other qualities which have been mentioned already, since none of them are objects in themselves. They are all attained for some other purpose. The object of sabr is, so that the desires of a person are crushed. The object of fear is, that it must function as a whip, and drive its possessor to the praiseworthy place desired. Zuhd is to assist a person to turn away from all those things which divert one away from **Allâh**. However, shukr is an object in itself. For this reason, it will not terminate in *Jannah*. In *Jannah*, there will be no need for repentance, fear, sabr and zuhd. However, shukr will be continuously uttered by the inhabitants of *Jannah*. **Allâh** states, "And their final speech will be, 'All praises are solely due to **Allâh**, the Sustainer of the universe.' "

To fulfil this great act of worship, three things are necessary. The first is knowledge. This will in turn lead to a special condition, which will eventually cause one to practise. Here, we will explain these three fundamentals of shukr separately.

---

[1] Hâkim (1/422), Tirmidhi (2486), Ibn Hibbân (315), Ibn Khuzaimah (1898)
[2] Bukhârî (4837), Muslim (2820), Tirmidhi (412)

**A) Knowledge** – One should possess knowledge of the bounty as well as The Benefactor. Together with this, one should realize that all these bounties have been gifted by **Allâh** ﷻ. All the means and causes for these bounties reaching us, are all in the control of **Allâh** ﷻ. Without His ﷻ Decision, neither can any atom move, nor can anyone receive anything. Once a person has properly understood this, then two qualities will be created 1) happiness with The Benefactor.  2) readiness to serve Him ﷻ and obey His ﷻ Commands. The first is referred to as hâl (condition), and the second is referred to as amal (action).

**B) Hâl** – One should be pleased with the bounty, since it is the gift from The Great Benefactor ﷻ. Together with this, one must portray a form of humility and servitude. If a king gifts a horse to one of his slaves, then the slave will be pleased, due to one of three reasons:

1) He has received something beneficial, by which he could fulfil many of his needs.

2) He is pleased, because this gift shows that the king has placed his gaze on him, and there is hope in future that he will attain something superior.

3) He will use the horse as his conveyance so that he may go into the presence of the king, and serve him.

The first type is not actual shukr, as a person is pleased with the bounty and not the provider of the bounty. The second type is included in the definition of shukr, but is weak when compared to the third type, which is the ideal shukr. In this case, the servant is happy with the bounty which **Allâh** ﷻ has bestowed to him, because this bounty is a means of reaching Him ﷻ, since it is only by means of His ﷻ Bounties will noble deeds be completed.

The sign that one has reached this stage is, that he does not show pleasure in such bounties, which will divert his attention away from **Allâh** ﷻ, but in fact becomes remorseful. Yes, one should be pleased with those bounties through which one's worldly worries are removed, and one attains peace of mind, so that this can assist him in remaining in the <u>dhikr</u> of **Allâh** ﷻ. The person who cannot reach this level of perfection, should aim for at least the second level. As for the first level, that is not even considered to be shukr.

C) **Action** – One should use the bounty bestowed to him by **Allâh** ﷻ in His ﷻ obedience and not in His ﷻ disobedience. This will only occur when one comes to know the Wisdom of **Allâh** ﷻ in His ﷻ Creation, and the object of each one's creation. For example, the eye is a bounty of **Allâh** ﷻ. The shukr of this bounty is that it must be utilized for studying the Book of **Allâh** ﷻ and other religious books; as well as gazing at the heavens and earth, so that one can take lesson from them and revere their Creator. The person should also conceal the faults which he sees in any Muslim, and abstain from glancing at strange women. Another bounty is the ear.

The shukr of this bounty is, that one should utilize it for listening to the dhikr of **Allâh** ﷻ, and for such talks which will benefit one in the Hereafter. He should abstain from listening to futile and evil speech. The tongue should remain engaged in the dhikr of **Allâh** ﷻ, and in praising Him ﷻ, abstaining from complaints.

If someone is asked about his condition, then he should not allow words of complaint to emerge from his mouth. Complaining of such a Mighty Being in front of a lowly and frail servant who can do nothing, is fruitless and places one in sin. If words of shukr emerge, then one will be regarded as obedient. The shukr of the heart is that it be used in contemplation, remembrance of **Allâh** ﷻ, Divine Recognition, sincerity, desiring good for the creation, beautifying it with noble character, and cleansing it of evil character. Similarly, all other bounties like the hands, feet, wealth, possessions, and honour, should be used in the obedience of **Allâh** ﷻ.

## FOLLOWING THE *SUNNAH*

Only that servant whose heart **Allâh** ﷻ has expanded for Islam, and whose heart **Allâh** ﷻ has imbued with wisdom and recognition, will be able to recognize the wisdom and secrets underlying each thing, and he will be able to see his Beloved (**Allâh** ﷻ) manifested in these things. As for the person who has not reached this stage, then it is necessary for him to follow the *Sunnah* and stay within the bounds of the shariah, by this, the secrets of shukr will be unveiled to one.

If a person gazes at a non-ma<u>h</u>ram (strange women), for example, then he has been ungrateful to the bounty of the eye, and the bounty of the sun. Without the eye, one cannot see; and without the sun, the eye is useless. All know that in the dark, the eye cannot glance at anything. The sun is in need of the sky for its existence. By one evil glance, it is as though one has been ungrateful for all the bounties in the heavens and earth.

## ALL SINS ARE IN REALITY UNGRATEFULNESS

This is the same with all other sins, since all bounties are linked to one another. If a person ponders deeply, he will be able to perceive this. Here we will suffice with only one example to highlight this. **Allâh** ﷻ has made gold and silver, so that it can serve as a means of establishing prices for all goods. If there was no wealth, then all dealings would have become difficult, as it would be difficult to establish how to sell material for saffron; animals for food; etc. since there is no compatibility between these items. The only similarity they possess is, that they are both commodities.

The scale of judging their value, is by determining their price in gold and silver. If one metre of material is equivalent to one dirham (silver coin), and one box of saffron is 50 dirhams, then one can determine that with 50 metres of material, one box of saffron can be purchased. In short, if this monetary system was not in place, then there would have been great difficulty in all monetary dealings. Money is thus a judge, which arbitrates in fixing prices. It is for this reason, that if any person has to lock away or bury this wealth, then it is as though he has locked up a judge of the Muslims, rendering all the laws, useless. Whoever has made utensils of silver and gold, then it is as though he has used the judge in sewing and farming, whereas other menial labourers could have fulfilled this task. This is even worse than locking it up. The person who began using this wealth as a means of increasing his finances in the form of interest, it is as though he is using the judge to cut his grass and sweep for him; whereas this is clear oppression, and causing a change in the Decree of **Allâh** ﷻ, due to which an announcement of war has been declared by **Allâh** ﷻ against him. The person who is not aware of this, will only understand the outer ruling of the shariah, but not the inner reality.

**Allâh** ﷻ states, "And those who hoard gold and silver, and they do not spend it in the path of **Allâh** ﷻ, then warn them of a painful punishment, the day when they will be burnt in the fire of Hell; then their foreheads, their sides, and their backs will be branded."

*Rasulullâh* ﷺ has stated, "He who drinks in gold and silver utensils, then it is as though he is swallowing the fire of Hell in his stomach."[1]

**Allâh** ﷻ states, "And those who consume interest, will stand up on the Day of Judgement just as the one whom shaitân has afflicted."

From these verses and the hadith we learn, that to hoard gold and silver – which acts as an arbitrator in the pricing of commodities -, to turn them into utensils and to earn interest on them, is prohibited and contrary to Divine Wisdom.

Those who have insight, and possess Divine Recognition, are aware of these finer details and secrets, as well as their proofs. Thus their knowledge is effulgence upon effulgence. The pious are only aware of the limits of the shariah, not having reached the depths of these laws. As for those who are ignorant and spiritually blind, they are deprived of knowledge of the bounds, as well as the finer details. Hell will be filled with such people.

**Allâh** ﷻ asks, "Can the one who knows that, that which has been revealed to you from your Sustainer is the truth be like the one who is blind?" In another place, He ﷻ states, "The one who turns away from My remembrance, then for him is a straightened life, and We will resurrect him on the Day of Judgement blind. He will say, "*O* my Sustainer, why have you resurrected me blind, whereas I used to see?" He ﷻ will reply, "In this manner Our Signs used to come to you, then you would forget them. In this way, you will also be forgotten today." The Signs here, refer to these

---

[1] Bukhâri (5634), Muslim (2065)

wisdoms and secrets in the creation which had been imparted by the *Ambiyâ* ﷺ, and explained in great detail by the scholars and jurists.

Remember, that there is no law in the shariah which is void of wisdom, secrets, and specialities. Those who know them recognize them. Those who are unaware of them, deny them. This denial is contrary to the action of shukr. Perfect shukr can only be attained by the person who possesses ikhlâs (sincerity), not possessing the slightest desire to show anyone else. Therefore, it will be appropriate that we mention sincerity and sidq (truthfulness) next.

# SIXTH PRINCIPLE

# IKHLÂS (SINCERITY)

Ikhlâs has a reality, a starting point and a level of perfection. The starting point is one's intention, since ikhlâs if found in the intention. The perfection of iklâs, is a level referred to as sidq. The reality of ikhlâs is to negate any kind of mixture in one's intention.

## 1) INTENTION

**Allâh** ﷻ states, "(*O* Muhammad ﷺ), do not repel those who call out to their Sustainer morning and evening, seeking His Being." From this verse, we learn that the object of any action is the Pleasure and Being of **Allâh** ﷻ. *Rasulullâh* ﷺ said, "Verily actions are based on intention."[1] In another hadith, *Nabî* ﷺ said, "The angels take up the records of the servant's action. **Allâh** ﷻ says, "Fling it away. He did not intend My Pleasure by it. However, record for him so and so action." The angels ask, "But he did no do any such action?" **Allâh** ﷻ replies, "Definitely he intended it, definitely he intended it."[2]

*Rasulullâh* ﷺ said, "People are of four types. The first type is he whom **Allâh** ﷻ has granted knowledge and wealth. He spends his wealth

---

[1] Bukhâri (1), Muslim (1908)
[2] Hilyah (2/313)

according to the dictates of his knowledge. The second type is he who sees the first and says, "If **Allâh** ﷻ had granted me what He ﷻ had granted him, I would have practised as he had done." The rewards of both are the same. The third type is he whom **Allâh** ﷻ has granted wealth, not knowledge. He wastes his wealth due to his ignorance. The fourth type is he who sees this person and says, "If **Allâh** ﷻ had granted me what He ﷻ had granted him, I would have practised as he had done." The sins of both are the same.[1]

It has been narrated that a man from the Banî Isrâîl passed by a rocky hillock during a time of famine. He said to himself, "If only these sand particles were food, I would have distributed it amongst the people." **Allâh** ﷻ sent revelation to the *Nabî* ﷺ of the time, "Tell him, '**Allâh** ﷻ has accepted your charity, appreciated your noble intention, and has granted you the reward of having spent in charity, all those sand particles, had it been food.' "

Understand well, that intention has a great part in one's action. *Nabî* ﷺ said, "When two Muslims face one another with their swords, then both the killer, and the one killed, will be in the Fire." *Nabî* ﷺ was asked, "We understand the reason for the killer being entered into the Fire, but why will the one killed also be entered?" *Rasulullâh* ﷺ replied, "He intended to kill his companion."[2] Another hadith states, "Whoever marries a woman having settled on a certain amount of dowry, but he has no intention to pay it, then he is a fornicator. Whoever takes a loan, and has no intention to repay it, then he is a thief."[3]

## THE REALITY OF NIYYAT (INTENTION)

Niyyat refers to an intention, which will lead to the ability to do something, and it arises from knowledge. It is obvious that firstly, knowledge is needed for any work. After knowledge, one must possess intention to act upon it. Thereafter, the ability to move the hands, feet, etc, to fulfil this

---

[1] Tirmidhi (2325), Ibn Mâjah (4228)
[2] Bukhâri (31), Muslim (2888)
[3] Ibn Mâjah (2410), Ahmad (4/322)

task is created. Thus, ability is the servant of intention. For example, you have within yourself the desire for food. However, this desire is so latent as though it is asleep. As soon as your eyes fall on the food, knowledge of the food is attained. The desire for food arouses. The hand then stretches towards it, and takes the food towards the mouth. The only reason the hand stretched out, was because of the strength within it, which was subservient to the desire of eating. The desire was created by the knowledge acquired by the senses, the eyes in this case.

Just as desire has been created in us for physical bounties, **Allâh** ﷻ has created within us desire for those enjoyments which are to come in the future i.e. the Hereafter. This desire is aroused by knowledge which is attained by the intellect. The strength within a person serves this desire, by making use of the limbs. This strong and fervent desire which compels a person to utilize his limbs is referred to as niyyat e.g. a person emerges from his house intending jihad. A person should now examine as to what factor propelled him to emerge? If the propelling factor is to acquire rewards in the Hereafter, then this is his intention. If the propelling factor is to acquire booty, fame, etc. then this will be his intention.

## MULTIPLE INTENTIONS

When you have learnt of the virtue, necessity and effect of intention, then you should make effort to try to increase your intentions, in all your actions, so that your reward is increased. In one action, multiple intentions may be made. One example will be explained here: Going to the masjid and sitting there is one act of worship. However, many different intentions can be made:

1) To realize that the masjid is the House of **Allâh** ﷻ. The person entering the House is actually visiting **Allâh** ﷻ. Thus intend this when entering. *Rasulullâh* ﷺ said, "Whoever sits in the masjid...then he has visited **Allâh** ﷻ. It is the right of the host, to honour his guest."[1]

---

[1] Tabrâni in Kabîr (6/253)

2) *Murâbitah* (waiting for salâh). You are keeping yourself confined in the masjid seeking **Allâh** ﷻ's Protection. You are thus following the command of **Allâh** ﷻ which is ورابطوا. The reward for this is separate.

3) I'tikâf. The meaning of this is to control one's eyes, ears and limbs from its normal movements, since it is a type of fast. *Rasulullâh* ﷺ said, "The monasticism of my ummah is to sit in the masjid."[1]

4) Solitude and exclusion of other thoughts- due to this, the concern for the Hereafter is created.

5) Seclusion for listening to and making the dhikr of **Allâh** ﷻ. *Nabî* ﷺ said, "Whoever goes to the masjid so that he can make the dhikr of **Allâh** ﷻ or remind others to do so, then he is like a warrior in the path of **Allâh** ﷻ."[2]

6) Benefitting people by your knowledge, being an example for those who are missing their salâh, or performing it incorrectly; commanding righteousness, prohibiting evil, due to which you will receive great rewards and be a partner in their actions.

7) Leaving of sins, due to shame in front of **Allâh** ﷻ. You are secluding yourself in His ﷻ House. Eventually, you will feel ashamed and will abstain from disobeying Him.

8) Benefitting some brother for **Allâh** ﷻ's Pleasure. This will be a treasury and boon for one in the Hereafter.

In this manner, for every action, a person could possess multiple intentions. By all of these intentions, one's action will increase in value, and will merge with the actions of the very close servants of **Allâh** ﷻ.

---

[1] Allâmah Irâqi says that he did not find this narration.

[2] This is actually the statement of Ka'b Ahbâr. In a hadith of Tabrâni and Ahmad, Abu Hurairah ؓ narrates that Rasulullâh ﷺ said, "Whoever enters this masjid of ours so that he can learn good or teach it, then he is like a warrior in the path of **Allah** ﷻ. Whoever enters for any other reason then he is like one who looks at that which is not his."

In like manner, remember that by multiple intentions of sin, one's actions will merge with the actions of shaytân. For example, if a person sits in the masjid with the intention of speaking nonsense, tarnishing the dignity of Muslims, laughing and joking, ogling at women and young boys who pass by, debating with contemporaries just for show and competition, merely to create honour for oneself in the hearts of those listening, etc. In this manner this, lone action will be regarded as a conglomeration of sins.

Another important point is, that one should not be unmindful of making good intentions in permissible actions. A narration states, " On the Day of Judgement, a servant will be questioned about every thing, even the antimony which he placed in his eyes, digging of sand with his fingers, and touching the clothing of his brother."[1]

An example of intention in permissible actions is, when a person uses some perfume on the Day of Jumuâh. His intention may be: to attain pleasure by its smell, to show off his wealth, to adorn himself to attain the stares and admiration of women. All of these intentions are futile and a cause of sin.

On the other hand, your intention may also be to follow the *Sunnah* of *Rasulullâh* ﷺ, honour the House of **Allâh** ﷻ, show reverence to the Day of Jumuâh, save the Muslims from any offensive smell, give comfort to them by a fragrant smell, and to close the doors of backbiting, which others will do if one emits a foul smell.

Nabi ﷺ has alluded to both these groups in a hadith, "Whoever applies fragrance for **Allâh** ﷻ's Pleasure, will appear on the Day of Judgement with his fragrance being more better than the smell of musk, and whoever applies fragrance for anyone besides **Allâh** ﷻ will appear on the Day of Judgement, with a stench worse than that of carrion."[2]

## 2) IKHLÂS

---

[1] Ibn Abî Hâtim in his Tafsîr (9/4050)
[2] Musannaf Abdur Razzâq (4/319)

**Allâh** ﷻ states, "And they have not been commanded, except that they worship **Allâh** ﷻ, making their worship sincerely for Him." In another place, He ﷻ declares, "(The hypocrites will be destroyed) except those who repented, corrected themselves, held firm onto the rope of **Allâh** ﷻ, and made their religion solely for **Allâh** ﷻ."

*Rasulullâh* ﷺ said, "Whoever will sincerely do any action for **Allâh** ﷻ for a period of forty days, **Allâh** ﷻ will make apparent fountains of wisdom from his heart onto his tongue."[1]

## THE REALITY OF IKHLÂS

Ikhlâs means to have intention for one thing only. This means that the propelling factor for an action is either show, or Divine Pleasure. The literal meaning of ikhlâs applies to both, since the word khâlis refers to that thing which is devoid of any adulteration. However, according to the terminology of the shariah, ikhlâs refers to doing an action solely for **Allâh** ﷻ's Pleasure. In the shariah, ikhlâs will not be used for inclining and intending anyone besides **Allâh** ﷻ. The word *ilhâd* refers literally to any inclination, whether it be towards good or evil. However, in the shariah, it is only used to refer to inclination towards evil. In like manner, if the object of worship is solely for His ﷻ Worship, then this will be ikhlâs.

If there is an adulteration of riyâ (show), or if a person also intends some worldly benefit through an act of worship, then this will not be referred to as ikhlâs. For example, if a person fasts since it is an act of worship and also so that he will attain some relief in sickness by abstention from food and drink, then he has gathered two intentions in one action. This will not be ikhlâs. Other examples are:
- A person frees a slave since it is a great form of worship, and also so that he is freed from the burden of clothing and feeding him

- A person performs Hajj as it is a noble action and beloved to **Allâh** ﷻ. Another intention made is that during Hajj, one is very active, and by activity, one's health and temperament will improve. Another reason could

---

[1] Musnadush Shihâb (466), Musnadul- Firdaws(5767), Hilyah (5/189)

be that he will attain some rest from his family members, safety from enemies, or he gets tired of residing in one place. He feels that by journeying, his heart will be comforted

- A person performs wudhu to attain cleanliness or to remove some dirt from the body

- A person sits for i'tikâf so that he will save on boarding expenses

- A person visits a sick person, so that he will be visited when he is sick

- A person gives charity so that the beggar will stop pestering him
All of these intentions are contrary to ikhlâs, and to be liberated from them is difficult. For this reason, some have stated, "In the ikhlâs of one moment, is eternal salvation."

Suleimân Dârânî ♦ said, "Blessed is that person whose one step is only for **Allâh** ♦."

Ma'rûf Kharkhî ♦ used to hit himself and say, "O *nafs*, be sincere, you will attain salvation."

Remember, however, that this adulteration takes on different forms. At times, these intentions overpower the intention of worship; at times these intentions are overpowered; and at times both intentions are equally made. In permissible actions, if the Pleasure of **Allâh** ♦ is intended even slightly, then according to the extent of the intention, one will be rewarded. However, in acts of worship, one must possess ikhlâs. If there is a contamination of some other intention, then one's ikhlâs will be nullified. If the contaminated intention is dominant, and the intention of worship is light, then the whole act of worship will be nullified.

## 3) SIDQ (TRUTHFULNESS)

This is the third fundamental of ikhlâs. It is the perfection and culmination of ikhlâs. **Allâh** ♦ states, "Our servants are those who are proven to be truthful in their promises." *Nabî* ♦ said, "Verily a man speaks the truth, and he keeps on intending truthfulness, until eventually he is written by **Allâh** ﷻ as a siddique (extremely truthful person)."[1] In the Qurân Karîm, **Allâh** ﷻ qualifies Ibrâhim ﷵ with the quality of siddique. The virtue of sidq is apparent, as by it one attains the rank of the siddiqîn (extremely pious).

Sidq is of six categories. Whoever attains perfection in all of them will be deserving of the title of siddique. Hereunder are the six categories:

1) Truthfulness in speech in all conditions, with regards to past, present and future matters. Perfection in this will be achieved by two actions:

a) Abstaining from ambiguity in speech. Even though the speech may be correct in itself, the listener understands something contrary to the reality. Thus abstain from this also. The reason why lies are prohibited is that crookedness is created in the heart, due to the crookedness of the speech. When the heart becomes crooked, the truth is not manifest to it. It is for this reason that such a person does not generally see true dreams. Even though ambiguousness does not derive such a result, it is similar to a lie, in this aspect, that the other person understands something contrary to reality. It is therefore appropriate for a siddîque to abstain from such speech, except in case of dire need.

b) Speaking the truth in one's speech with **Allâh** ﷻ e.g. in salâh, one utters with the tongue "I turn my face to the Being who created me." If in the heart, there is no other thought besides that of **Allâh** ﷻ, then one is truthful in his speech, otherwise not. Another example is when one utters in Surah Fâtihah, "Only You (ﷻ) do we worship, and only You (ﷻ) do we seek assistance from." If in the heart lies desire for gold and the love of wealth, then this is also falsehood, since one is claiming that he is a servant, and **Allâh** ﷻ is his object of worship, whereas he is actually a slave of wealth and the world, in his heart.

---

[1] Bukhârî (6094), Muslim (2607)

2) Truthfulness in intention – A person must possess such ikhlâs, that his intention must not be anything besides worship, and the desire of doing good. There should not be any contamination in the intention.

3) Truthfulness in determination – A person normally determines, that if he is blessed with wealth, then he will give it in charity; and if he is given rulership, he will rule justly. This is referred to as *azm* (determination). Some people's determination is strong, whilst others are shaky and weak. A strong determination is referred to as truthful. An example of this is found in the life of Umar ﷺ who said, "My being brought forward, and my head being cut off, is more beloved to me than my being appointed as a leader over a nation, in which Abû Bakr ﷺ is present."[1]

The amount of determination in even the truly pious, differs. The highest level is, when one is pleased to lose his life, but is not prepared to compromise on his ideals.

4) Truthfulness in fulfilling one's determination – Many people are determined to do an action, however, they become weak and lazy when the time arrives for implementation. For example, a person was determined to spend in charity if he possessed money. However, when he now becomes the owner of a huge sum of wealth, he does not possess the courage to spend. A person was determined to rule justly, if he was the ruler, but when the occasion arises, he is not able to rule justly; whereas this is the time of examination. To determine something in the heart is not as difficult as implementing it. For this reason **Allâh** ﷻ states, "Amongst them are those who promised **Allâh**, "If He (ﷻ) grants us wealth from His (ﷻ) Grace, then definitely we will spend in charity.".... "Then **Allâh** ﷻ created hypocrisy in their hearts ... because of their breaking their pact with **Allâh** and because of their lies."

5) Truthfulness in action – A person's inward and outward must correspond i.e. the external must be the same as the internal e.g. a person who walks slowly, shows that he is a man of dignity, whereas he possesses no dignity in his heart. He does this merely to show people that he is

---

[1] Bukhâri (6830), Ibn Hibbân (413), Ahmad (55/1)

dignified. This is referred to as riyâ. If the object is not show, but a person walks in this manner due to unmindfulness and inattentiveness, then though this will not be referred to as riyâ, it will also not be sidq, but in fact deception and lies. For this reason, *Rasulullâh* ﷺ made the following duâ, "O **Allâh** ﷻ, make my internal better than my external; and make my external righteous."[1]

6) Truthfulness in the maqâmât (stages) of dîn – i.e. in hope and fear, in love and Divine Pleasure, in Tawakkul (Trust in **Allâh** ﷻ) and zuhd etc. one must attempt to reach its peak. In the beginning stages, only the name of these qualities exists in one. Eventually as a person progresses, he reaches a stage where true fear, true love, etc. are created. Thus **Allâh** ﷻ states, "The true believers are only those who believe in **Allâh** and His Messenger ﷺ, after which they have not a trace of doubt; and they strive with their wealth and lives in the path of **Allâh** ﷻ. They are the truthful ones."

By attaining perfection in these six categories, one will be worthy of being called siddîq. Whoever has a portion of them, will be granted this level of sidq. A portion of sidq is to establish in the heart that **Allâh** ﷻ is Razzâq (Sustainer), and to place trust in Him. Therefore it will be appropriate to mention the quality of tawakkul next.

---

[1] Tirmidhi (3586)

# SEVENTH PRINCIPLE

# TAWAKKUL   (TRUST IN ÂLLÂH ﷻ)

**Allâh** ﷻ states, "Only upon **Allâh** ﷻ should the believers place their trust."
"And only upon **Allâh** ﷻ place trust, if you are believers."
"Verily **Allâh** ﷻ loves those who place their trust in Him."
"Whoever places his trust in **Allâh**, He is sufficient for him."
"Verily those whom you worship leaving aside **Allâh** ﷻ cannot grant you sustenance, so seek sustenance from the side of **Allâh** ﷻ."

*Nabî* ﷺ said, "If you place your trust upon **Allâh** ﷻ as you ought to do, then He ﷻ would have granted you sustenance just as He sustains birds, which depart famished in the morning, and return with a full belly."[1]

In another hadith, *Rasulullâh* ﷺ said, "Whoever turns his complete attention to **Allâh** ﷻ, **Allâh** ﷻ will suffice for all his needs, and grant him sustenance from where he never imagined. Whoever devotes himself to the world, **Allâh** ﷻ will hand him over to it."[2]

## REALITY AND FUNDAMENTALS OF TAWAKKUL

Tawakkul refers to a condition which is created when one regards **Allâh** ﷻ to be Unique, the Only Doer of everything, and Independent, having **NO** partner in any quality of Perfection. The effect of this becomes apparent in one's actions. Tawakkul is of three fundamentals a) knowledge b) hâl (condition) c) action. We will explain each one of them separately.

a) Knowledge – This is the fundamental quality. By this is meant tawhîd, which is confirmation of "There is none worthy of worship besides **Allâh** (ﷻ), He (ﷻ) is alone, He (ﷻ) has no partner, for Him (ﷻ) is

---

[1] Ibn Hibbân (730), Tirmidhi (2344), Hâkim (4/318)
[2] Shua'bul Imân (1044), Tabrâni in Awsat (3383)

Sovereignty, and for Him (ﷻ) is all Praises. He (ﷻ) possesses Power over everything." In this, one affirms that **Allâh** ﷻ is Perfect in His ﷻ Power, Generosity and Wisdom, due to which He ﷻ is worthy of Praise. Whoever affirms this with sincerity and truthfulness, then true îmân will become entrenched in his heart. Now the quality of tawakkul will definitely be created, on condition that these words were uttered from the depths of the heart. This means that the reality of these words dominate the heart to such an extent, that there remains no place for any other thought in the heart.

b) Hâl – This means that you should hand your matters over to **Allâh** ﷻ and your heart should place trust in Him ﷻ. You should not turn to anyone besides **Allâh** ﷻ, at all. Your example should be of a person who hands his affairs to a lawyer who is intelligent, compassionate, and cares for you. Now seated in your house, you will remain in ease and contended, not even mulling over it, and not seeking the assistance of any person, since you know fully well that this lawyer is extremely intelligent and your well-wisher, and that he will never allow your opponent to overpower you. Similarly, when you are fully aware that sustenance, death and life, and all matters of creation, whether small or big, are within His ﷻ Control; He has no partner, and neither is there any limit to His ﷻ Generosity, Wisdom and Mercy; then why are you not content and why do you not raise your gaze from others?

## TWO CAUSES FOR LACK OF TAWAKKUL

After possessing knowledge of this, and then too, one lacks this quality, then he should realise that the cause of this must be one of the following two reasons:

1) Weakness of yaqîn (conviction)- This can be due to doubt in the fact that **Allâh** ﷻ is The Sustainer ﷻ, The Most Powerful ﷻ, The All-Hearing ﷻ and The All-Seeing ﷻ . (May **Allâh** ﷻ save us!) Another reason can be that a person has complete conviction, but the effect of this belief has not as yet affected the heart. This is just like a person who has full conviction that death is soon to come. Despite his firm belief that he is definitely going to die one day and leave this world,

he still acts without fear and lacks total concern for this idea. The reason is that the full effect of this conviction has not yet entered the heart.

2) By nature, the heart of a person is weak and cowardly, due to which his heart becomes subservient to such thoughts and imaginations which are completely false and non-existent. This is just like how a person fears to lie next to a dead person, whereas everyone knows that the dead one cannot do anything. Still too, one will not be able to fall asleep, and will feel afraid. This is actually obedience to thoughts and phantoms which plague the mind, which does not allow the weak heart to act on matters of conviction e.g. some people have a dislike for eating honey merely due to the fact that they feel that the colour of honey is similar to that of excreta, even though they are convinced that the item before them is honey. A similarity in colour is of no consequence. Still too, one will not eat it. This is the effect of his imagination, which is difficult for man to stay away from.
Likewise, it is possible that one's conviction in tawhîd is complete, and he has no doubt whatsoever. However he is bound to use means, and he cannot attain complete trust, which is referred to as tawakkul.

c) Action – it is the opinion of some ignoramuses, that tawakkul refers to abstaining from earning and leaving out all forms of effort, but rather sitting and doing nothing. If one is sick, he must not use medication. One must be able to place himself in places of danger, without any thought, like jumping into a fire, or placing his hand in the lion's mouth, then only is he worthy of being called a mutawakkil (i.e. a person of tawakkul). This notion is completely incorrect. To do such an action is actually harâm (prohibited) in Islâm. Islâm on the other hand has mentioned the virtues of tawakkul. Then how can it be possible, that the very same thing which Islam regards to be as impermissible is encouraged and codoned? Man's effort is generally due to one of four things:
A) Effort to acquire something beneficial which was not attained before
B) Effort to protect and look after whatever one has
C) Effort to save it from future harm
D) Effort to remove present harms

The first two types (A and B) are referred to as jalbe-manfa'at (acquiring benefit). There are three causes for this

a) Yaqîn - By using the means, the acquirement of the benefit will be realised definitely.
b) Ghâlib zann - One possesses an overpowering thought that he will attain some benefit
c) Mauhûm - One imagines that he will derive some benefit.

An example of the first type is when a hungry man does not stretch out his hand towards the food placed in front of him. He says, "I have full trust that **Allâh** ﷻ will feed me." Another example is of a person who wants children, but he does not have sexual relations with his wife; or a person wants crops, but he is not prepared to plant seeds. This is complete ignorance, since the results of using these means are definite, which **Allâh** ﷻ has decreed by His ﷻ Law. There is no change in this System of **Allâh** ﷻ. Tawakkul in these things will be in two ways:

1) To know that the hand, food, ability to eat, planting the seeds, the energy to have relations, etc. are all Signs of the Power of **Allâh** ﷻ.

2) Not to have trust in these means with the heart. Trust must be kept in **Allâh** ﷻ. To have trust on means from the depths of the heart, is completely incorrect. How could one possess such trust, when the hand can suddenly become paralyzed, the food may be destroyed, and insects or the heat may destroy the seeds? Then no benefit will be attained at all.
Keeping these two points in mind, there is no harm if one uses the means. It will not be regarded as going contrary to tawakkul.
An example of the second type is when one takes provisions for a journey. If these provisions are not taken, then it is not definite that one will pass away. However, the dominant feeling is that by travelling in the jungle without any provisions, will lead to destruction. To utilize such means is not contrary to tawakkul, but in fact has always been the path of our pious predecessors. Yes, one will still have complete trust in the Grace of **Allâh** ﷻ that He ﷻ has protected one from thieves, saved the food from rotting, kept one alive and granted him the power to eat.

An example of the third type is, when a person works extra hard feeling that he will acquire extra wealth. This is referred to as *hirs* (greed). Due to this quality, a person at times acquires doubtful food. This is also contrary to tawakkul. The proof for this is, that *Nabî* ﷺ described those with the quality of tawakkul, as those who do not brand themselves (a form of treatment used in those times), and they do not use amulets and charms. He ﷺ did not describe them as those who do not live in the cities and do not earn a living. From here we learn that to use such means whose effects are imaginary, is contrary to tawakkul e.g. using of charms, and treatment of sickness by branding oneself. As for those causes which definitely or generally bring about an effect — e.g. keeping provisions for a journey, or stretching one's hand towards food and chewing it etc. — are not contrary to tawakkul.

## FUTURE PLANNING AND STORING

Planning and making effort for the future (tadbîr) — included in this is to keep grains, or to store for the future. However, if a person is granted wealth, and he starts saving up for more than a year, then his tawakkul will be destroyed. If he keeps food for a day and distributes the rest, then he will be perfect in the quality of tawakkul. If he stores food for forty days, then there is a difference of opinion. Sahl Tastarî ﵀ states that this is contrary to tawakkul, whereas Khawâs ﵀ states that one's tawakkul will still be intact.

If a person has a family, then it will be permissible for him to save up provisions for them for a full year, as *Rasulullâh* ﷺ did with his ﷺ respected wives; he ﷺ would grant them expenses for a full year. However, his ﷺ own condition was such that if he acquired some food in the morning, he ﷺ would not keep it for his evening meal.

Saving more than a year's expenses, even for one's family members, is contrary to tawakkul. Firstly, this will be regarded as possessing long hopes, whereas one has no guarantee of the next moment. Thus how can one gather food for the next time? It is for this reason that the more a person abstains from possessing inordinate hopes, the higher his status will be. However, since the System of **Allâh** ﷻ is such, that every year, He ﷻ grants a renewed sustenance and new plantations, there is some allowance for a person to store up provisions - between these two bestowals - due to family responsibilities, so that there is no worry and distress, for those who are of a weak nature. Gathering food for even more than this period, is a sign of extremely weak îmân (belief). As for storage of furniture and household appliances, there will be no harm if kept, and stored for more than a year, as these are not bought every year, and the necessity of these items are continuous. Yes, keeping clothing for more than a year is contrary to tawakkul, since there is no continuous need for it. Winter clothing is not utilized in summer, and vice versa. Based on this, *Rasulullâh* ﷺ remarked regarding a poor person who was being buried, "Verily he will be resurrected on the Day of Judgement, with his face shining like the full moon. Had it not been for one quality, it would have shone like the radiant sun. When the winter months would come, he would store his summer clothing, for the following summer."[1]

The last two types (C and D) are referred to as daf'e-madarrat (removal of harm). Examples of this are; running away from a carnivorous animal, moving away from a falling wall or flood waters, repelling sickness with medication etc. These are also of different levels. These can be deduced by analogy from the three types mentioned above i.e. yaqîn, ghâlib zann and mauhûm.

Abstaining from storage of anything is commendable, for those whose conviction is strong, and whose hearts are firm. As for the weak-hearted, this condition is not appropriate for them. In fact, if their hearts become agitated by not keeping anything back, then it is necessary for such a person to abstain from this level of tawakkul, and to gather his goods, so that the heart could be at ease, and he could worship open-heartedly. Correction of worry and concern, which will lead to greater harms, will take precedence.

As for those whose îmân is strong, and they possess internal comfort, it will be permissible for them to travel without taking any provisions, on condition that they are able to stay hungry for seven days, and suffice on grass, since this is readily available in the countryside. If a person of weak îmân has to do this, then he will be a sinner, since he will be flinging himself into destruction. To intentionally thrust oneself into harm is prohibited. In like manner, if a strong person binds himself in a cave wherein there is no grass, and no human beings pass by there, then this

---

[1] Imâm Zubeidi in Ithâf (9/503) has attributed this narration to the author of Al-Qût, with the sanad to Shahar ibn Haushab from Abû Umâmah ﷺ.

will not be permissible. Even though it is within the Power of **Allâh** ﷻ to send sustenance to such a place, it is contrary to His ﷻ System and Habit.

If such a person has to receive sustenance here, this will be referred to as a karâmat (miracle). Since it is inappropriate for a servant to force his Master ﷻ to do acts against His ﷻ System, this will not be permissible for even those who are strong in îmân. In the countryside and jungle, permissibility was granted, as the System of **Allâh** ﷻ is that these places are not devoid of grass, and many people pass by these places. Thus when one's îmân is strong, there is no strong likelihood of harm to oneself. So there is no sin on one. Sitting in a cave all alone, is actually trying to go against **Allâh** ﷻ's System. This is not permissible.

In short, if a person turns away from open and clear means of livelihood, and suffices on the grass in the jungle and country-side, trusting on **Allâh** ﷻ's Kindness and Wisdom, then this is better and more appropriate.

# EIGHT PRINCIPLE

# MAHABBAH (LOVE)

**Allâh** ﷻ states, "He ﷻ loves them, and they love Him ﷻ."

*Nabî* ﷺ said, "None of you can have true îmân until **Allâh** ﷻ and His(ﷻ) Messenger (ﷺ) are more beloved to him than everything else."[1] In another hadith, *Rasulullâh* ﷺ said, "Love **Allâh** (ﷻ), because of the bounties which He (ﷻ) blesses you with, and love me, because **Allâh** (ﷻ) Loves me."[2]

Abu Bakr ﷠ said, "Whoever has tasted the Love of **Allâh** ﷻ, then this will prevent him from seeking the world, and create dread in him from all humans."

---

[1] Bukhâri (6941), Muslim (43)
[2] Hâkim (3/149), Tirmidhi (3789)

Hasan Basrî ﷺ said, "Whoever recognizes **Allâh** ﷻ will love him. Whoever recognizes the world, will be disinclined to it. A believer does not engage in such futile acts, that he becomes unmindful. When he ponders, he becomes grieved."[1]

The philosophers and mutakallimîn deny the love of **Allâh** ﷻ. They thus interpret it in the following manner, "It is not possible for us to have any compatibility with that Being ﷻ which has no equal; neither can our intellects fathom Him ﷻ completely. The only meaning of having love for Him ﷻ is that we obey His ﷻ Commands." Since these deprived people are ignorant of the reality of things, they feel that it is only possible for us to love those who are of our jins (genus and species). Their minds cannot fathom reality. Here briefly, we will mention the reality of love.

## THE REALITY OF LOVE AND THE SIXTH SENSE

Every enjoyable thing is beloved to man. The meaning of beloved, is that the heart is inclined towards it. When this inclination becomes very intense, then this is referred to as *ishq*. The meaning of hatred, is when the heart of man is dis-inclined from something, since it causes distress and harm. If the hatred and dislike intensifies, then this is referred to as *maqt*.

When this is understood, then ponder: Whatever we can perceive with our senses, is either in accordance with our desires, contrary to it, or neither in conformity nor contrary. Whatever is in conformity to our desires is beloved and enjoyable; whatever is contrary to it is disliked and detested; and whatever is not contrary nor in conformity does not create enjoyment nor dislike- one remains in a condition of equilibrium.

Enjoyment always occurs after perception, and that is is of two types:
 1) external perception
 2) internal perception.

The external perception is attained by the five senses e.g. the eye enjoys pleasure in looking at beautiful objects, the ear attains delight in listening

---

[1] Ahmad in Zuhd (1595)

to well-structured beautiful-sounding poems, the tongue and nose feel enjoyment in tasting delicious food, and in smelling wonderful fragrances, and the whole body derives joy in touching soft and delicate objects. All of these things are beloved to the soul i.e. the *nafs* is naturally inclined to them.

Similarly, man has been granted a sixth sense, which is an internal perception. The location of this sense is the heart. This sixth sense is sometimes referred to as aql (intellect), nûr (illumination), or the sixth sense. In short, no matter what it is called, this internal perception, just like the external senses, gains enjoyment from those things which are in conformity with it. Thus *Rasulullâh* ﷺ said, "From your world, three things have been made beloved to me: fragrance, women, and the coolness of my eyes lie in salâh."[1]

By perfume, the sense of smell derives pleasure. By beautiful women, the sense of sight and touch develops delight. However, the enjoyment of salâh is not perceived by any of the external senses. The enjoyment is felt by the sixth sense, which is internal, the location of which is the heart. It is for this reason that whoever's heart is corrupt, will never attain enjoyment in salâh. Only the person whose heart is sound, will really experience this joy. The specialty of man is due to this sixth sense, since all animals equally possess the other five qualities. Thus animals are also desirous of beautiful forms, articulate voices, wonderful smells, tasty food and touching delicate objects.

## INTERNAL BEAUTIFUL FORMS

Just as the outward eyes derives pleasure by looking at beautiful women, the internal eyes derives pleasure from internal good qualities, on condition that the eyes of the heart are open. Perhaps you might not understand internal beauty and its enjoyment. Therefore I say to you, "Introspect! Do you possess love for the *Ambiyâ* ﷺ, the *Sahâbah* ﷺ, the *awliyâ* ﷺ and ulemâ? Do you not find in your heart any difference between a just, knowledgeable, honourable, compassionate king and an ignorant, stingy,

---

[1] Hâkim (2/160), Nasaî (7/61)

harsh, foul-mouthed oppressor? If there is any difference, then I ask you, "What is the reason that your heart is attracted to one person, and is appalled by the other?

If you ponder, you will come to realize, that this is the internal sense which is deriving pleasure from these beautiful qualities. Similarly, when you hear of the truthfulness of Abû Bakr ﷺ, the political acumen of Umar ﷺ, the generosity of Uthmân ﷺ and the bravery of Alî ﷺ, then such happiness and joy as well as an inclination to these personalities is created, which cannot be denied. A more apparent example is that of people, who possess such feeling and connection with the imams of their madhabs that they are prepared to even sacrifice their wealth and lives in defense of them, whereas these people have not physically seen them. If they had seen them, perhaps they would not have been pleased with their looks, since the enjoyment of the eye is a different form of enjoyment.

There is a world of difference between these two forms of enjoyment. If they possessed good looks, and their forms were thereafter disfigured, then too, love for them would have remained, due to their internal beautiful qualities. It is apparent that this enjoyment is attained by the sixth sense of a person, which is located in the heart. It is the heart which derives pleasure from the teachings of these great personalities.

## CAUSES WHICH LEAD TO LOVE

If you ponder over the qualities due to which love for them is attained, you will find that there are three qualities 1) Knowledge 2) Power 3) Freedom from faults and weaknesses.

1) As for their knowledge, they possessed knowledge of **Allâh** ﷺ, His ﷺ Angels, His ﷺ Books, His ﷺ amazing Creations, and the finer details of the shariah of the *Ambiyâ* ﷺ.

2) As for their power, they were able to control themselves by harnessing their carnal desires, remaining steadfast on the straight path, and they were able to control the creation of **Allâh** ﷺ by their policies and guide them towards the truth.

3) As for their purity, their internal was free from ignorance and stinginess, jealousy and evil character.

A combination of knowledge, practice and noble character, creates such beauty within a person which animals can never comprehend. It is only man who possesses this sixth internal sense of the heart, by which he can derive pleasure.

When you possess love for these imams of the madhabs, due to these qualities, then it is obvious that the love you will possess for *Nabî* ﷺ will be far greater than the love one possesses for all the other *Ambiyâ* عليهم السلام and ulemâ, since these qualities are found to the greatest extent in the being of *Nabî* ﷺ.

Thereafter, look from *Nabî* ﷺ towards the Creator ﷻ and Dispatcher ﷻ of *Nabî* ﷺ, the Being ﷻ who has favored His ﷻ Creation by sending the *Nabî* ﷺ to convey the message of Islâm to them.

It is evident that the knowledge, strength and purity of the *Ambiyâ* عليهم السلام has no comparison whatsoever, with the Limitless Knowledge, Infinite Power and qualities of Perfection of **Allâh** ﷻ. It is only the Being of **Allâh** ﷻ, who is free from all imperfections and blemishes. Besides Him ﷻ, there is no other being free of every type of fault and weakness. If no fault can be seen in any of the creation, then too humility, neediness, servitude and meekness are major blemishes. These are even found in the *Ambiyâ* عليهم السلام, since no human individuals are exempted from these qualities. All know that these great personalities are in need of food and drink, they cannot grant sustenance or life to anyone, nor can they give life and death to any being. Can there ever be any comparison between the power of the *Ambiyâ* عليهم السلام and the Power of **Allâh** ﷻ? Look at the everlasting Knowledge of **Allâh** ﷻ! It is an everlasting ocean which has no shore. There is not an atom which is beyond the confines of His ﷻ Knowledge. The heavens, the earth, the Arsh (Throne), Kursî (Chair), Lowh (Protected Tablet), Pen, every tree and stone, in short, even those objects which are not found in one's thought, are all present in the Knowledge of The Knower of Unseen ﷻ. In short, whatever qualities are found in the *Ambiyâ* عليهم السلام are in reality a shadow of the Qualities of **Allâh** ﷻ. When your heart inclines towards the shade, despite it being temporary and being the shadow of the sun, then why does it not incline towards the starting and emanating point i.e. the sun? When you possess so much of love for the *Ambiyâ* ﷺ, whose qualities have all been created by **Allâh** ﷻ, then why do you not possess love for the Creator and Originator of these qualities i.e. **Allâh** ﷻ?

## THE LOWEST LEVEL OF LOVE IS LOVE FOR ONE'S BENEFACTOR

If your internal perception still cannot recognize the Beauty and Grandeur of **Allâh** ﷻ, and you have still not developed ishq (intense love) for Him ﷻ , then at least count His ﷻ Favours and Bounties upon you. It is obvious that you can never enumerate them. Do not be worse than a dog, since it possesses great love for any person, who shows kindness to it.

Ponder over this. Is there anyone who is your benefactor besides **Allâh** ﷻ? Is there any enjoyment, joy, bounty which has been created by any being besides **Allâh** ﷻ? Ponder over your limbs, and how amazingly it has been created! Love Him ﷻ because of His ﷻ Favours for you. This is a lower level. This means that if you do not love Him ﷻ as the angels due to His ﷻ Beauty and Grandeur, then love Him ﷻ as the general creation loves others, due to their benevolence. In a hadith, *Rasulullâh* ﷺ said, "Love **Allâh** ﷻ due to His Bounties ﷻ which He ﷻ grants you as sustenance, and love me due to **Allâh** ﷻ loving me."[1] This is a very weak level of love, since one's love and dislike will increase and decrease with an increase and decrease of bounties. This person is like a slave who portrays love and does work, just for a wage, and to fill his belly. The highest and most perfect level is to love **Allâh** ﷻ, due to His ﷻ Qualities of Beauty and Grandeur ﷻ, the Being ﷻ who has no equal. For this reason, **Allâh** ﷻ revealed to Dâwûd ﷿, "Verily the most beloved of My (ﷻ) lovers is the one who worships Me (ﷻ), without any desire for recompense, but only so that he can fulfill the right of Providence."

---

[1] Hâkim (3/149), Tirmidhî (3789)

In the Zabûr, it was mentioned, "Who can be a greater oppressor, than the one who worships Me for *Jannah* or *Jahannum*? If I did not create *Jannah* or *Jahannum*, would I not be Worthy of being worshipped and obeyed?"

Once Îsâ ﷺ passed by a group of worshippers who had become emaciated? He ﷺ asked them, "What has withered your body?" They said, "We fear the fire, and we have hope of *Jannah*." Îsâ ﷺ remarked, "You fear the creation, and you place hope in the creation." He then passed by another group in the same condition. On being questioned, they replied, "We worship Him ﷺ, due to love for Him ﷺ, and due to honour for Him ﷺ." He ﷺ commented, "You are in fact the true friends of **Allâh** ﷺ. It is with people like you that I have been commanded to sit."[1]

## SIGNS OF THE LOVE OF ALLÂH ﷺ

The signs which portray the love of **Allâh** ﷺ are many, which cannot be enumerated here. At this juncture, only a few of these will be mentioned:

1) Granting precedence to the commands of **Allâh** ﷺ over one's desires, abstaining from sins, and keeping the bounds of the shariah in place.

2) Having desire to meet **Allâh** ﷺ, and to be void of dislike for death – If one desires death, then the only reason is so that one can acquire more *ma'rifat* (recognition). The more *ma'rifat* is gained, the better it is, so that more enjoyment can be attained when meeting the Beloved ﷺ. *Ma'rifat* is the seed of witnessing the Beauty of **Allâh** ﷺ. The more seed planted, the more crops will grow. Similarly, the more one attains *ma'rifat*, the more enjoyment he will experience when beholding the Beloved ﷺ.

3) Being pleased with the Decision of **Allâh** ﷺ - Whatever conditions pass one, whether favorable or not, one does not complain, whether by tongue, or heart.

Now it is appropriate that we explain the meaning of radhâ (being pleased with the Divine Decision), so that man is not deceived into thinking that

---

[1] Abû Nu'aym in Hilyah (7/10)

he possesses the reality of the Love of **Allâh** ﷻ, since acquiring this reality is not easy.

# NINTH PRINCIPLE

# RADHA BIL QADA (PLEASED WITH THE DECREE OF ALLAH ﷻ)

**Allâh** ﷻ has stated, "**Allâh** ﷻ is Pleased with them, and they are pleased with Him (ﷻ)."

*Rasulullâh* ﷺ said, "When **Allâh** ﷻ Loves a servant, He (ﷻ) tests him. If he exercises patience, He (ﷻ) chooses him. If he is pleased with Allah's (ﷻ) Decree, He (ﷻ) makes him His (ﷻ) Chosen Servant." [1]

Once *Rasulullâh* ﷺ asked a group of Sahâbah ﷺ, "Who are you?" They replied that they were believers. *Nabî* ﷺ then asked them, "What is the sign of your îmân?" They replied, "We are patient in times of difficulty, we are grateful in times of ease, and we are pleased with Divine Decree." *Rasulullâh* ﷺ remarked, "You are (true) believers, by the Lord (ﷻ) of the Ka'bah."[2]

**Allâh** ﷻ sent revelation to Dâwûd عليه السلام, "O Dâwûd عليه السلام, you intend, and I (ﷻ) intend. Only that will occur, which I (ﷻ) intend. If you happily accept that which I (ﷻ) intend, then I (ﷻ) will be sufficient for you in that which you intend. If you are not pleased with that which I (ﷻ) intend, then I (ﷻ) will tire you in that which you intend, then too, only that which I (ﷻ) intend will come to pass."[3]

A group of people has denied this concept of being pleased with Divine Decree. Their objection is that being pleased with something contrary to one's desires, cannot be fathomed. Yes, it is possible for one to bear this

---

[1] Musnadul-Firdaus (971)

[2] Tabrâni in Awsat (9423)

[3] Hâkim Tirmidhî has mentioned something similar to this in Nawâdirul-ûsûl (1981)

condition patiently. However, this denial of theirs is a sign of weakness of intellect. Just as they are deficient in understanding the Love of **Allâh** ﷻ, they are deficient in understanding this concept as well.

## LOGICAL PROOFS ILLUSTRATING PLEASURE IN DIFFICULTY

To exhibit pleasure in difficulties, and to be pleased when matters go contrary to ones temperament is possible, due to the following three reasons:

1) Seeing one's beloved and an excess of love causes one to be unmindful of pain. Thus, if the beloved hits the lover, he does not experience discomfort. When a person is overcome by desires or anger, then we witness that the body is wounded, the head is hurt, blood flows, and the body becomes saturated with blood, but then too, one does not experience pain. At times, you may have noticed that when you were completely absorbed and immersed in something beloved to you, and whilst walking, a thorn settled in your foot, you experienced no pain or difficulty.

However, when the anger dissipates, or the enthusiasm and love fades, then the pain is now felt e.g. when one receives the item he was desirous of, or when one loses hope in ever receiving it. When one does not feel pain, due to this miniscule amount of love, then where there is excessive love, the feeling of even gigantic difficulties will not be felt. In the world a person becomes enamoured, and is inclined to another human being – who is permeated with filth and dirt. This beloved can only be seen with the eye, which causes so many errors. At times, it sees something huge as small, something far as close, and something ugly as beautiful. When this is the condition with a mortal being, then why is this feeling impossible for that Being ﷻ whose Beauty is Everlasting, whose Grandeur ﷻ is Perpetual, who can never die and has no form of imperfection, and who can be perceived with internal vision, which is much clearer and truthful than the outer eye?

Based on this, when Junaid Baghdâdî ﷺ asked Sirrî Saqatî ﷺ, "Does a lover feel the pain of difficulty?" he replied in the negative. He then asked him, "Even if he is struck with a sword?" "Even if he is struck seventy times with a sword," came the reply.

An ârif once mentioned, "I love all things which He (ﷻ) has Created, due to love for Him (ﷻ), so much so, that if He (ﷻ) loves the Fire, I would have loved to enter it." The meaning of this is that due to love, he would not feel any pain in the burning of the fire also.

Umar ibn Abdul Azîz ؓ said, "For me no pleasure remains except in that which **Allâh** ﷻ has Decreed."[1]

The child of a sufî went missing for three days. He was asked, "Why don't you make duâ to **Allâh** ﷻ to return him back to you?" He answered, "My objecting to His ﷻ Decision is much more severe on me than my child being lost."

2) The second reason why it is possible for one to be pleased with **Allâh** ﷻ's Decision, is that one feels difficulty, and dislikes it naturally. However, since his intellect informs him of a great result i.e. reward in the Hereafter, he accepts this difficulty happily. An example of this, is when a doctor gives a patient bitter medicine to swallow, or encourages him to take an injection. Swallowing bitter medication, or taking an injection causes discomfort and pain. Nonetheless, since the patient is aware of its beneficial effects - that it will lead to good health - he is pleased with the doctor, and in fact, feels obligated to him and appreciates him. A business-man is pleased with all the difficulties and encumbrances he has to undergo, even though it is completely against his temperament. Since his intellect has explained to him the great benefits and results of this difficulty, this dislike and hardship converts into love and desire. When one does not regard difficulties to be difficulties, just for attaining the temporary benefits of this world, then why should it be surprising when one is pleased to bear difficulties and hardships, in attaining the felicity and success of the Hereafter?

---

[1] Shua'bul Imân (225)

A pious woman once slipped. Her toenail fell out. Instead of moaning and wailing, she began smiling. People asked her, "Are you not feeling pain?" She replied, "The enjoyment of the reward I will receive, has removed from my heart the bitterness of its pain."

In short, whoever believes from the bottom of his heart, that he will receive such a great reward from **Allâh** ﷻ for every difficulty he bore; that this difficulty will bear no comparison to the reward, will find himself happy and pleased, even in difficulties.

3) A person understands that there are amazing secrets and workings of **Allâh** ﷻ in every action. In every amazing incident and new event, there is not one, but hundreds of mysteries hidden, some of which only a person of great insight will be able to fathom. Looking at these benefits and wisdoms, a difficulty does not remain a difficulty. Whatever is happening in this temporary world, which is regarded to be a cause of worry, concern and anguish by an ignorant person, is seen in a different light by people of understanding. The surprise of this person, is like that of the surprise shown by Mûsâ عليه السلام to Khidhr عليه السلام, after staying in his company, as explained in Surah Kahf. Whilst sitting in a boat of poor people, Khidhr عليه السلام damaged it by removing a board from it. Musâ عليه السلام in surprise asked him why he committed such an act of excess. Thereafter, Khidhr عليه السلام killed an immature youngster. Again Musâ عليه السلام, in astonishment, objected, that since when had the blood of an innocent youngster become permissible.

Continuing ahead, they reached a certain area where the inhabitants did not even care to host them. In the morning, whilst leaving the area, their gaze fell on a wall which was about to collapse. Khidhr عليه السلام repaired this wall. Musâ عليه السلام was again taken aback, objecting that he should not have favoured such an unfriendly community, who cared not in the least bit for their guests. After this third objection, the two of them parted ways, in accordance to their agreement.

It is clear that the only reason Musâ عليه السلام was surprised with these incidents, was that he was not aware of the underlying secrets and wisdoms of these incidents. Thereafter Khidhr عليه السلام informed Musâ عليه السلام that the boat belonged to some poor sailors. The king at that time, was unjustly seizing ships that were in an excellent condition. He thus damaged the ship, so that these poor people's means of livelihood would not be taken away.

The child who was killed was naturally irreligious, and there was a strong fear that on reaching adulthood he would lead astray his believing parents, since they would not be able to resist his demands, due to their parental love for him. This child was thus taken away, and another child was to be bestowed to them, which would be pious, and a cause for their success in the Hereafter. As for the wall, it belonged to two orphans, whose father was pious. Underneath this wall was buried his wealth, which he had left behind for these two children. Thus, he straightened the wall, so that these two children could retrieve the wealth after attaining maturity. If the wall had to fall now, the wealth would have been usurped by others. After these explanations, the amazement of Musâ عليه السلام was eradicated.

An incident is mentioned of a pious man who would always utter in every problem, "Goodness is in that which **Allâh** ﷻ Ordained." He used to reside in a village. He possessed a donkey on which he would load his goods; a dog that would guard his house; and a cock that would wake him up in the morning. One day, a fox came and grabbed the cock, taking it away. When he saw his wife disheartened, he said to her, "Goodness is in that which **Allâh** ﷻ Ordained." Thereafter a wolf came and killed the donkey. Again, he uttered these words to console his wife. The dog thereafter fell sick, and died. Once again, he uttered, "Goodness is in that which **Allâh** ﷻ Ordained." His wife was astonished at him, that there was so much of loss caused to them, but he continued to say that there must be goodness in these actions.

One morning, they woke up to find that all the houses around them had been attacked the night before. All the people were imprisoned, and all the children made into slaves. The soldiers had recognized the houses in the darkness of the night by the braying of the people's donkeys, the barking of their dogs, and the crowing of their cocks. The pious man then said to his wife, "You have seen now that goodness is in what **Allâh** ﷻ has Ordained. The animals of the people were the cause of their problems. If our animals had not died before this, then you and I would also have been taken away as prisoner."

A *Nabî* ﷺ was once sitting worshipping **Allâh** ﷻ in the cavern of a mountain. Nearby a stream flowed. Once, a person riding a horse came to this stream. He removed his money-belt and placed it on the floor before drinking water. He then went away, forgetting this belt in which was a thousand dînârs (gold coins). After a short while, another person came and took this belt away. Then a poor man came, carrying a bundle of wood on his back. He removed this bundle from his back, and sat down to drink and rest. The horseman, in the meantime, returned very agitated, looking for his money-belt. He caught hold of the poor man and started beating him, asking for his bag. When the poor man denied any knowledge of the bag, he brandished his sword, and killed him. The *Nabî* ﷺ, having witnessed this whole incident, remarked, "O **Allâh** ﷻ, this incident was most amazing.

This poor man did not take the bag but was killed for it, and the other oppressor who stole the bag, was not taken to task." **Allâh** ﷻ revealed to him, "Remain engaged in your worship. Knowing the mysteries behind Divine Workings is not your work. The reality of this matter is that this poor person had killed the father of the horseman. I (ﷻ)thus allowed retribution to take place by the son of the murdered person. The horseman's father had once stolen one thousand gold coins from the person who took the bag. I thus returned it from his estate."

In summary, whoever believes in these wisdoms and deeper secrets, will not be in the least bit surprised at the Actions of **Allâh** ﷻ. In fact, he will be surprised at his own ignorance and foolishness. He will not question Divine Decisions by using words like, 'why' and 'how'. He will be pleased with the decisions which **Allâh** ﷻ has determined.


## THE CORRECT MEANING OF RADHÂ BIL QADHÂ

Commanding righteousness is a compulsory duty. Those who abstain from it, cannot be said to possess the quality of radhâ bil qadâ, since radhâ (happiness) and dislike are two opposing qualities. Two opposing traits cannot combine in one place. It is obvious that whatever you dislike and regard as evil, you will definitely possess hatred for it. Whatever you regard as good, you will be happy and pleased with it. Thus, in one action, and in one aspect, a person cannot be happy, as well as displeased. Yes, this is possible in two different aspects; e.g. someone is your enemy as well as the enemy of your enemy. If you kill your enemy, then this will be a cause of happiness for you, since he was your enemy. However, it will also be a source of sadness, in one aspect, that the enemy of your enemy has died. You would have liked your enemy's enemy to stay alive, so that he could cause your enemy more harm.

Similarly, disbelief and sins have two angles. The first is that they have occurred by the Will and Intention of **Allâh** ﷻ, since no atom in the world can move without the Command of **Allâh** ﷻ. This is referred to as qadâ and taqdîr. From this aspect one should not be displeased but should be pleased, since every working of **Allâh** ﷻ is according to Wisdom. From another angle, a person should have hatred and dislike for these actions, since disbelief and sin are perpetrated by a disbeliever and sinner, which is a sign of enmity and disobedience to **Allâh** ﷻ. **Allâh** ﷻ has commanded us to dislike those in whom the signs of **Allâh** ﷻ's opposition is found. Fulfilling the Command of **Allâh** ﷻ and possessing dislike for a disbeliever is also part of being pleased with the Law of **Allâh** ﷻ.

By way of example, your beloved says to you, "I am going to test your love and ardour. I will force my slave to swear me, and then I will hit him. Whoever shows dislike to this slave of mine, I will regard him to be my lover, and sincere devotee; and whoever likes him, I will regard him to be my enemy." Now perchance, if the slave swears your beloved in front of you, will you possess love or hatred for him? At the time of listening to him uttering these vulgarities, will you be pleased or displeased? It is obvious that you will feel displeased, since he is attacking the honour of your beloved. Committing such an action, shows that he has enmity for your beloved. The enemy of your beloved, especially when he openly exposes his enmity and dislike, is worthy of being hated and disliked. However, in one aspect you will not be upset, since you have understood that the action of the slave has occurred by the intention and will of the beloved. In fact, your conviction on the strength of the beloved will be created, that he is able to take any work from any of his slaves, so much so, that if he commands them to utter vulgarities at his own pure being, they possess no right to disobey and turn away from this command. Regard the disbelief of a disbeliever in the same light. Since, it is occurring by the Will and Intention of **Allâh** ﷻ, one will not be displeased from this angle.

Together with this, one will be displeased with this person's disbelief, since **Allâh** ﷻ's Pleasure is not in such an act, and since disbelief is a sign of being disliked by **Allâh** ﷻ and being **Allâh** ﷻ's enemy. For this reason, advice will be proffered to him, and the message of truth will be conveyed to him, because the enemy of your beloved will also be your enemy.

## RADHÂ BIL QADHÂ IS NOT CONTRARY TO DUÂ AND THE USE OF MEANS

Radhâ bil qadhâ does not mean that one should abstain from duâ, usage of medication, and abstention from worldly means and agencies. For example, an arrow is shot at you. If you have the ability to fend it off by your shield, then you should do so, not allowing it to afflict your body. You should not be under the notion that if you leave it to strike your body, then you will have been pleased with Divine Decree. This is ignorance and baseless thinking. Duâ and saving oneself from harm, has been commanded in the shariah. One is not allowed to defy the laws of his Beloved ﷻ.

The meaning of radhâ bil qadhâ, is that one should use whichever means **Allâh** ﷻ has stipulated for the attainment of certain objectives, so that He ﷻ can become pleased with you, using the system He ﷻ has kept in place. If you have to abstain from adopting these means, then you will be regarded as one opposed to the Beloved, and the enemy of His ﷻ Pleasure. For example, a thirsty man comes across water, but he does not stretch his hands forth. He thinks to himself that he is pleased with his thirst, since thirst is the Divine Decree of **Allâh** ﷻ, and he must remain pleased with these Decrees. Such a person will be regarded as irrational. He will be asked, "Are you trying to create a fissure in the systems placed by **Allâh** ﷻ and in his structures. Or do you want to cross the limits of the shariah?" What you have understood is not the meaning of radhâ. The actual meaning of radhâ is, that a person should not object to any condition which overcomes him, inwardly or outwardly, verbally or in the heart.

Together with this, he should fulfil the Commands of **Allâh** ﷻ, and he should not exceed the system which **Allâh** ﷻ has created in the world for that work, i.e. he should remain within the limits sets by the shariah, trying to attain the Pleasure of **Allâh** ﷻ. For example, when he is commanded to make duâ, then he should fulfil this duty so that humbleness, tranquillity and softness is created in the heart, and he attains that ability in his heart, by which illumination and Divine Manifestations may enter. He should then use the means to attain the object. However, after utilizing the means, if the objective is not attained, then no anxiety or sorrow should be experienced. One should be pleased, and should realize that the means in reality, is not the actual cause. It was **Allâh** ﷻ's Will that one did not attain the object. *'I should thus be pleased with the Decision and Decree of **Allâh** ﷻ.'* Thus, despite adopting the correct means and avenues, if the object is not attained, there is no need for any grief, sorrow or worry.

# TENTH PRINCIPLE

# REMEMBRANCE OF DEATH

The nine principles which we have discussed are of different levels. Some are objectives in themselves, like the stage of radhâ and love; whereas others are means to the objective e.g. tawbah (repentance), sabr (patience), fear, and zuhd (abstinence). The aim of these is to gain Divine Proximity, and all of these are aids to achieve this quality. Qurb (Divine Proximity) is attained by love and recognition (*ma'rifat*). However, these two qualities will not be attained until the love of those besides **Allâh** ﷻ is removed from the heart. This will be removed by means of tawbah, fear, sabr and zuhd, thus they are also of importance.

Amongst the aids which assist in gaining Divine Proximity, one is the remembrance of death. Therefore, it seems appropriate to mention it here.

By remembrance of death, the love of the world departs from the heart. When this connection is terminated, the Love of **Allâh** ﷻ will be attained.

## CONCERN FOR DEATH IS THE CORNERSTONE OF REFORMATION

**Allâh** ﷻ states, "Say, 'Verily the death from which you are running away, will definitely overtake you.' "

*Rasulullâh* ﷺ said, "Remember in great abundance, the destroyer of pleasures." i.e. death.[1]

Aishâ ؓ said, "Once I asked *Rasulullâh* ﷺ, 'Will anyone be resurrected with the martyrs?'" He replied, "Yes, the person who remembers death twenty times a day."[2]

*Rasulullâh* ﷺ said, "Death is sufficient as admonition."[3]
In one hadith, *Rasulullâh* ﷺ is reported to have stated, "If the animals knew about death as much as man knows, then you would not find fat animals to eat."[4]

"I leave for you two advisers, one silent and the other talking. The silent advisor is death, and the talking one is the Qurân."

Death is terrifying, and the conditions following it, are even more severe. Thinking about death and discussing it, creates an aversion for the world, and makes one loathe it. Detestment for the world, is the source of all goodness; just as love for the world is the root of every evil. Thus, when the heart dislikes the world, then all goodness is attained. This will only be created when a person has concern and fear for death, thinking of the difficulties awaiting him.

---

[1] Tirmidhî (2307), Ibn Hibbân (2992)
[2] Tabrâni
[3] Musnad Shihâb (1410)
[4] Musnad Shihâb (1434), Shuabul-îmân (10073)

# THE MANNER OF PONDERING OVER DEATH

Sit some time in solitude. Remove all other thoughts from the heart, and then ponder over death, with full concentration and determination. First think of your friends and family members, who have departed from this temporary abode, one after the other. Think of where have the shapes and forms of these people gone? What great ambitions and hopes have they taken with them into their graves? Think of their greed and aspirations? All their expectations of wealth and fame, were hidden in their hearts. All of these are now hidden beneath the sand. Their names have faded into oblivion. Then think of the deceased people's bodies. How beautiful they looked? How delicate were their bodies. Now they have disintegrated, and have become the sustenance of insects and worms. Think of each limb. What has happened to that mouth which could not remain quiet for even a short while? Where are those hands which were in motion all the time? Whose sustenance have the beautiful eyes and neck become? In short, by pondering in this manner, one will become fortunate, as it has been narrated, "A fortunate one is he who takes lesson from others."

## LENGTHY HOPES

How sad it is that we are unmindful of such an important and frightening matter as death. Millions of people, on this same land we are treading, have come and passed on, but we think that we will remain forever. The dangerous and terrifying journey of death stares us in the face, but we are completely unmindful. This neglect has created lengthy hopes in us. If this ignorance is removed, then the thought of death will become a reality for us. For this reason, *Rasulullâh* ﷺ advised Ibn Umâr ﷺ, "When you wake up in the morning, then do not be concerned about the evening. When the evening arrives, do not concern yourself with the morning. Prepare in this life of yours for your death, and in your good health for illness, because, O Abdullah, you do not know what your name will be tomorrow"[1] (i.e. whether you will be among the living or the dead). Be concerned all the time for that event that has no specified time. Throw dust over your

---

[1] Hilyah (1/312) in a marfu' form. In Bukhârî and Tirmidhî, this hadith is narrated as a statement of Ibn Umar ﷺ.

hopes, and do not allow your aspirations to increase. Only **Allâh** ﷻ knows what our condition will be in the next hour.

Once Usâmâh ﷺ bought a slave girl for a hundred gold coins, promising to pay after two months. *Nabî* ﷺ said, "Are you not surprised at Usâmah, who is promising to pay after two months? Verily Usamâh possesses long hopes. Whenever my eyes open, I think that my eyelids will not meet because I will leave this world. Whenever I lift my hand, I do not know whether I will be able to place it down before death. Whenever I eat a morsel, I feel that I will not be able to swallow it, before my soul is seized." Then *Nabî* ﷺ said, "O children of *Adam* ﷺ, if you possess intelligence, then count yourselves from amongst the deceased. By the Being (ﷻ)in whose Control my life lies, that which you have been promised is coming, and you will not be able to escape it."[1]

*Rasulullâh* ﷺ said, "The first of this ummah will gain salvation by yaqîn (conviction) and zuhd (disinclination from the world), and the last portion of the ummah will be destroyed due to stinginess and inordinate desires."[2]

In another hadith, *Rasulullâh* ﷺ is reported to have stated, "Does every one of you desire to enter *Jannah*?" When the Sahâbah ﷺ answered in the affirmative, *Nabî* ﷺ said, "Shorten your hopes, place death in front of your eyes, and be ashamed in front of **Allâh** ﷻ as you ought to be."[3]

---

[1] Hilyah (6/91), Shuabul Imân (10080), Musnad Shâmiyyîn of Tabrânî (1505)
[2] Daylamî in Musnad Firdaws (6853)
[3] Hilyah (8/185), Zuhd of Ibnul Mubârak (317)

# CONCLUSION

Upto this juncture, whatever you have read, was to caution you and create within yourself enthusiasm towards **Allâh** ﷻ. If you have not paid attention, or have been listening superficially as you listen to fairytales, then you have failed to benefit, and you have oppressed yourself. **Allâh** ﷻ states, "Who can be a greater oppressor than the one who has been admonished with the verses of his Sustainer (ﷻ), then he turns away, and forgets that which his hands have sent forth." If you have listened with concentration, and you have pondered with an open heart, then definitely, you will gain benefit. You will then be able to leave and abstain from those things, which are a barrier towards the straight path.

## GREAT BARRIER FOR REFORMATION- LOVE OF THE WORLD

The greatest barrier in the Path to **Allâh** ﷻ is the love of the world. This creates unmindfulness of **Allâh** ﷻ, and does not allow a person to think of the Hereafter and the Day of Judgement. Therefore daily, after Fajr salâh, which is a time when the mind is clear, and the stomach is empty, sit for a few minutes in solitude, reflecting over your condition. Think of your beginning, and eventually your final stages. Take a stock of your *nafs*, this will prove to be extremely beneficial. Address the *nafs* in the following manner, "*O nafs!* , I am a travelling business man." My profit is everlasting success and proximity to **Allâh** ﷻ, whereas my loss is in everlasting failure and being veiled from **Allâh** ﷻ. My life is my capital. My every breath is a valuable gem and a huge treasury, by which I can purchase eternal felicity. When my life comes to an end, my business will terminate. Then I will not be able to do anything. Today is the time for me to work. **Allâh** ﷻ has granted me this opportunity. If I wish, I may make profit in this business of mine. If I am raised from this world, I will then wish to be returned, and to be granted just one day in which I could do some noble deed.

*O nafs!* Today is the day I have been granted respite from my Sustainer. Now fulfil your promise and watch what you are doing. If you regard this respite as an opportunity, and you do not procrastinate, then you will earn much profit today, and you will not undergo any sorrow. If tomorrow you are still alive, then keep these points in mind again."

In short, as long as you are alive, regard every day as a new day, and do not be deceived by the Forgiving Nature of **Allâh** ﷻ, since this is only a thought. It is quite possible that your thought may turn out to be false. It is not binding on **Allâh** ﷻ to forgive you, nor does He ﷻ owe it to you, which you can demand. Even if you are forgiven, you will be deprived of the rewards of the pious servants; and after death all your sorrow will be of no consequence. Whatever was to take place, has occurred. Whatever time has elapsed, will never return. Each breathe of a person is a great boon and a valuable gem.

Thereafter if the *nafs* asks you, "What should I do, and how should I value my time?" then say to it, "Concern yourself not with those things which will separate from you at the time of death, and hold firm onto that which will remain eternally, and will never leave you i.e. attain recognition of **Allâh** ﷻ and become accustomed to His ﷻ Remembrance."

Then if the *nafs* asks, "How can I escape from the world? Its connection with the heart has become strong and firm. Breaking this bond will be difficult." Answer in the following manner, "Cut off connection from the world, from the inner recesses of the heart. Search for the worldly connection which is strongest. Slash this sickness from its roots. If the love for wealth is dominant, then remove it. If the desire for status is stronger, then eradicate it.

The explanation and cure for these spiritual sicknesses have already been explained. Study them, and after placing trust on **Allâh** ﷻ, brace yourself, be firm, and act contrary to that which your *nafs* desires. Then see whether you will attain salvation from these sicknesses or not.

*O nafs!* You are ill. This life of yours should be spent in abstinence. The spiritual expert doctor, *Nabî* ﷺ, - whose truthfulness you are fully aware of, has stated that enjoyments are harmful for you, whereas bitter medicine is advantageous and beneficial for you. Do you not bear the difficulties of travel, with this hope in mind that once you reach your destination, you will be able to rest comfortably? If you are tired due to the difficulties of the road, then remember that the caravan may soon leave, and you will be left all alone in the jungle; where either you will be consumed by a predatory animal or you will get lost, which will lead to your destruction.

*O nafs!* What desire do you possess of this world? If you desire wealth, and if we assume that you possess it, and you are a wealthy person, so what? If you look around, you will find many Jews and Christians wealthier than you. If you desire honour and status, and you attain it, what will be its result? If you glance around, you will find thousands of ignoramus non-believers, and lowly, mean disobedient servants of **Allâh** ﷻ who have far more status, and honour than you. These people have such status, and sit on high posts of position, that if they wish, they can capture you and lock you up in prison. *O nafs!*, if you are not afraid of the calamities and problems that plague one, when one desires to achieve status and honour, and you are not afraid of the difficulties that plague one after attaining prominence, then how can you be prepared to partner these lowly and despicable people in their qualities? Is such a worthless and valueless object worthy of being sought, which every wretched and miserable person can attain, and has already attained? Even if you strive for fifty years, you will not attain this rank of his.

*O nafs! If you turn away from this world, and turn towards the Hereafter, you will become an outstanding and unique person in time. There will be none to rival you. O nafs! What is now worthy of acquiring? Remember well that there is no better well-wisher for you than me? Do not look and listen to anyone in this matter. Answer, keeping in mind the result of this world and the Hereafter- what are you inclined towards?*

In this way, if you continue to debate and argue with your *nafs*, then one day, your *nafs* will become obedient to you, and will lead you on the straight path. If you are intelligent, then realise that this debate is far more important than debating any of the groups of falsehood, whether it be the innovators, the Mu'tazilâ, etc, since the wrongs and errors of others will not cause the least harm to you. However, your wrongdoings will definitely affect you. You will be forced to bear its consequences. Therefore, first kill that blood-thirsty enemy, who resides within you. Once you have been saved from him, then it will be appropriate to take stock of others. It is surprising that no thought is given to this enemy. In fact, it is given whatever it desires, and is obeyed as soon as it commands. To fulfil its desires and requests, the brains are racked and many schemes and plans are contrived.

Can there be any person more foolish, than the one who is concerned with removal of flies from the face of another by fanning him, whilst a poisonous snake is sitting below him, waiting to attack and destroy him? Your condition is that you are so concerned with debating others and placing them on the correct path, that you are totally unconcerned of debating your own *nafs*, and being wary of its destructive nature of your worldly and religious life.

## SPECIALITY OF THE *NAFS*

Understand well, that as long as one does not struggle against the *nafs* for a long period, it will not become straight. As long as this does not occur, neither will you be able to remember **Allâh** ﷻ correctly, nor will you attain enjoyment in your supplications. You will not turn towards the Path to **Allâh** ﷻ (called sûlûk), and you will not have the worry to walk the straight path. Therefore, regard this debating as compulsory upon yourself. Whenever you have the opportunity, commence this deliberation. Whenever the *nafs* opposes you, reprimand it, and impose a penalty on it which is effective. The characteristic of the *nafs* is that of a dog – as long as it is not beaten, it will not learn manners.

If you desire to learn the manner of debating, arguing, and punishing your *nafs*, refer to "The book of muhâsabah and murâqabah" in Ihyâ-ul-ûlûm. This book does not allow us to mention these chapters.